Marc Yeats

# MUSIC, PAINTING, LANDSCAPE AND ME

Vision Edition

Copyright © 2024 by Marc Yeats
www.marc-yeats.com

## Vision Edition
www.visionedition.com

Vision Edition 025-MC

ISBN 978-1-7397815-8-3

Cover Design by Marc Yeats

# CONTENTS

**ACKNOWLEDGEMENTS** v

**INTRODUCTION** 1

**CHAPTER ONE – THE LIST**

Origins and Nature 9

The 'Lived Experience', Neuroscience and Ontology 10

Science: Truth and Objectivity 13

Metaphysics and More 16

Fuzzy Logic 21

Interpretation, Objectivity, Meaningfulness and the Artist's Statement 22

Equivalency of Meaningfulness and Fuzzy Values 27

Transduction, Transmission, Meaningfulness and Autoethnography 28

Memory and Resonance 33

Affect 36

Titles, Intention, Indeterminacy and Superposition 38

Composer, Performer, Audience: Intentionality, Interpretation, Transmission, Convention, Deterritorialisation and Meaningfulness 42

Polyphony for the Eye, Polyphony for the Ear 61

Polyphony, Assemblage and a 'Sense of Place' 63

Flux, Jelly, Indeterminacy and Fuzzy Sets 64

Observation and Quantum Mechanics 75

Writing for Answers: Hermeneutics and the Perpetual Symbol 77

Hallucination 79

**CHAPTER TWO – 'MAPPING'**

Introduction 87

The Berkshire Downs 96

The South Downs National Park and Lymington Marshes 100

The Suffolk Coastline 104

**CHAPTER THREE – FOR THE LOVE OF CHALK AND OTHER MATTERS**

The White Stuff 109

PK Coupling, Behaviour and Embodiment 111
Sensed Sound, PK Coupling and Proprioception 114
Expanded Proprioception 115
Performance: Embodiment and PK Coupling 118
PK Coupling: Possibilities and Assumptions 120

## CHAPTER FOUR – STYLE, SPONTANEITY, SERENDIPITY AND MISTAKES

Style 123
Spontaneity 126
Serendipity and Mistakes 136

## CHAPTER FIVE – AN ENVIRONMENT OF POSSIBILITIES

Introduction 139
Music Composition 143
Tempo Transformations 147
Pitch Transformations 148
Constructing Compositions 149
Making Paintings 153
Becoming 160
Technology, Photography, Prints and the Feedback Loop of Image Generation 166
Shared Making Processes 169
Gathering Thoughts: Functional Relationships 172

## CHAPTER SIX – THE CONSOLIDATION

Introduction 175
Ontology and Being 177
Science or Ontology? 180
Symbolic Forms 182
Truth and Fact 185
Subjectivity and Truth 186
The Ultimate 'Why?' 189

**BIBLIOGRAPHY** 191

**INDEX** 197

# ACKNOWLEDGEMENTS

For many years, I harboured thoughts of writing a book that delved into my dual identity as an artist and composer. However, these thoughts remained unrealised until 2021, shortly after completing my doctoral studies at the University of Leeds' School of Music. The idea of comprehensively exploring my artistic practices began crystallising during this period. I started gathering notes and musings, laying the groundwork for what would eventually become a deeper investigation into my creative processes.

I recognised the potential value of this exploration for myself and others, so I applied to Arts Council England's Developing Your Creative Practice (DYCP) scheme. I proposed using the grant and the allocated time to research further and refine my ideas. In August 2021, I received the encouraging news that my application had been successful. The grant awarded me forty-five days over nine months, during which I developed key book components, including the introduction, chapter outlines and a sample chapter. These elements allowed me to extend my exploration beyond the boundaries of my doctoral research and the academic frameworks that typically define PhD inquiries. I aimed to deepen my understanding of creative practice by examining the behaviours, ideas and misconceptions intertwined with creating through the lens of my experiences.

The DYCP grant was instrumental in developing The List, the book's first and most comprehensive chapter. This chapter and the confidence gained from writing my doctoral thesis empowered me to tackle the rest of the book.

During this period, my friendship with Markus Wenninger, a multifaceted artist described on his Twitter profile as an enthusiast of flute, chirography, Feldenkrais, kinaesthetic, yoga, pedagogy, neuroplasticity, snuff and skateboarding, grew profoundly. Our acquaintance dates to 2011, with Markus performing and recording many of my compositions for clarinet and flute and the multitracking of smaller timecode-supported polytemporal ensemble pieces. Throughout the writing of The List, Markus served as an invaluable sounding board through our ongoing correspondence, aiding in navigating my uncharted territories of thought and experience. His insights into hermeneutics, interpretation and embodiment, along with introductions to concepts like PK Coupling and the philosophies of Jacques Derrida and Ernst Cassirer, significantly enriched the book's exploration of embodiment, communication and perception. In recognition of his passion and contribution, the book is dedicated to Markus.

My gratitude extends to the music organisations Sound and Music and The British Music Collection, who supported me during and after the DYCP grant period. Their backing was instrumental in publicising the project and creating a video diary series documenting my two-and-a-half-year writing journey.

Once the book was completed in draft form, three friends—composer Dr Sadie Harrison, Leadership & Conflict Resolution Master Facilitator Carmel Gardener and located audio designer, writer and declamatory poet Ralph Hoyte—offered their perspectives on the manuscript. Their feedback was instrumental in refining aspects of the presentation and format, underscoring the book's strengths and areas for reconsideration. In addition, Professor Stephen Davismoon, Executive Dean, Faculty of Creative Arts and Humanities at Liverpool Hope University, composer, sound-designer, educator and writer; Dr Alexander Murdin, Director at ruralrecreation.org.uk; Professor Ian Pace, pianist, musicologist, writer and composer, and Professor of Music, Culture and Society at City, University of London, along with The Cross-Eyed Pianist (Frances Wilson, writer and publicist) have reviewed the book. Their endorsements are hugely appreciated and feature on the back cover.

A special mention must be made of my partner, Mark Hewitt, whose patience and enthusiasm have been a constant throughout my frequently speculative philosophical musings and the book's development. His unwavering support, particularly during my 'wobblier' moments, has been a cornerstone of this project.

Lastly, I thank John Palmer and Vision Edition for their patience, enthusiasm and belief in this project. Their professionalism and guidance in helping me to prepare the manuscript for publication have been crucial in bringing this book to completion.

# INTRODUCTION

Writing this book has been a journey of personal discovery and 'becoming'. It is a journey realised through words used to intimate disparate thoughts, assumptions, conclusions, confusions, contradictions, speculations, musings and countless open questions that have passed through my mind at different points in life or have presented as continual emergent themes that have never entirely found resolution. Some of those questions have arisen through the activity of writing this book where, because of amassing various threads and data about my entire practice in one place for the first time, newly observed perspectives and relationships have emerged to generate yet more questions. In attempting to answer those questions, *Music, Painting, Landscape and Me* is an observation of my life and work as a composer and painter positioned entirely within and through my opinion of its precursors, actions, operations and outcomes. It is, if you like, a self-portrait that attempts to situate its content within objective and verifiable fields of knowledge but where, despite this intention, the text is dominated by subjective components.

Much about the modus operandi of my artistic practice is passionate, immediate and fluid regarding its speed and intensity of execution. I operate with confidence in this territory. However, when writing, I take a more cautious approach to expressing my ideas in words. When I'm creating music or painting, words are unnecessary. I rely entirely upon a direct relationship between physicality, thought and its embodiment in my work through the action of making. I find this a clear and straightforward relationship.

I write from the perspective of a composer and painter who believes his work asks questions and seeks to solve problems by making itself. Many of those questions concern my relationship to and concepts around perceived internal and external realities, their embodiment and possible transmission to others through my work. More precisely, I ask what compels me to make paintings and music compositions per se and why the processes, methods, concepts, rituals, antecedents and behaviours I have developed and acquired cause me to make work the way I do. I also ask what influence concepts of affect and a 'sense of place' play in the outcomes I produce and how those may be embodied into the work and transmitted to others. Crucially, I ask how music and painting are connected and how both relate to my engagement with the concept of landscape.

And regarding landscape, 'sense of place' is a term I refer to continually throughout *Music, Painting, Landscape and Me*. This is perhaps unsurprising as my fascination and engagement with the landscape are very much rooted in my relationship to physical places, their topographical configurations, geology, surface patterning through human interventions such as farming and land management, as well as the flora and fauna that inhabit those locations and the weather conditions and consequent light effects that articulate them as sensory and visual phenomena. But for me, the term 'sense of place' goes beyond the observable physicality of a location and dives into the less clear realms of physical sensations I experience when in those landscapes, as well as the affective response such physical configurations trigger. I discuss those responses and affects at some length as the book unfolds, explaining how I believe they relate to my practice both as a generative force that, through a desire to recreate similar sensations, compels me to make paintings and music and how those artefacts unite configurations of sound, colour, texture and structure between the physically perceived world and my interior experiences and constructions of landscapes. I attempt to explain such phenomena where possible, but my attempts often must be revised. Nevertheless, before proceeding, I would like to define what is meant when referring to a 'sense of place'.

As the description above explains, a 'sense of place' is a complex and multidimensional concept that characterises the relationship between people and places. The term is used widely in several fields, particularly geography and anthropology, where its meaning gravitates towards places that are held affectionately or through attachment rooted in upbringing or cultural associations conjuring impressions that may be positive or negative such as homelands, belonging, *"the land of my forefathers"*, childhood locations, such as holidays, schools or in urban and rural studies around communities, place-making and place-attachment. For my purposes, I think of a 'sense of place' as a feeling or perception associated with a physical location or any 'conceptual builds' I have constructed in my imagination or memory associated with those specific places and their landscapes. Anthropologists Steven Feld and Keith Basso define a 'sense of place' as: *"the experiential and expressive ways places are known, imagined, yearned for, held, remembered, voiced, lived, contested and struggled over [...]"*. When discussing a 'sense of place' throughout *Music, Painting, Language and Me*, it is this definition I refer to.[1]

My 'reading' of landscape, its forms and structures and their relationships to one another; the 'sense of place' I associate with those landscapes; how I interpret my artwork, the artwork of others and more generally, the world about me involves semiotics and hermeneutics. Semiotics, the systematic study of signs and their meaning production and hermeneutics, the study of the interpretation of signs and their meaning, are referred to throughout the book. Semiotics is an enormous subject only touched upon in *Music, Painting, Landscape and Me*. I reference the work of Charles Sanders Peirce, who defined a sign as *"something which stands to somebody as something"*. His significant contribution to semiotics was:

*The categorisation of signs into three main types: (1) an icon, which resembles its referent (such as a road sign for falling rocks); (2) an index, which is associated with its referent (as smoke is a sign of fire); and (3) a symbol, which is related to its referent only by convention (as with words or traffic signals). Peirce also demonstrated that a sign can never have a definite meaning, for the meaning must be continuously qualified. [...] Sign Theory, or Semiotic, is an account of signification, representation, reference and meaning. Although sign theories have a long history, Peirce's accounts are distinctive and innovative for their breadth and complexity and for capturing the importance of interpretation to signification.*[2]

Terms such as icon and referent and 'signifier' and 'signified' ('signifier' meaning any material thing that signifies a tree, house, boat, face, word, feeling, sensation, music notation etc. (Peirce's *"something which stands to somebody"*). 'Signified' is the concept that any 'signifier' refers to (Peirce's *"as something"*) is used frequently to describe the symbolic nature and status or specific aspects of my visual and sonic work, their internal symbolic relationships and the relationship to each other.

Although everything can be meaningful, no sign means everything to everyone. Signs are differentiated from one another. They exhibit differences. If all signs pointed to all possible meanings, signs would have no meaning, as there would be no differentiated meaningfulness to distinguish them. Therefore, it is reasonable to assume there is an upper and lower limit to

---

[1] Feld, Steven and Basso, Keith H., p. 11.
[2] Britannica, The Editors of Encyclopaedia, 'Semiotics' in *Encyclopedia Britannica* (21 May 2020), https://www.britannica.com/science/semiotics [accessed 11 September 2022].

the arbitrary nature of all possible meanings that signs and sign relations can signify, rather than an infinite array of potential meaningfulness, enabling us to bring meaning, signification and organisation to phenomena, thoughts, concepts, words, music and painting. It is that signification which helps confine constructed meaningfulness within a given artefact, so it is not entirely arbitrary or means anything at all despite the significant bandwidth of possibility its signification inhabits for the interpretant. Therefore, although a book may hold multiple and iterative meaningfulness for any reader, the words it contains are not arbitrarily meaningful. Within this understanding, all my references to meaning, meaning construction, interpretation, hermeneutics, authorship, codification and de-codification take place throughout this book.

Related to semiotics, hermeneutics, the study of interpretation, plays a role in many disciplines where meaning, belief, historical documentation, actions and the meaning of human experience as preserved or embedded in the text, the arts and artefacts, generally require interpretive treatment. The *Stanford Encyclopaedia of Philosophy* says that hermeneutics

*Concerns the meaning of interpretation—its basic nature, scope and validity, as well as its place within and implications for human existence; and it treats interpretation in the context of fundamental philosophical questions about being and knowing, language and history, art and aesthetic experience and practical life.*[3]

Additionally, the notion of the hermeneutic circle, as developed by several philosophers, including Hans-Georg Gadamer, underpins much of my hermeneutic activity. The hermeneutic circle is used as a metaphor to explain the process of generating an understanding of a text or artefact through the hermeneutic investigation of each part that builds towards an understanding of the whole work. As understanding unfolds and meaningfulness is established, a new position or insight associated with that content would subsequently inform every other aspect of the work being examined as an iterative recontextualisation of the whole. The process is recursive until such time (if any) as a position of understanding is reached. The process could also continue as a lifelong hermeneutic discovery through interpretation, with each new experience influencing previously established meaningfulness across a spectrum of experience and knowledge. Hermeneutics and the hermeneutic circle are essential in my approach to building significance, meaning, understanding and expertise by interpreting my paintings and compositions.

Hermeneutics drive the iterative contextualisation necessary for completing my work and how I interpret the work of others and the world around me in general. Hermeneutics enables me to construct meaningfulness. I do not happen upon meaning as if it were something lying around waiting to be discovered; I build meaning and become aware of it. Something becomes meaningful when I think of it or say it is meaningful. The act of thinking renders meaning. This meaning-building is not a projection but an immanent hermeneutic consequence of being in and engaging with the world, of receiving and processing information neurologically.

Within painting and music, for example, the meaning I construct from the vast relationships of signs I encounter is not necessarily objective meaningfulness because meaningfulness generated in this way may lack the material descriptive coherence present in the natural sciences

---

[3] Theodore, George, 'Hermeneutics' in *The Stanford Encyclopedia of Philosophy*, Edward N. Zalta ed., (winter 2021) https://plato.stanford.edu/archives/win2021/entries/hermeneutics [accessed 11 September 2022].

associated with phenomena such as weight, density, length, frequency, mass or what have you to establish factual truth. Science can support verifiable, measurable, objective descriptions concerning what something *is* and how it operates. Descriptions generated through engagement with art objects rely primarily on subjectivity and personal perspectives, such as opinions and feelings that may have no internal coherence, cannot be measured and are not independently verifiable. Science deals with establishing facts. Art deals with establishing meaningfulness. It is challenging to have a proper, intrasubjective discussion about meaningfulness or what something *is* when its descriptors share no equivalence from person to person or context to context. The internal coherence of descriptors within the natural sciences enables ideas and concepts to be exchanged, analysed, developed and theorised objectively as fact, independent from opinion and subjectivity.

Concerning the arts and living more generally, my interpretation arises through hermeneutics, engagement, investigation, meaning construction and building an understanding of the phenomena surrounding me. In the broadest sense, the study of such phenomena from the first-person perspective is known as phenomenology, a philosophical position adopted as a primary mode of inquiry concerning the study of the structures of experience and consciousness through the objects of direct, immanent experience. Phenomenology seeks to determine the essential properties of those structures through systematic reflection to situate and explain experience within the objective domain as far as possible. It is the 'science' of phenomena distinct from the nature of being. Different from the seventeenth-century French philosopher René Descartes's approach to understanding the world as a logical place that holds definite and fixed meaning, known as the Cartesian or scientific approach to understanding, phenomenology considers that our experience of the world is not as logical or scientific owing to the role our senses play in interpretation and how interpretation is filtered through our bias, preconceptions, prejudices and social and historical contexts that are together described as the 'lenses' through which we perceive and think. The Cartesian approach considers those emotions and filters as distractions that obscure the true meaning of reality. In contrast, phenomenology attests that meaning can only be conditioned and come into reality through our senses, emotions and consciousness so that both objective (Cartesian) reality and experienced reality are brought together through phenomenology to generate our understanding of the world in such a way that our interpretation is part of what the world means.

Having described and explained definitions and philosophical approaches behind the writing of *Music, Painting, Landscape and Me*, it would be misleading to allude to semiotics, hermeneutics and especially phenomenology as comprising a rigorous methodological approach to answer questions posed in this book. I am indeed using those approaches, often quite loosely, to uncover and reflect upon my 'lived experiences', particularly those situated in subjectivity, often through analysing parts of my experience to gain interpretation and a sense of meaning concerning my entire practice and I undertake those actions in as interrogative and open a manner as possible. In many ways, owing to my cultural situatedness within Western philosophical thinking, my starting point is rooted in logocentrism, an understanding of words and language as a fundamental expression of an external reality.

The term 'logocentric' derives from the Greek term Logos. It encompasses thought, reason and law, with its predispositions towards notions of logic, purity, objectivity, science and fact above its dualities of chaos, contingency, subjectivity and the fluidity of meaningfulness. Despite this predisposition, when engaging in hermeneutics and auto-phenomenology, there are limits to how objective and analytical I can be when observing myself through myself. Therefore, I feel any attempts to systemise this investigation through some empirical measure to record phenomena and my subsequent hermeneutic actions to establish meaningfulness, in other words, to be methodologically rigorous, are thwarted and would only contribute to mainly additional irrelevant text that amounted to a subjective organisation of subjective content (a picture of cats herding cats comes to mind). Nevertheless, I endeavour to describe phenomena and concepts, thoughts and actions as precisely as I can and, similarly, describe the conditions of interpretation I instigate through my actions.

This text, phenomenologically and hermeneutically speaking, sits between analysis and description. As such, what is revealed will not necessarily be sufficiently objective to apply beyond my experience domain. However, this does not mean that the presentation, analysis and discussion brought about by such investigation are not helpful to many others interested in its subject area including the nature of consciousness, communication, interpretation, meaning generation, performance, neuroscience, walking, New Music, painting, landscape, quantum physics and philosophy, or from the perspective of practice researchers and makers of paintings and music compositions with similar or different modalities of operation to my own. To this end, the book is directed towards any reader with interest in its wide-ranging subject areas.

As I use my practice to ask questions and seek solutions, I consider my actions as research. To be more specific, practice research. In his article *Creative Practice as Research: Discourse on Methodology*, Lyle Skains writes that within practice research, "*the creative artefact* [in my case, compositions and paintings and perhaps even this book] *is the basis of the contribution of knowledge*".[4] Practice research is the "*method applied to original investigations seeking new knowledge through practice and its outcomes where claims of originality are demonstrated through the creative artefacts*".[5] In academically situated practice research, creative artefacts are produced alongside a commentary or exegesis exhibiting a critical discussion around any claims, research questions and outcomes and how they address those questions. The artefact and the critical interpretation offer a cohesive, contextualised and fuller understanding of the research undertaken and the artefact itself.[6]

I am undertaking practice research outside an academic framework. I am not presenting the artefacts I produce and their examination as singular contributions to knowledge even though each holds this status. Rather, I'm looking across my entire practice as the contribution to knowledge alongside *Music, Painting, Landscape and Me* as the commentary on that work and the practice necessary to produce it, sometimes critically situated, sometimes subjectively, as an artefact, attempting to answer my questions. Skains again:

*Put simply, in practice-based research the creative act is an experiment (whether or not the work itself is deemed 'experimental') designed to answer a directed research question about art and the practice of it, which could not otherwise be explored by other methods. We create art to connect with others, to connect with ourselves and often just for the sake of it. We experiment with our art in order to push boundaries, to ask questions, to learn more about our art and our role within it. This is nothing new. What emerges, then, from this methodology, is the exegesis that accompanies the creative work: that knowledge that has remained implicitly within the artist, made explicit and*

---

[4] Skains, R. Lyle, pp. 82-97.
[5] Ibid, p. 86.
[6] Ibid, p. 86.

*seated within the context of the scholarly field.*[7]

I consider myself a practice researcher, but first and foremost a visual artist—a painter of abstracted landscapes—and a composer of New Music. In addition, I would self-identify as something of a thinker, a ruminator, a problem solver and an inventor. I am a maker and a builder of sonic and visual structures. I am an appropriator, a self-referential, self-borrowing material generator. This is where my skills lie.

I would be a different artist entirely had I devoted my life to the knowledge acquisition necessary to grasp the implications, context, condition and outcomes of my actions and work as a composer and painter viewed precisely through the natural sciences of physics, biology and chemistry; and the humanities, psychology and social sciences through both subjective and objective viewpoints to answer my questions. Rather than build knowledge in those areas through appropriated learning, I have, from a very early age, been exclusively compelled to learn experientially—autodidactically—through the practical production of work and acquisition of skills necessary to make work, what is colloquially known as 'learning on the job', as a life-long circumstance conducive to getting lost in the act of making art at the expense of asking why and how that art is being made. Only now, at sixty, has the compulsion to investigate and contextualise what I do across the entire range of my artistic practice taken root within the notion of writing a book to 'think aloud' and attempt to work out and answer my questions. It is only now that I want to draw the creative threads of my practice together into a cogent whole.

I appreciate that the results of my research through practice are first and foremost manifested as embodied knowledge expressed in its terms semiotically in the work I produce. I also understand that this embodied knowledge is not necessarily directly commensurate with expression through words and that any attempts on my part to interpret and transduce a sense of meaningfulness in my practice through words risks transforming significance in the process, not least because interpreting the symbolic nature of music and painting in this manner creates another symbolic entity that itself invites a further layer of interpretation that contrary to bringing the intended clarification I seek may only serve to obfuscate it further.

Difficulties around situating any phenomenological self-analytical processes describing and transmitting meaningfulness in the objective realm still need to be solved. I am also mindful that the interpretation of my paintings, music and writing by others will generate a different significance and meaningfulness to my own. Above all else, I appreciate that 'mesearch' offers only one perspective on my actions, outcomes and conclusions. Despite my familiarity with the subject, this perspective may not be the best, most elucidating or contextually situated. At its most self-indulgent, autoethnography can result in auto-hagiographic writing.

Consequently, anything I write will, by its very nature, be biased and somewhat myopic. It should be taken with a healthy pinch of salt. With such challenges and limitations in mind, fixing and transmitting exact meaning from me to the listener, viewer or reader, not to mention the added sonic artefacts players bring to the performance of music through interpretation, remains an unlikely ambition. Considering those factors, the question of why I am writing a book like this is pertinent.

---

[7] Skains, R. Lyle, p. 86.

Ideally, I should be happy to present only my work as a singular statement demonstrating what I think, feel and do, where my compositions and paintings stand on their own two feet to transmit whatever meaningfulness they possess or trigger through interpretation without further intercession on my part. I have been contented with this position for many years. However, as I grow older, I find this position unsatisfying because I wish to communicate about my work in ways that go beyond what the work itself can say through the symbology of paint and sound. I wish to expand this meaningfulness into words. This is why I am writing a book.

Up until now, the questions I pose and the answers I discover in my work find expression through the symbolic forms of music and painting. The significance conveyed or interpreted is presented within those symbolic realms. To communicate within the realm of words, I must transform questions, concepts and responses from the 'languages' of painting and music into word-based forms. This process opens new dimensions of interpretation and expression.

This transformation is a learning experience, allowing for fresh perspectives on my work and providing alternative ways to articulate my thoughts. My motivation in undertaking this task stems from the belief that my questions about my creative practice will resonate with many who engage in artistic pursuits. By using words to convey those thoughts, I aim to offer a valuable alternative to relying solely on my music compositions and paintings as the exclusive sources of information about my practice.

Ultimately, putting my thoughts into writing is an effort to consolidate and satisfy my curiosity regarding why and how I pursue my artistic endeavours. It also seeks to explore whether there is a way to convey the connection I perceive between music, painting, the landscape and myself that extends beyond my personal experience.

I consider the travelling of this path—the journeying—a 'becoming'. In writing this book and embodying thought as word, I gather a lifetime of rumination and observation drawn from external and internal worlds as perceived through the 'I' and filter those phenomena through the lenses of science, philosophy and ontology (the branch of metaphysics dealing with the study of the nature of being) to develop an interpretation of my practice. Consequently, 'mapping' takes place that gradually constructs a more precise concept of my practice as an artist. This is the process I refer to as 'becoming'.

'Becoming' through writing is an act of self-building, of constructing an internality and externality of words that signify the objective aspects of my practice and the subjectivity that drives, defines, articulates and generally makes that practice possible. This book attempts to explain my raison d'être for being a painter and composer as much as it describes aspects of my methodologies and the concepts and phenomena that populate them. In providing this primarily phenomenological description, the book presents the reader with connected and disconnected homogenous, heterogenous and sometimes arbitrarily situated texts that offer an interplay of many mechanisms and networks touching on physics, quantum mechanics, chemistry, biology, philosophy, ontology, metaphysics, psychology, emotion, intellect, behaviour, capacity, gathered experiences, self-awareness, free will, consciousness and of course, the techniques and processes necessary to make the work. The text reflects this complexity and invites the reader to assemble their understanding of my artistic practice as a do-it-yourself interpretive construction.

Although I stopped writing *Music, Painting, Landscape and Me* when I felt I had shared as much of my research and its findings as was known to me, the writing is never truly finished.

With all life journeys, the story continues until the end of life. Like the book, I am a work in progress. Things change. Opinions, concepts and perceptions all change. Claims I make at the outset of writing change through hermeneutics, the writing process and research outcomes. I learn. My position alters, sometimes radically so. I contradict myself through developed understanding. I am experiencing and learning constantly. My world is invented each day anew. This is the 'becoming'. It remains unclear when 'becoming' attains the status of 'the become', not as a condition of transcendence but as the completion of a stage of journeying. As ever, questions beget yet more questions. Words generate more words. Truth and fact, outside the science domain, remain elusive. Meaningfulness is all around, but how much of that meaning is shared? The search continues.

# CHAPTER ONE

## THE LIST

### Origins and Nature

The List is an introduction to *Music Painting Landscape and Me*. It serves as an enormous upbeat to the following chapters, setting the context and territory within which they are situated. It is the outpouring of a noisy brain, full of questions that ask why and how I am an artist. Those questions lead me into various areas ranging from quantum mechanics and neurology to philosophy, metaphysics, hermeneutics, inspiration, spontaneity and serendipity. Commenting on those subjects creates a sprawling entity shaped by a lifetime of thinking. There is repetition, not for its own sake, but because of the inevitable return to loci reached via differing perspectives. Now homogenised into a textually approachable format, it originated as a stream-of-consciousness scrapbook and sketch pad, organised as a collection of thoughts and questions added in a numbered list format, hence its name.

Positioned at the beginning of this book, The List enables me to define terms and frame questions before moving forward into the specific focus of each chapter. For the first time, I lay bare this thought and show the background against which I function as an artist. Whether I can answer those questions in the following chapters remains to be seen. It sets the scene. It does not provide the answers.

While the primacy of objectivity and fact is recognised, The List also values knowledge and learning rooted in embodiment and experience. No singular vision, theory, perception, philosophy or concept is extolled as an all-encompassing truth. It is not trying to be 'right', present a fixed position, or construct a theory. It documents thought processes, insights, possibilities, curiosities and interests, bringing together materials I consider helpful relative to the topics under discussion. Its writing and development expand through intellectual spasms. It is self-reflexive and open. It embodies my thought, its structures and processes as situated within the semiotic realm of words knowing full well the pitfalls around assumptions of how meaningfulness is constructed, transmitted and received within concepts of authorship, intentionality, originality and hermeneutics.

Above all else, The List is my enthusiastic manifesto to maintain an open mind. Its scope ranges from isolated utterances and passing thoughts through to extended paragraphs that occasionally give rise to subjects developed to the scale of an independent chapter, all accommodated within its flow. It will remain a work in progress. Incompletion is its raison d'être. It is potential but not a conclusion. It is open-ended and defines its limits only by its capacity to create new relationships within and outside of its meaningfulness network where the reader may build new hermeneutic plateaus, expanding meaning beyond my original intention or concept. It reflects my process of learning.

Although arboreal in design, The List aspires to the notion of the rhizome as set out in Gilles Deleuze and Félix Guattari's 1987 book, *A Thousand Plateaus: Capitalism and Schizophrenia*, at times exhibiting the potential for simultaneous connectivity to and within any other part of this book.[8] It strives to connect the heterogenous with the homogeneous and embrace flux and

---

[8] Deleuze, Gilles and Guattari, Félix, (1987) pp. 1-25.

instability concerning its meaningfulness. To help or hinder this process, I have incorporated several of my poems into the text as an alternative way to express ideas I find difficult to capture using regular syntax, offering open and closed propositions to reflect the complexities of experience. The poems show my preoccupation with many of the issues highlighted in *Music, Painting, Landscape and Me*, stretching back across decades, some to childhood. The poems use vague language to hint at things, allude to and look indirectly upon issues of time, permanence, flux and a whole gamut of 'lived experiences'.

## The 'Lived Experience', Neuroscience and Ontology

I write predominantly about the work I produce as a physical product and the demonstrable processes I undertake to make work from a phenomenological position and, when not describing a process, frequently from the perspective of the 'lived experience', an orientation that is very real and factual to me but does not qualify as independently verifiable fact.[9] It is essential that I am clear about the terms I use and where fact moves into opinion.

Is there any experience that is not 'lived'? No. All experience is 'lived' and passes through consciousness. I use the term to separate the objective and empirical natural sciences—physics, chemistry and biology and the understanding of life and living from the human sciences—history, philosophy, sociology, psychology and the arts, where those experiences may be considered through phenomenology, reflection and opinion.[10] Within my use of the noun 'experience' and depending upon the (hopefully) clear context in which the word is used within the text, experience, including the term 'lived experience', encompasses:

*A direct observation of or participation in events as a basis of knowledge; the fact or state of having been affected by or gained knowledge through direct observation; a practical knowledge, skill, or practice derived from direct observation of or participation in events or a particular activity; the length of such action; [and of specific significance here] something personally encountered, undergone, or lived through; the conscious events that make up an individual life; the act or process of directly perceiving events or reality.*[11]

My practice involves behaviours, processes and phenomena with objective and subjective components that may be considered through the 'lived experience'. I wish to identify and analyse those components. Within my practice, science describes structures and systems such as nerve impulses, muscular actions, neuroplasticity, biochemical transmission, the relationships between physical bodies and, for example, their forces in classical physics that are essential to know, yet, owing to the phenomena studied, offers little insight into 'being' an artist experientially. As being is an ontological matter, science does not describe it. Nevertheless, with being, awareness and consciousness central to my artistic practice, it is essential to establish, as far as possible, what science, particularly neuroscience, has to say about those conditions. I shall begin, then, with the question, what is consciousness?

According to Anil Seth, Professor of Cognitive and Computational Neuroscience at the University of Sussex, the question of what consciousness is has been side-lined until recent

---

[9] I do not use the term 'lived experience' to indicate any aspect of identity politics.
[10] Within the field of qualitative phenomenological research, 'lived experience' is used to distinguish the human sciences from the natural sciences. Dilthey, Wilhelm p. 61.
[11] 'Experience', in Merriam-Webster.com Dictionary, *Merriam-Webster*, <https://www.merriam-webster.com/dictionary/experience> [Accessed August 2022].

decades. In his 2017 YouTube video lecture, *the Neuroscience of Consciousness* he says: "*A good landmark [of where not acknowledging consciousness ended] is this paper by Francis Crick and Christof Koch, published in 1990 [where] they start their paper by saying that it is remarkable that most of the work in cognitive sciences and the neurosciences, makes no reference to consciousness or awareness at all*".[12]

Seth writes that consciousness, self-awareness and the mind were rarely mentioned in neuroscience research for fear of opening up a metaphysical can of worms or a 'plughole' as he describes it, mainly, I imagine, concerning ontology, the branch of metaphysics that in the first instance deals with the nature of being and secondly, categorises domains to show their properties and the relationships between them.[13] Now, there are research programmes dedicated to exploring consciousness from the neuroscientific perspective, Seth's work among them. However, despite this innovative research focus, mind and consciousness remain largely unexplained. I do not doubt that this position will change in the future. Among those researching consciousness, there is a tendency to use what is already known of the vast and complex mechanisms explaining brain operations to extrapolate a theorem identifying what consciousness and the nature of being are.

Neuroscientists are still determining if current research approaches will lead them to where they want to be in understanding consciousness. Like all research processes, findings and theories must be rigorously tested and peer-reviewed before any meaningful or valuable conclusions that unite an individual's day-to-day experience of self-awareness and consciousness—of being—with neuroscience is found. In addition to the neuroscience perspective of consciousness, there is the unexplained observer effect. The observer effect is a fact in quantum mechanics where observing a situation or phenomenon necessarily changes it. Consciousness's implications and role in this phenomenon are not yet fully understood.

As if to emphasise the disconnection between science, in this case, physics and the production of a valuable explanation for consciousness, an August 2022 article in the *Big Think* titled *Ask Ethan: How Do Fundamental Particles Create Consciousness?* Ethan Siegel, an astrophysicist and science communicator, makes considerable attempts to answer the question posited by a reader. The bulk of the article itself is given over to explaining as much as is possible in non-specialist yet still heavy technical terms, the nature, properties, behaviours and relationships of sub-atomic particles and how together in a great soup of probabilities and governing rules, the complex material of the universe including life itself arose. As something of an anti-climax for me as a reader and after so much 'objective' explanation, a few paragraphs are given over at the end of the article to deliver the answer to the question concerning what consciousness is and how it arose. I quote:

*The emergence of life from non-life certainly occurred, but we're still puzzling out precisely how it occurred on our planet. However, the forces of electromagnetism and gravity, given the conditions that arose naturally and the presence of complex molecules, seem to be all that's required. Similarly, life has survived, thrived and evolved over billions of years, giving rise to the diverse set of organisms that exists today, including us. As far as we can tell, what makes a 'living' alive is simply*

---

[12] Seth, Anil, *the Neuroscience of Consciousness, The Royal Institution,* YouTube video lecture <https://www.youtube.com/watch?v=xRel1JKOEbI&ab_channel=TheRoyalInstitution> [accessed 15 August 2022]. Timepoints 4:25-5:15, referencing Francis Crick and Christof Koch. *Towards a Neurobiological Theory of Consciousness* in *Seminars in the Neurosciences*. Vol. 2. (London: Saunders Scientific Publications, 1990).
[13] Ibid, Timepoints 30:48-30:56.

*the presence of electricity: the flow of electrons. Although there are many with wild ideas about what consciousness is and what its connection to the quantum realm might be, it's possible—perhaps even likely—that simple electricity (i.e., the flow of electrons throughout a brain and nervous system in animals) is enough, given the right external configuration of atoms and molecules, to create the phenomenon we identify as consciousness.*[14]

It is clear from the written qualifications, terms such as *"as far as we can tell"*, *"it's possible"* and *"perhaps even likely"*, that this answer is pure speculation built on and projected from the foundation of theoretically verifiable material knowledge. For a scientist, this is a reasonable assumption and leap of faith when theorising about consciousness. In short, it suggests that consciousness arises entirely from the elements around it, where the whole (consciousness) is greater than the sum of the parts. This is difficult to counter as a proposition and would appear an obvious conclusion to reach considering that such an explanation would apply, in theory at least, to every aspect of our material universe, including our construction, as being constituted of the elements, forces, behaviours and rules governing the known universe. However, the summation of the parts to generate a whole, in this case, consciousness, illustrates a route to consciousness arising rather than an explanation of what consciousness is per se and, indeed, fails to help me understand what consciousness is from a condition of *being* conscious. I also feel that the response should be more clearly framed as guesswork and separated from the extensive preparatory work drawn from particle physics that, in my view, seeks to set up a plausible foundation and expectation to support the likelihood of what follows as the answer to the question posed. Furthermore, I find the statement *"it's possible—perhaps even likely—that simple electricity (i.e., the flow of electrons throughout a brain and nervous system in animals) is enough, given the right external configuration of atoms and molecules, where the ingredients may be known but exactly how they relate and operate with each other to create the phenomenon we identify as consciousness"*, misleading and disappointing as it suggests that electricity in organic tissue alone may in some way correspond to the phenomena of consciousness. I cannot help then thinking if electricity is perhaps itself a precursor to or form of consciousness, somewhat facetiously, that when I switch on a light, a washing machine or my computer, the electricity whizzing through its circuitry is somehow generating a form of consciousness, self-awareness and free-will not so different from my own. I jest, of course, but such fanciful notions of the potential for electricity operating outside of organic tissue to support consciousness have implications for the emergence of self-awareness within cybernetics and artificial intelligence. Thinking of consciousness in terms of *"simple electricity"* in combination with organic nervous matter does not help me to rationalise or comprehend my sense of being conscious in any meaningful way, nor does it provide me with a frame of reference I can use to understand and articulate consciousness away from any subjective inclinations I hold about the matter. I am made of the stuff of the universe. Yes indeed. But I had worked that out already. All else remains speculative.

Despite the efforts of neuroscience and science in general to explain life, consciousness and awareness, there are, perhaps unsurprisingly, no terms or concepts that sufficiently explain the nature of being outside those provided by an ontology. I use ontological terms to describe *my* nature of being in this book. Using this language does not demonstrate my wholesale belief in all ontological concepts or metaphysics widely. Nevertheless, I keep an open mind knowing that answers to the why and wherefore of my artistic practice and 'lived experience' does not

---

[14] Siegel, Ethan, *Ask Ethan: How Do Fundamental Particles Create* Consciousness [accessed 11 August 2022].

sit comfortably in the scientific realm, being difficult to reconcile as fact pragmatically. This is why my writing will incorporate subjectivity and expressions of self-awareness, but also because, as previously mentioned, as an artist and like everyone else, the phenomena I experience cannot be removed or separated from the mechanisms through which I experience and comprehend them. It is challenging in the extreme to separate my 'lived experiences' into what is objective and subjective phenomenologically. This difficulty makes objectively verifying my ontological condition impossible, particularly considering the knowledge and resources I possess as an artist. I cannot wire myself up for investigation and collect and analyse my data within the perfect theoretical framework. This is not my modus operandi.

My research takes place through making music and paintings, hermeneutically reading paintings as music and music as paintings and, in many ways, reading my artwork and music as landscapes in the way I read and engage with physical landscapes. It also operates through walking as an act of composition in both aural and visual capacities within physical landscapes and through thinking and writing about those processes. In short, it takes place through the experience and activities I generate and the numerous incommensurate semiotic systems I have devised or assimilated to express thought through action as embodiment. This is how I establish meaning. It arises from the act of interpretation. The knowledge I absorb as a research activity, like the music and paintings I make and other practices I list above, is filtered through my perceptive, cognitive, intellectual, biological and emotional filters. Those filters disbar any concept of absolute objectivity and make all cognition ultimately a subjective activity when writing about myself from the position of myself. Even theorising or analysing data, including reading the work of others, is undertaken through those filters. I assume that, like many, I interpret what I want from what I read as my bias filters and privileges information that confirms my position. Within this environment of comprehension and despite a lifetime of research through making, observing, learning and thinking, I have not yet come close to answering many questions about the mechanics of being an artist and why I do what I do; about embodiment, affect, 'sense of place' and the transmission of those conditions across media and from person to person. Some areas now have clarity. Many others remain opaque. What is clear is that much of what I think and write falls between science and ontology as two expressions of reality. But science isn't as unshakable in its factual basis as one might initially believe.

## Science: Truth and Objectivity

Knowing the difference between fact and fiction and opinion and science is not essential to being an artist or making art. However, understanding aspects of science is important to master some practical elements of craft and in more neurological, biochemical, behavioural and experiential terms if you wish to comprehend what you are doing on multiple levels and discuss how art is made in interpersonal terms. In those circumstances, I need scientific understanding to help differentiate what I know from what I don't know.

From my perspective, my artistic practice looks like a vast puzzle, its pieces scattered on a table. A few have found their place. A tiny part of the picture is clear—science has contributed a number of those areas of clarity as has a basic understanding of semiotics and hermeneutics— but much of the picture is absent from view and many of the parts are scattered here and there. Some are lost. I think of this incomplete puzzle as a void, as what I call 'the missing middle'. Concepts of absolute immutable certainty in science are not accepted among all scientists, with some noted individuals disputing notions of scientific proof and fact as even being possible beyond the framework and confines of their investigative and theoretical constructs. Perhaps this is partly because each level of understanding and knowledge and the analysis of observations and data filtered through new theoretical models opens a vista onto the subsequent development that, in turn, has the potential to destabilise the former. Science and its internal speculations, propositions and constantly adaptive theories do not offer me enough certitude to extrapolate its contribution to filling 'the missing middle'. Nature abhors a vacuum. With no content, I fill the void with my subjectivity.

Although valuable to me, many of the phenomena I discuss here, including subjective matter, the 'lived experience', consciousness and being, are categorically different from the type of phenomena science examines to establish agreed facts and meaning. The phenomena science examines are termed intersubjective objects. In his 1992 article, *The Logic of Scientific Discovery*, João Paulo Maia writes:

*One result of this view is that specialists in the philosophy of science stress the requirement that observations made for the purposes of science be restricted to intersubjective objects. That is, science is restricted to those areas where there is general agreement on the nature of the observations involved. It is comparatively easy to agree on observations of physical phenomena, harder to agree on observations of social or mental phenomena and difficult in the extreme to reach agreement on matters of theology or ethics (and thus the latter remain outside the normal purview of science).*[15]

But as the collapse in positivism demonstrated, even scientists became aware that their work was framed by the limits and perceptions of their knowledge and imaginations and the lenses associated with them. Dr Asad Zaman, writing an opinion piece called *The Rise and Fall of Logical Positivism* in an October 2015 edition of the *Express Tribune* tells me:

*Among philosophers, positivism had a spectacular crash. Many of the central ideas of positivism proved to be indefensible on closer examination. Even the fundamental concept of factual and objectively verifiable could not be sensibly defined. For example, my feeling of happiness is observable to me and as factual as the sun shining in the sky, but it is not observable and hence subjective to others. Even the lifelong advocate, Ayer, came to realise that positivism was wrong and said so in a public interview.*[16]

For example, the influential philosopher of science, Thomas Kuhn, denied that it is possible to isolate the hypothesis being tested from the influence of the theory in which the observations are grounded. He argued that observations always rely on a specific paradigm and that it is impossible to evaluate competing paradigms independently. By "*paradigm*", he meant a consistent "*portrait*" of the world, one that involves no logical contradictions and is consistent with observations made from the point of view of the paradigm. More than one logically consistent construct can paint a usable likeness of the world, but there is no common ground to pit two against each other, theory against theory. Neither is there a standard by which the other can be judged. Instead, the question is, which portrait is considered by some to promise the most useable and consistent outcomes in terms of scientific "*puzzle-solving*".[17]

With so much unknown and still unproven scientifically, it is difficult not to wonder where speculation and scientific fact are situated and which is which. There are questions at the very heart of science concerning the validity of scientific truth and how concepts of scientific truth

---

[15] Maia, João Paulo, p. 12. [accessed 12 August 2022].
[16] Zaman, Asad, [accessed July 2022].
[17] Bird, Alexander, [accessed 2 August 2022].

and proof are commonly understood. In a 2017 article *Scientific Proof is a Myth*, published online in *Forbes Magazine*, the PhD astrophysicist, author and science communicator Ethan Siegel explains:

*You've heard of our greatest scientific theories: the theory of evolution, the Big Bang theory, the theory of gravity. You've also heard of the concept of a proof and the claims that certain pieces of evidence prove the validities of these theories. Fossils, genetic inheritance and DNA prove the theory of evolution. The Hubble expansion of the Universe, the evolution of stars, galaxies and heavy elements and the existence of the cosmic microwave background prove the Big Bang theory. And falling objects, GPS clocks, planetary motion and the deflection of starlight prove the theory of gravity. Except that's a complete lie. While they provide very strong evidence for those theories, they aren't proof. In fact, when it comes to science, proving anything is an impossibility.*[18]

In this article, Siegel goes into detail and presents numerous examples to present his case. My primary takeaways can be summarised as follows: We can't observe or measure everything. Even if the Universe weren't subject to the fundamental quantum rules that govern it, along with all its inherent uncertainty, it wouldn't be possible to measure every state of every particle under every condition all the time. At some point, we must extrapolate. This is incredibly powerful and useful, but it's also very limiting. Siegel explains:

*Our best theories, like the aforementioned theory of evolution, the Big Bang theory and Einstein's General Relativity, cover all of these bases. They have an underlying quantitative framework, enabling us to predict what will happen under a variety of situations and then go out and test those predictions empirically. So far, these theories have demonstrated themselves to be eminently valid. Where their predictions can be described by mathematical expressions, we can tell not only what should happen, but by how much. For these theories in particular, among many others, measurements and observations that have been performed to test these theories have been supremely successful. But as validating as that is—and as powerful as it is to falsify alternatives—it's completely impossible to prove anything in science […]. Even in theoretical physics, the most mathematical of all the sciences, our 'proofs' aren't on entirely solid ground. If the assumptions we make about the underlying physical theory (or its mathematical structure) no longer apply—if we step outside the theory's range of validity—we'll 'prove' something that turns out not to be true. If someone tells you a scientific theory has been proven, you should ask what they mean by that. Normally, they mean 'they've convinced themselves that this thing is true,' or they have overwhelming evidence that a specific idea is valid over a specific range. But nothing in science can ever truly be proven. It's always subject to revision. This doesn't mean it's impossible to know anything at all. To the contrary, in many ways, scientific knowledge is the most 'real' knowledge that we can possibly gain about the world. But in science, nothing is ever proven beyond a shadow of a doubt.*[19]

With the possibility of nothing being beyond doubt in science, I feel compelled to question the validity of what I have considered fact, truth and meaning as reliable, stable concepts. I am living in the postmodern and post-truth era. I am told by some that truth and meaning are dead and experts unreliable. I am, most likely, thinking as a postmodernist, situated at some point in that broad church of approaches between the endless growth and entanglements of Deleuzian 'becoming' and Derrida's deconstructionist, nihilistic post-truth scepticism, where truth and absolute value cannot be known. Everything, it seems, must be questioned.

---

[18] Siegel, Ethan, *Scientific Proof is a Myth* (2017) [accessed 8 August 2022].
[19] Ibid.

Against this background, my immanent experiences, embodied knowledge, analysis of my actions, the material reality of my work and the subjectivity through which all those conditions are considered, I cannot categorically state that *Music, Painting, Landscape and Me* is a work of fact. From the positivist perspective, this book is a work of fiction. And I agree, much of what I write sits outside of science fact. This fiction is not a purposeful invention, a mirage, an imagining or a conceit. Its intention is not to lie or create falsehood masquerading as truth; it is fiction owing to the unverifiable nature of much of its content. What I write is 'my' truth but not 'the' truth. Because of this, I consider the recognition and relationship between aspects of the many dualities I encounter; the assumed known and unknown; the self and others; physical objects and sensation, for example, all necessary to be open to the potential of the entire understanding of myself, the world around me and my operation and practice as an artist and composer ideally moving through and between them seamlessly. It is about bridging the gap between the relationship of interiority and exteriority, at the very least.

## Metaphysics and More

Metaphysics and ontology, in one form or another, will inevitably be part of the mix and reflect in the book's character to some degree. I cannot eradicate this science/metaphysics duality to constantly come down on one side in favour of the other without independent consideration solely because of the categorisation of the phenomena, condition, sensation or experience. I don't have the answers or an omniscient perspective to judge. I can, however, access the thought of others and trust in their learning. Though I would like to think that the choices around the knowledge I embrace is informed through reason, I suspect decisions, rationalised and selected through my lenses, will be subjective.

It is worthwhile defining metaphysics to understand a concept referred to throughout this book in various capacities. Many definitions for metaphysics are available and most define them in broadly similar terms but using different language. I found the definition from PBS, The Public Broadcasting Service, an American public broadcaster and non-commercial, free-to-air television network, an excellent overview and introduction to the subject. This definition taken from their glossary of terms explains that:

*Metaphysics is a type of philosophy or study that uses broad concepts to help define reality and our understanding of it. Metaphysical studies generally seek to explain inherent or universal elements of reality which are not easily discovered or experienced in our everyday life. As such, it is concerned with explaining the features of reality that exist beyond the physical world and our immediate senses. Metaphysics, therefore, uses logic based on the meaning of human terms, rather than on a logic tied to human sense perception of the objective world. Metaphysics might include the study of the nature of the human mind, the definition and meaning of existence, or the nature of space, time and/or causality.*

*The origin of philosophy, beginning with the Pre-Socratics, was metaphysical in nature. For example, the philosopher Plotinus held that the reason in the world and in the rational human mind is only a reflection of a more universal and perfect reality beyond our limited human reason. He termed this ordering power in the universe 'God'.*

*Metaphysical ideas, because they are not based on direct experience with material reality, are often in conflict with the modern sciences. Beginning with the Enlightenment and the Scientific Revolution, experiments with and observations of, the world became the yardsticks for measuring truth and reality. Therefore, our contemporary valuation of scientific knowledge over other forms of knowledge helps explain the controversy and [scepticism] concerning metaphysical claims, which are considered unverifiable by modern science.*

*Recently, however, even as metaphysics has come under attack for its apparent lack of access to real knowledge, so has science begun to have its own difficulties in claiming absolute knowledge [...]. For example, since the act of scientific observation itself tends to produce the reality it hopes to explain, the so-called 'truths' of science cannot be considered as final or objective [...]. What becomes apparent, therefore, is that the process of human interpretation in the sciences, as elsewhere, is both variable and relative to the observer's viewpoint.*[20]

In some contexts, metaphysics can be viewed as pre-science as a way of conceptualising the universe and our place within it before science has a handle on the actual nuts and bolts. I am reminded that around 400 BC, the Greek philosopher Democritus developed the term 'atom', meaning indivisible, to describe the tiniest particles of matter the Greeks considered possible. This thinking was born out of metaphysics. It wasn't until the scientist John Dalton adopted the term again in the 1800s that the notion of the atom became part of the first modern atomic model. Where science illuminates, metaphysics passes into the shadows.

Also relevant to my use of metaphysics is a definition put forward by the French philosopher Jacques Derrida, one of the prominent figures associated with poststructuralism and postmodern philosophy. Derrida is best known for deconstructionism, a philosophical approach developed through close readings of the linguistics of Ferdinand de Saussure and Husserlian and Heideggerian phenomenology that, among other insights, attests that concepts and meanings associated with linguistic signs (words) are arbitrarily related to reality and categorise and group phenomena and experience in ways neither natural, necessary nor in principle, exactly duplicated from language to language. Derrida explains that meanings can only be understood correctly concerning the differences and contrast of the associated meanings of other words. Consequently, for Derrida, meaning and meaningfulness are derived through an infinite and indefinite play of differences between words and not in relation to an a priori idea or fixed intention existing beyond language, acting as the immutable, self-sufficient transcendental meaning or centre of words, meanings or concepts that invests them with absolute authority beyond all question. Before writing about Derrida's use of the term metaphysics, it is helpful to contextualise his work further concerning structuralism, a philosophy and approach that emerged from linguistic studies in the middle of the Twentieth Century. It investigates the fundamental patterns of social activity through its concern with relationships rather than individual things. Alternatively, it defines objects by the relationships they are a part of rather than by their attributes when viewed separately.

In broad terms and about the arts, structuralism urges consideration of all forms of culture, such as literature, poetry, film, theatre, the visual arts and music, as cultural texts situated within a type of language system. Drawn from the work of de Saussure, those cultural texts are methodically analysed with one another and broader cultural activity to find corresponding patterns and meaningfulness. Structuralism understands phenomena using language as a metaphor. Using 'logocentric' principles, language is a self-referential system defining itself in terms of itself and where words explain other words to produce meaning as a set of structures. It challenges us to think about how a specific piece of art and its narratives and genres derive meaning in its terms and how much it depends on tropes and conventions found in a larger

---

[20] 'Metaphysical' in 'Glossary Index', *The Public Broadcasting Service* (PBS) website:
<https://www.pbs.org/faithandreason/gengloss/metaph-body.html> [accessed 10 August 2022].

'language' of human culture. This approach contextualises meaning by analysing and identifying similar or different norms and tropes to highlight meta-narratives and overarching structures.

However, postmodernism encourages us to consider that narrative texts and genres, as human constructions tied to language development, use and understanding, may be prone to flaws and biases similarly embedded in language, communication and thought. In 1966, Derrida made a ground-breaking contribution to literary theory with his paper titled *Structure, Sign and Play in the Discourse of the Human Sciences*, presented at a structuralism conference at John Hopkins University in Baltimore.[21]

Derrida's work proposed a complete deconstruction of the structuralist theory. It explores how the concept of structure is deeply entrenched in everyday language and has formed the foundation of Western civilisation, ranging from, for example, metaphysics to epistemological thinking and where this concept is identified through the belief that all structures have had a fixed origin or centre crucial to their legitimacy and validity. However, Derrida highlights the fallacy of blindly adhering to structures by demonstrating that they are not a concrete, all-encompassing force of knowledge but rather a series of substitutions and determinations of the centre. In essence, structures are not transcendental but are constituted by a linked chain of centre replacements.

As mentioned, logocentrism is a philosophical school of thought in the Western world that relies on fixed, transcendental meanings of words and signs. However, according to Derrida, a centre cannot be considered a universal truth within a system and is susceptible to changes. Derrida attests that centres operate within and outside the structure, making the 'logocentric' viewpoint arbitrary. The idea that words are standalone metaphysical entities is flawed since they vary based on the specific language and context in which they are used in speech by individuals. Derrida's theory of 'différance' emphasises the perpetual supplementary nature of signs and centres, highlighting the difference and deference of signs within a language. The 'signified' object is not fixed and the semiotic relationship between the sign and the 'signifier' is coincidental. Rather than serving as an independent entity, words are part of a larger system that is constantly evolving.

In Derrida's deconstruction of logocentrism, the concept of the transcendental 'signified' as an external point of reference that is the origin of origin is crucial when considering the infinite referentiality of the centre. This signifies a sign that is a source of ultimate signification and does not derive meaning from any other sign, much like the a priori truths of philosophical logocentrism. However, Derrida argues that positioning words or signs as the centre of a system is inherently flawed. A 'signifier' has no universal truth; its meaning is solely based on the user or context's perceived meaning of the signs.

Consequently, poststructuralism urges us to consider if language might fail us and convey something wholly different from what we had in mind. The underlying suspicion that we are not fully in control of the linguistic system, that it is imperfect, illustrated by expressions such as *"if you see what I mean"* or *"in a manner of speaking"*, remains a central concern of poststructuralism. Those concerns encompass communication and meaning transmission and generation from an author, through artwork or text, to a receiver across all cultural texts, including music and painting. Furthermore, owing to those inherent biases and flaws,

---

[21] Derrida, Jacques, 1978.

poststructuralism emphasises the uncertainty of knowledge, particularly knowledge situated in and expressed through language and posits that 'truth' is not a fixed concept, but a perspective based on cultural, political, social and economic situatedness. The *Stanford Encyclopaedia of Philosophy* explains that:

*Although Postmodernism is indescribable, it can be characterised as 'a set of critical, strategic and rhetorical practices employing concepts such as difference, repetition, the trace, the simulacrum and hyperreality to destabilize other concepts such as presence, identity, historical progress, epistemic certainty and the univocity of meaning.*[22]

Within culture and society generally, poststructuralism encourages us to move away from 'logocentric' notions of definitive meaning and meta-narratives to explore the multiple meanings that, for example, in the arts, in a book, film, painting or musical composition or its notation as another form of cultural text, might invite. Roland Barthes' 1967 article *The Death of the Author*, discussed later in The List, critiques earlier scholars' concerns with analysing cultural texts with the aim of determining meaning based solely on the assumed perspective of what an author meant the work to signify.[23] It asks if, with language being an imperfect, flawed and biased means of communication, it is even feasible to comprehend a work authentically to what the author intended. Searching for this authored authenticity will involve reading 'between the lines' or in music, reading beyond what is 'signified' in notation to discern the author's intentions. This action inevitably entails a range of assumptions concerning intentionality but also dismisses and confines the text's many inherent, rich and profound interpretive possibilities. This interpretive limitation results in poststructuralism's disinterest in an author's original and intended meaning, amplified by the conclusion that it is doubtful that any cultural text has an objective or final meaning because it could be interpreted in many ways. Consequently, poststructuralism is frequently accused of failing to give the author of the text sufficient priority, bypassing what might have been their preoccupations, intentions, beliefs, experiences and contexts for writing to elevate the reader's interpretations to the status of what the text means.

To celebrate the richness of the text itself without necessary reference to knowledge concerning the intentionality of the author, Derrida wrote in his 1967 book *De la Grammatologie*, "*il n'y a pas de hors-texte*", which roughly translates as "*there is nothing outside the text*" or "*there is no outside text*".[24] Scholarly debate around the exact meaning of this phrase continues. Still, it is generally held to mean that the text in front of us encompasses everything, in which case we should consider all potential circumstances that might impact the interpretation of it.

Derrida was intrigued by the idea that a text's meaning can depend as much on what is missing from it as on what is included. This realisation informed Derrida's definition of metaphysics regarding language and cultural texts. In his 1988 book *Limited Inc*, Derrida puts forward a definition of metaphysics that says:

*The enterprise of returning 'strategically', 'ideally', to an origin or to a priority thought to be simple, intact, normal, pure, standard, self-identical, in order then to think in terms of derivation, complication, deterioration, accident, etc. All metaphysicians, from Plato to Rousseau, Descartes to Husserl, have proceeded in this way, conceiving good to be before evil, the positive before the*

---

[22] Aylesworth, Gary, [accessed 11 Sept. 2022].
[23] Barthes, Roland.
[24] Derrida, Jacques, 1967.

*negative, the pure before the impure, the simple before the complex, the essential before the accidental, the imitated before the imitation, etc. And this is not just one metaphysical gesture among others, it is the metaphysical exigency, that which has been the most constant, most profound and most potent.*[25]

This thinking is part of what informs Derrida's concept of deconstruction. Derrida points out that through logocentrism, Western thinking and its language are built around metaphysical hierarchies that privilege notions of purity and presence, that which is and is apparent, at the expense of complexity and contingency that are themselves considered to be atypical and aberrant and therefore able to be side-lined and subordinated into dualisms and oppositions. Derrida identifies the aberrant and atypical within this dualistic hierarchy as the biases often hiding in plain sight within languages. This privileging has ignored the essential differences between things that make presence possible. Crucially, it ignores the role of absence. For example, the concept of good is not viable without an idea of evil, order without chaos and sound without silence, where those oppositions are mutually dependent for their significance and where it is impossible to think of one without knowledge of or a concept (perhaps hidden in the background) of the other. What is thought, written and spoken depends upon a network of supporting meanings, oppositions and contexts; of things absent from the text that are of equal importance, bringing meaning and significance to what is present. Any attempt to subordinate those absences through various hierarchical dualities results in a metaphysics of presence, as Derrida describes it. This thinking is significant because society uses language as the medium to reach consensus concerning what reason, truth and scholarship are—poststructuralism questions whether such concepts can ever be objectively decided upon.

Using its three key features, the illusion that a word has its origin in the structure of reality and that, in so doing, makes that word's 'truth' present to the mind, known as logocentrism; the reduction of meaning to set definitions that are expressed as writing (referring to Derrida's phrase fragment, there is nothing outside of the text) and as discussed, how the reduction of meaning to writing embeds within it oppositions and binaries that comprise concepts (mind and body, nature and culture, speech and writing, male and female, inside and outside, presence and absence, for example, known as 'différance', Derrida's concept of deconstruction enables an ongoing process of questioning the accepted basis of meaning through a close reading of texts. This reading demonstrates that any text comprises irreconcilably contradictory meanings rather than a unified, logical whole.

Over and above metaphysics, the metaphysics of presence and questioning received knowledge and fact through a post-structuralist lens, much of my understanding of the universe remains 'logocentric' and built upon my trust in the learning and science of others who have dedicated their lives to such matters. Nevertheless, some areas of scientific thought are frequently challenged or supplemented by new theories, not least in neuroscience and quantum mechanics. Exciting times indeed. Keeping pace is challenging. Time and trial determine the most relevant research and theories but building any house of fact upon the shifting sands of knowledge require degrees of trust in a stable foundation I do not possess. I work with what I know and what I have—my collection of today's facts—some of those, like old friends, have been with me for some time and like my expectations around the truth of how gravity, friction, tension and magnetism work from my day-to-day operational perspective as a human, are unlikely to alter radically. Still, I leave the door of possibility and change open to replace today's and yesterday's facts with tomorrow's as necessary. Facts are, I believe, ultimately time-sensitive.

---

[25] Derrida, Jaques, 1988, p. 93.

As science constantly questions itself, it can self-regulate and develop, sometimes through epoch-defining spasms.

Even with this illumination, sometimes, I cannot find any useful or convincing answers to my questions in either science or metaphysics. In those situations, my questions are placed in a 'don't know' box where I wait for clarification. Those are my 'missing middle', my unanswered questions (no musical pun intended). They exist in a state of flux between various possibilities, some known and many unknown, often in partial truth.

## Fuzzy Logic

'Fuzzy Logic' is connected to conditions outside simple black or white or true or false dualities. It is a mathematical system for analysing phenomena that exist in a state of flux—a partial truth—between various possibilities and positions. Could 'Fuzzy Logic' be useful as a tool or method to manage the analysis and description of objective and subjective phenomena in a mathematically orientated way? What, then, is 'Fuzzy Logic?' According to Daniel Johnson, an AI and Robotics professional:

*Fuzzy Logic is defined as a many-valued logic form which may have truth values of variables in any real number between 0 and 1. It is the handle concept of partial truth. In real life, we may come across a situation where we can't decide whether the statement is true or false. At that time, fuzzy logic offers very valuable flexibility for reasoning. Fuzzy logic algorithm helps to solve a problem after considering all available data. Then it takes the best possible decision for the given the input.*

*Characteristics of fuzzy logic include: a flexible and easy-to-implement machine learning technique; processes that help mimic the logic of human thought; the generation of logic that may have two values which represent two possible solutions; and is a highly suitable method for uncertain or approximate reasoning; for example. Although, the concept of fuzzy logic had been studied since the 1920s.*[26]

*The term Fuzzy Logic was first used in 1965 by Lotfi Zadeh, a professor at UC Berkeley in California. He observed that conventional computer logic could not manipulate data representing subjective or unclear human ideas. The fuzzy algorithm has been applied to various fields, from control theory to AI. It was designed to allow the computer to determine the distinctions among data which is neither true nor false. Something like the process of human reasoning. Like Little dark, Some brightness, etc.*[27]

All my work could be considered in terms of a little dark and some brightness along a spectrum ranging from total dark to total brightness alongside multiple other descriptors and values between 0 and 1. For example, when writing about my practice, I start with what can be identified as known values. This approach situates its subjective materials between three phenomena. The first and last are predominantly material and physical if one excepts the reality of an exterior world. They are: 1) the landscape and 3) the artefact. Sandwiched between them is 2) a combination of subjective and objective components I describe as me, the artist and the processes I use to conceive of and physically make work. Those phenomena range from fuzzy

---

[26] Johnson, Daniel, *Fuzzy Logic Tutorial: What is, Architecture, Application, Example* from the website *Guru99* <https://www.guru99.com/what-is-fuzzy-logic.html#1> [accessed 30 July 2022].
[27] Ibid.

to crisp. The processes of making also fall mainly into three associated stages: 1) experience and absorption of the landscape; 2) the serendipitous and consolidating process of making undertaken to produce actions embodied in the work; and 3) through those actions, creating a referent association, emotion or affect that triggers a sense of that landscape and a 'sense of place' through the artefact. Those process stages can be broken down into discreet subsets of activity where action and outcome may be crisp or fuzzy.

The notion of truth values pervades my landscape experiences and, as such, will influence my writing about those experiences and how they manifest in my work. I will consider those implications later in The List. Despite the wide variety of truth values, one constant statement in my practice is that I make things that remind me of places. This assertion is the binding glue between any relationships I describe concerning music, painting, landscape and me. Because of this, sound and vision feel interrelated and correlated as sound induces visual interpretation and visual stimuli produce interpretation through sound. But how can I verify if this assertion is factual? To do this, I need to examine what happens when I make work and what is communicated between and through what I make to others.

## Interpretation, Objectivity, Meaningfulness and the Artist's Statement

*to comprehend*
*is to see the surface*
*to intuit*
*is to live the paradox*
*that drives existence to its beginning*[28]

We are all hermeneutic islands building our kingdoms of meaning. Where is the overlap between us?

That communication and transmission of ideas exist seems obvious. We speak, write, listen, instruct, build and work together as individuals and in society. But exactly how much we understand communication as a precise, shared delivery of information and how much of our comprehension is based on assumption and guesswork, evidenced by our continual need to test our understanding of what has been communicated through further communication and verification, remains to be seen.

When audiences engage with artforms that utilise written or spoken language, there can be a general agreement about what is being transmitted concerning meaning more widely. Certainly, a book, for example, is seldom considered to mean anything whatsoever. Although meaning is flexibly interpreted, it is often iterative and related to a broader context of meaningfulness that though not specific, is not arbitrary. But what about non-word-based transmission as in painting, music, dance or sculpture; is meaning construction here an interpretive free for all?

Does it matter? Is the artist's inability to transmit what they consider to be the imbued and assumed qualities of an artefact, including meaningfulness, a 'sense of place' and notions of specific affective properties as a fixed condition, detrimental to its value as art? Many things, not least meaningfulness, feel like they are in motion. Everything feels in flux. All my actions, thoughts, internal and external and everything I make and experience is adaptive to this flux. Everything, it seems, is transforming and 'becoming'. This is not transcendence. It is not a

---

[28] Yeats, Marc, 14 Poems (12th November 2005). Forthcoming publication on Vision Edition.

metaphysical concept. It is movement. It is forward motion. It is a perpetual unfolding. I find those processes and meaning construction challenging to articulate pragmatically using words. For this reason, I choose to express such thoughts and feelings through non-word-based language-type systems such as music composition and painting. Whatever is or is not irreducible to words, everything is reducible to hermeneutics.

Figure 1. *Chalk Downland near Winchester.* Pencil drawing. Marc Yeats (2015).

To this end, I interpret everything. So, when, for example, I ask myself, "*What am I doing here?*" or "*What does this or that colour convey in a painting?*", I answer: "*Almost anything*" or, more accurately, "*Whatever I think it means at the time I think it*". Colours, as with sounds and all components of any artwork in their multiplicity of relationships and temporal contexts, elicit extremely complex sensations, realisations, significance and meaning in and of themselves. If I attempt to describe those meanings or emotions using words, I multiply the richness of possible meaningfulness beyond that of the artefact. Description generates new states of interpretation owing to the array of possible definitions those words singularly and in combination generate. But even this interpretive reading is not fixed. The same artwork may trigger a differently orientated series of responses, emotions and meaningfulness on another occasion leading to very different experiences and word-based descriptions. Interpretation is always in motion. It cannot be fixed. It remains in a powerfully affective flux within the hermeneutic matrix of each of us, its parameters governed by the morphing filters through which perception operates, influenced by the individual's ever-changing contextual, psychological and emotional interiority.

As an artist, I send messages that are lost in translation. However, despite fluctuating meaningfulness and the various transmission means, those messages remain messages even though my intended significance is adapted or overwritten by and to suit the receiver because of their interpretation. This is what our neural setup—our programming—does; it interprets the world around us to create meaning and reality through a continual hermeneutic act. That we communicate through any degree of shared meaningfulness is a miracle, considering the scope of possible variables.

Figure 2. *Adam's Grave No. 1*. Digital print. Marc Yeats (2022).

As a case in point, that transmission has occurred when a musician interprets one of my drawings, for example, Figure 1, is obvious enough as they have produced a new artefact in sound stimulated by what is embodied and 'signified' as meaningfulness in the drawing. But give that drawing to two musicians and you shall hear two different pieces. Both have transmitted their interpretation as a sonic fact. Both interpretations are built around and transmit different meaningfulness even though what is materially 'signified' in the drawing— its surface, lines, structures and textures—are objectively identical.

An examination, for example, of Figure 2, that can equally be read and performed as a musical score will show what is physically embedded in the surface of the painting. Apart from any meaningfulness associated with the marks, structures and colours seen here, what is embodied as material fact is the artist's intentionality to place this colour here or that line there, for instance. Those observable and objective aspects of intentionality are also aspects of embodied knowledge, not least owing to the self-evident and apparent understanding of technique manifest in the painting through the artist's actions.

From the viewer's perspective, transmission from artist to artwork has occurred as an artwork has been materially produced. Transmission has also occurred from the artist, via the artwork, to the viewer through what is embodied. What is embodied—its meaningfulness—comprises observable material facts as the objective component of the transmission but also where those objective components trigger emotional responses as part of the viewer's immanent and subjective experience. Nevertheless, the exact nature of that transmission cannot be pragmatically analysed. Similarly, meaningfulness is self-evident owing to the production of work and what has been 'signified'. There can be no signification without meaningfulness. The hermeneutic act renders the relationship 'real' and meaningful because the artefact has been interpreted—mediated by the viewer, listener or performer and brought into self-evident material existence.

Synaesthesia poses interesting questions concerning interpretation, embodiment and transmission. The afferent/efferent couplings within more-or-less fixed neurological relationships between sound, colour, texture, taste and smell among synaesthetes who paint, compose or both paint and compose, though more stable than within the general population remain particular to them.[29] Also, synaesthetes are all wired in different ways. Because of this, the meaning and significance of the relationships between afferent and efferent stimuli each experience, though meaningful to the individual, remain personal, with the challenges of transmitting that meaningfulness through what is embodied or symbolised in their artistic work just as challenging as it is for non-synaesthetes. I have often wondered if synaesthesia is a sensory enhancement, evolutionary advancement or sensory aberration. Is it significant beyond those with synaesthesia, showing how the brain could or should function ideally? Is it a perceptual limitation? Does it prevent the free association of ideas, materials and sensations owing to the pre-formatted nature of such relationships so crucial to the creative process?

Synaesthete or not, the transmission of fixed meaning through symbolic embodiment does remain the Holy Grail of many artists regardless of the impossibility of realising this goal. Despite its impossibility, I sometimes find it hard to let go of such ambition as I reach out and communicate with others. It is impossible to transmit specific, high-resolution meaningfulness within abstract painting and music, with only the broadest, most course categorisation of meaning transmission achievable. What I describe as course meaning transmission will likely operate where a work's symbolic component is iconic or referential and situated within a familiar cultural framework shared between maker and receiver or composer, performer and listener. Interpretation will be entirely open outside of those potential frameworks and conventions of meaningfulness.

I am not a synaesthete. As far as I know, the correlation between my afferent and efferent neurological activity is not fixed. This implies that any correlations I may detect will be transitory. Or perhaps not. Perhaps those correlations are more embedded through a lifetime of practice and recurring behaviours than I realise. This book examines those possible correlates, for example, as they manifest and transmit in my practice as a painter and composer. Unfortunately, autoethnography as a method of investigation is flawed. As the maker, listener and viewer, any objective assessment of what is transmitted is redundant as I already know what intentionality and meaningfulness are involved. That I recognise such transmission in my work is unsurprising. I constantly take a position on the effectiveness of my actions as I develop compositions and paintings towards completion as a recursive and assimilative process. Those

---

[29] Afferent and efferent signals are two fundamental types of information flow in the nervous system. Afferent or sensory signals travel from peripheral receptors towards the central nervous system (CNS), conveying information about external stimuli or internal conditions. On the other hand, efferent signals, or motor signals, travel from the CNS to the periphery, initiating muscle contractions or glandular activities, thereby orchestrating voluntary and involuntary responses to stimuli. These signals enable the nervous system to perceive and effectively respond to the surrounding environment.

actions are a back-and-forth transmission of significance. I generate meaningfulness through the operations I carry out and the materials and structures I embed those operations within. I create the rules of engagement, the rules of significance and meaningfulness. Those rules are mutable and transferrable in my hermeneutic and semiotic terms as an artist between any media I choose. I can legitimately read and interpret one artform as another through a range of conscious and unselfconscious hermeneutic processes that though challenging to articulate using words, exist as objective things because they are manifest as material artefacts.

But are those realisations objective or subjective conditions? Are they both? In this regard, I am judge, jury and executioner. This is my plight and challenge. Away from the point of immanent experience, phenomenology is, I believe, subjective no matter how objectively one approaches it or how 'scientific' the frameworks of analysis are. For example, a blow-by-blow analytical account of each step of my making process, considering all the objective and subjective drivers for those actions, including their ongoing assessment and recursive adaption, is beyond my scope as an artist and I assume difficult to analyse meaningfully. The artist attempting to analyse each action in real-time would disrupt the act of making as a fluid activity that unites objective and subjective processes. Therefore, the artist's actions would become self-conscious, unnatural and not representative of the act of making. Observing the act of making in this way will change outcomes, precluding any objective analysis. One cannot remove oneself from the equation. The very act of observing the phenomena changes that phenomenon—the act of setting up the analytical framework to observe phenomena filters and changes outcomes. Like data, its analysis will produce different results as the investigative method is modified. It is more than possible to produce the results you expect to see or want to see through manipulation, whether manipulation is wilful or subconscious.

As discussed, products of the mind, such as meaning and affect, are not absolute values and cannot be examined with the same certainties as numbers in a data set. However, the creation of the artefact is a fact, be that a painting or a composition a) as a material body (including a score or music when it is instantiated into sound through the physicality of sound waves, sonic vibrations, ear drum vibrations and bone conduction for example and b) as the physical and material embodiment of the actions of the maker (or in music, the composer and performer who share authorship) that are themselves embodied within the fabric of the artefact itself. Those are material outcomes, real measurable things in the physical domain, whatever processes brought them into being. When making art, hermeneutics renders thought solid through action, through the mind and body.

With meaning and significance constructed by the receiver, I am reluctant to express views around what I consider meaningful in my work, knowing that such concepts are my own and are challenging to transmit value for value. Taking this position explains my hesitancy to write artists' statements explaining my work. Of course, artists are free to discuss and disclose what they consider are their antecedents, backstories, political motivations, impulses or inspirations necessary for making work from their own perspectives to help establish meaningfulness and context. Audiences and viewers are often interested and delighted with such communication. However, being uncomfortable expressing subjective ideas to establish meaningfulness and delighting in the generative and multivalent capacity of the human mind to interpret and create significance, I avoid explaining anything other than the processes of making, much of which can be described objectively. I appreciate that those processes carry their own meaningfulness. However, this meaningfulness may be categorically different from the ontological condition of the thing being made. Away from emotional considerations, processes are the techniques through which a work passes as its meaningfulness is developed. For example, making involves establishing meaningfulness and significance at every step of the way. Here, hermeneutics equals action as interpretation and directs the artist to take decisions and evaluate their outcomes, how those sit contextually within whatever is already present in the artefact and any future steps necessary to move the work towards completion. This is meaningfulness construction on a massive, ongoing, recursive and assimilative scale that is immanent, dynamic, reflexive and reactive. In short, attempting to describe what a cake *is* and how it tastes through a detailed analysis of its recipe and baking alone—its making techniques—will not tell you anything about the experience of eating the cake, only how to make that cake. Only when eaten will the nature of 'cake' be fully meaningful.

## Equivalency of Meaningfulness and Fuzzy Values

As discussed, there is no pragmatically demonstrable equivalency between what is 'signified' in my work and its meaningfulness. However, if I were disposed to believe equivalency did exist, I often muse how this could be proven. Such an investigation would involve a considerable amount of work. Results would only be subjective away from the broadest associations and definitions and even those general associations will likely have differing meanings. There seems little point in going down that route to try and identify meaning to demonstrate some internally consistent symbolic 'language' that almost certainly cannot be reduced to thought 'signified' by the written word. Therefore, I use the medium of paint or sound for communication. Yet, like the presence of certain words or phrases, consistent and recognisable mark-making and sound gestures repeatedly feature throughout my work in symbolic form. Symbols are combined in multiple ways to clarify or generate meaning. I cannot extract or point to specific meanings from individual symbols. Still, I appreciate that their meaning as a body of symbols emerges in combination to create relational networks. This approach is similar to how words are combined to generate meaning. Single words possess a range of possible meanings that require conditioning from other words before their specific context and meaningfulness can be ascertained. As words are conditioned, they generate more words to condition those words and so on. Therefore, words are generative. They operate through relation, where the relationship between words defines their meaning rather than any a priori meaning at the conceptual heart of any given word. It is the act of generating and combining symbols that externalise and embody whatever meaningfulness I attempt to transmit to others. With meaning constructed using non-word-based symbols, I cannot control what meaningfulness is interpreted or rely upon any of the more-or-less agreed-upon definitions words are considered to have to suggest meaning. This process describes, to some extent, what embodiment is.

This kind of content cataloguing of mark-making and corresponding values between different phenomena expressed in and across artwork is very much what Paul Klee undertook in his notebooks; Volume 1, *The Thinking Eye* and Volume 2, *The Nature of Nature*.[30] They make beautiful artefacts and are of the utmost importance as a presentation of the principles of design ever made by a modern artist. While I hugely admire this collection of lectures, thoughts, musings, illustrations and diagrams as the work of an exceptional mind, I do not feel that following a similar route regarding the presentation of my work and an attempt at disclosing its symbolic significance is relevant, valuable or effective in respect to the music and paintings I make and the practices they involve that are radically different to those of Klee. Klee deals predominantly with constructions, mainly geometric. My mark-making and pictures are related to entanglements, rhizome-like tentacles, kinetically charged gestures, seemingly

---

[30] Klee, Paul, 1992.

unstable relationships, ambiguities, degrees of visual complexity, wildness and chaotic networks. My work proceeds through layering and erosion.

I assume that any attempt I make to catalogue some affective impact correspondence, for example, where 'x' mark-making corresponds to 'y' configurations of sounds or whatever, is a fool's errand. It is too easy to fall into the trap of believing that an understanding of a work through the comprehension of its meaningfulness and affective detail if such qualities can be disentangled, is inevitable, not least because affect is most likely drawn from a work's wholeness—from its internal relations—and not its components in isolation. As affect is a phenomenon generated in the individual, cataloguing those signs will only be meaningful to that individual. Outcomes will be personal and subjective. Despite the attraction of assigning significance to each aspect of a work in isolation to gain overall understanding, I imagine any artist attempting such an action would (perhaps unwittingly) use subjectivity to measure subjectivity, probably through a pseudo-scientific (objective) framework. Results rendered using this approach would prove disappointing.

There is a risk in analysing and creating any potential ontology of mark-making or sonic gestures where there is an ambition to make those conditions correspond in value, that in so doing, the results may obscure the conclusions. Here, the processes of organising any data may take on an objectivity of its own; the objectivity of creating lists, if you like, to become the focus and justification for the research because the act of cataloguing and ordering relies on an objective, even mathematical sequencing of data that can mislead the researcher into thinking they are undertaking work that will lead them to similarly objective outcomes. In this case, well-organised data are everywhere. Still, it does not follow that any answers to the questions asked will arise purely from the meticulous management of that data, particularly if the information is drawn from subjective sources. In such a scenario, seeing the woods for the trees may not be possible.

## Transduction, Transmission, Meaningfulness and Autoethnography

Transduction is a concept I frequently refer to throughout this book. I use the term to describe the process of making work in different media that utilise the same generative sources and, by implication, perhaps share and transmit similar levels of meaningfulness between both, from my perspective as the maker. Simply, it involves converting material or substance from one form to another. It is a sophisticated transformative process. I'm drawn to the medical definition of transduction in the *Merriam Webster* dictionary. I am happy to interpret this with a degree of latitude for my creative purposes and my understanding of other artists and performers who similarly use the term. *Merriam Webster* writes that transduction is: *"the action or process of converting something and especially energy or a message into another form and 'the transfer of genetic material from one organism (as a bacterium) to another by a genetic vector and especially a bacteriophage".*[31]

Having quoted this definition, it is essential to distinguish between quantifiable, demonstrable scientific transduction as a process and my word usage concerned with converting significance or meaningfulness through hermeneutic actions as processes of reading or transmission between composition and painting, for example. In such instances of 'artistic and performative'

---

[31] 'Transduction', in Merriam-Webster.com Dictionary, *Merriam-Webster*, <https://www.merriam-webster.com/dictionary/transduction> [accessed 12 August 2022].

transduction, it is rarely possible to factually demonstrate or 'say' the transformative process between source and outcome as the exact mechanism is unclear.

The German physicist Werner Heisenberg (1901-1976) explains this distinction as played out in areas of the scientific community where presumed facts are highly valued and all else conveniently ignored. He writes that *"the positivists have a simple solution: the world must be divided into that which we can say clearly and the rest, which we had better pass over in silence. But can anyone conceive of a more pointless philosophy, seeing that what we can say amounts to nothing? If we omitted all that is unclear, we would probably be left with completely uninteresting and trivial tautologies"*.[32]

A central assertion in *Music, Painting, Landscape and Me*, is my conviction that it is possible to transduce music to painting and vice versa. With music and painting using incommensurate symbolic systems and materially different categories of phenomena to embody thought, the overarching question is how do I achieve this transduction? How, for example, do I signify a sense of time passing and time passing at different psychological speeds in painting as I do in music? In painting, I am aware of the pictorial and cliché portrayals of specific fixed times of the year, the time of day, but how is the concept of moving through time—as time in motion—so intrinsic to music, 'signified' symbolically in a media that is itself physically fixed and set in its temporality?

Paintings offer their visual information immediately, with colour, structure, forms and textures apparent in that moment of observation. Nevertheless, exploring the surface of a painting beyond this initial perceptual 'grab' of data takes time for the eye to navigate as it maps content and builds meaningfulness. This assimilation is a temporal activity. Still, unlike music, where only the very moment that sound is produced shows what the music *is* at that point in time and where everything that has passed as sound is immediately consigned to memory, the entirety of a painting is ever present as a physical entity in any singular moment of time. Even examining a musical score full of Western classical music notation requires reading as a visual entity and time to build a conceptual image where sound is imagined and, once again, outside of what is immanently conceived, notions of form and structure are constructed from remembered materials. I appreciate that there is no empirical equivalence between the meaningfulness of a painting and a piece of music or where a painting has been transducted to music or vice versa that I can 'say' in objective terms. The temporal difference between both media is irreconcilable as a pragmatic act of transduction.

For example, in my polytemporal music, where different strands of musical activity move at independent speeds to one another simultaneously, perception of those differently occurring speeds is possible. Polytemporality changes my perception of time on a strata-by-strata level, in as much as those layers that move at comparatively quicker speeds may be perceived as fast time passing and those moving more slowly as slow time passing. Those thoughts around the perception of time reminded me of a Twitter conversation with Markus Wenninger, a friend, colleague and performer based in Germany, when he was recording several layers of a timecode-supported polytemporal piece for later combination in a recording, where I wrote: *"Yes. It's like a perceptually based temporal flux. The rate of temporal movement differs depending upon where your experiential focus is fixed—on which horizons of activity and how the flow of surrounding strata contextualises them"*.[33] The perception of time, of psychological

---

[32] Jaeger, Gregg, p. 128.
[33] Twitter conversation between Marc Yeats and Markus Wenninger, 1 May 2022.

or felt time, differs categorically from the exactitude of measured time. Experienced time feels flexible.

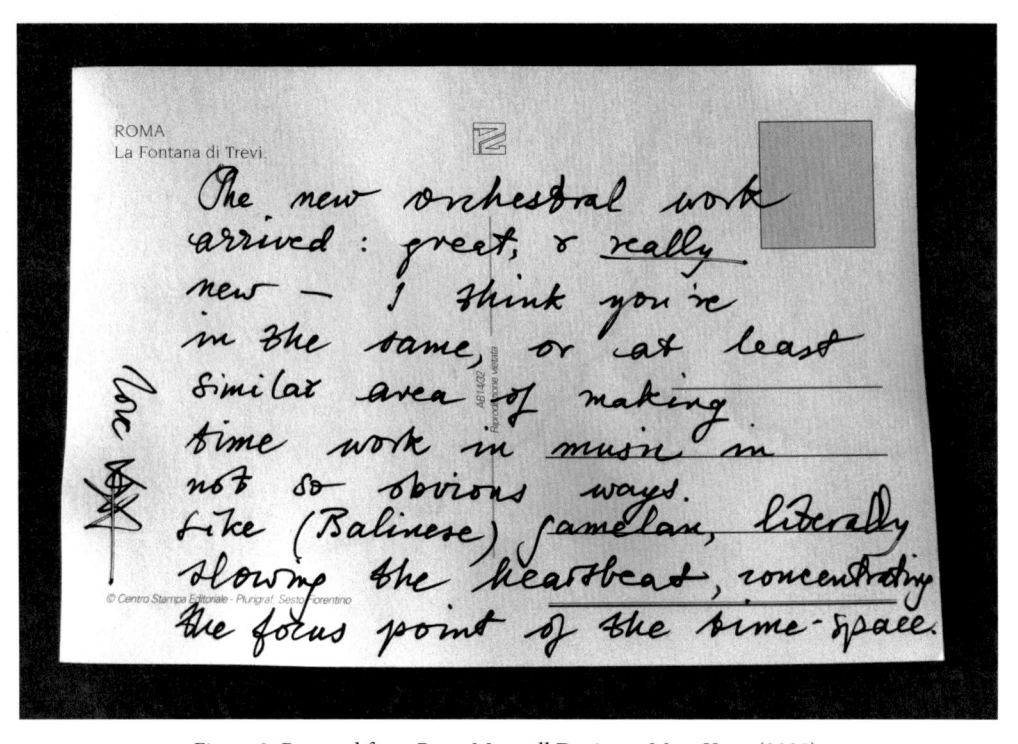

Figure 3. Postcard from Peter Maxwell Davies to Marc Yeats (2005).

In 2005, I composed and dedicated a new piece of orchestral music called *The North Sound* to the late composer Peter Maxwell Davies for his seventieth birthday. This was a conducted and synchronised piece of music. After spending time with the score, Max wrote his initial thoughts on a postcard as seen in Figure 3. His thoughts gravitated around my use of musical and perceptual time—an aspect of the composition that fascinated him. Unfortunately, the piece has not been performed, so neither Max nor I could experience how this musical time element could be experienced in performance. I would have been fascinated to hear if Max's assumptions around how his experience of conceptual time, predicted solely upon his examination and understanding of the score, felt when compared to the experience of listening to the piece live in real-time. Unfortunately, I shall now never know.

I digress. But my point remains, how can I transduce the temporal richness of my musical artefacts into paintings? I explore this matter further in 'Mapping' and For the Love of Chalk and Other Matters, discussing the relevance and correlation between proprioception—the awareness of the position and movement of the body in space, kinetics—the biological study of the rate of reactions—and embodiment and performance transducing sensory information into action to make art, among other functions. For now and with artistic transduction "*rarely possible to factually demonstrate or say*", I conclude that it, like transmission taking place,

<https://twitter.com/markuswenninger/status/1520667663688773633?s=21&t=faeFGfqpPInY3Wb8kXMkHA> [accessed 12 August 2022].

validates itself regardless of the exact mechanisms involved because the outcomes of transduction, like transmission, are present as a material reality embodied within any artefacts produced—transduction results from hermeneutics. The action and its outcome are its truth.

*though we mark it*
*cut it*
*count it*
*are never fixed*
*in the continuum of experience*
*lies infinite space without line, dimension, or division*
*save our mutilations*
*to stop this riot and hang on*
*for dear life*
*is measured*
*by fear of passage*
*to the other side of time*[34]

However difficult it is to transmit consistent concepts of meaningfulness from the artist to the receiver, I have noticed that viewers of paintings that I would describe as landscapes have, without conscious preparation on my part and notwithstanding those responses having been influenced by foreknowledge of my titles, any available text relating to the work or my practice more generally, been consistently identified as landscape paintings, often accompanied by landscape-related emotional responses. However, the more those somewhat generic landscape impressions are unpacked, for example, if I ask a viewer to expand on what they think the painting is about or what they see, their interpretations diverge from my own, sometimes radically. Considering those responses, I can't know how much the viewer learns of my work and practice in advance or how they position my work contextually within the broader genre of contemporary landscape painting. Consequently, I cannot draw objective conclusions from their anecdotal nature. For now, I shall assume that fundamental landscape qualities are embodied, transmitted and recognised but that the shared significance of such qualities dissipates with more detailed scrutiny. Interestingly, I have found no similar correlations of meaningfulness reported from those listening to my music. Impressions and perceptions are completely open, with only occasional reference to landscape-like qualities being noted. This may be owing to my compositions' non-mimetic nature and absence of referent symbols.

With significance largely personal, why should I bother to communicate what I consider is the meaningfulness of my work and why challenge my opinions? With no absolute meaning, as post-modernist thought would have it, isn't my truth, my interpretation, all that matters? Such attitudes can and have produced bad autoethnography. This August 2022 article in *Times Higher Education* titled *Masturbation Journal Paper Exposes Deeper Problems in Research* written by William Matthews, a fellow in the anthropology of China at the London School of Economics and Political Science highlights some of the issues at stake in autoethnographic research.[35]

The challenge with autoethnography is in attempting to separate what are *"objective empirical observations from subjective interpretation"*. Matthews writes that *"the best ethnographic research meets this [challenge] by focusing on what can be objectively documented, assessing this*

---

[34] Yeats, 27 Poems (9th November 2005). Forthcoming publication on Vision Edition.
[35] Matthews, William, [accessed 20 August 2022].

*comparatively and being explicit about crucial details and where subjective interpretation begins*".[36] However, such distinctions become increasingly difficult to disentangle when one undertakes an autoethnographic 'research' project from the perspective of the self-observing the self, affectionately known as 'mesearch', no matter how meticulously 'data' is catalogued. Matthews goes on to write:

*Since the introduction of 'postmodern' approaches to anthropology and the turn to a focus on reflexivity, in attempting to address genuine issues, anthropology has tended towards abandoning any pretence to objectivity in the first place. For some, this means that because objectivity cannot be achieved, it shouldn't be attempted at all. It is then a short step to subjectivity becoming a 'method' and source of knowledge in its own right. [...] What it produces is equivalent to a diary [that] in itself it is not research in any meaningful sense.*[37]

As well as *Music, Painting, Landscape and Me*, being a work of fiction, it may also be a diary, as Matthews describes.

Despite my appreciation of the futility of such things, my desire to fully comprehend what is transmitted in art and to correlate, unify and fix meaning and understanding, is embedded within me. It is also demonstrated in common parlance among art lovers and experts through phrases that declare an 'understanding' of art or music. What exactly does this mean? Does it imply understanding the process of making, techniques and methods; grasping theoretical concepts; understanding the physics of optics and sound and the chemistry of pigment; materiality and the agency of actors; the historical, social or personal circumstances through which work is conceived and made; the current historical, social or personal events through which the work is engaged; appreciating the effect and affect of secondary encoding and the co-authorship of performers in music; understanding a work's affective components through decoding, translation, transduction and transmission; understanding the viewer's perceptual limitations and filters; appreciating how our neural network is built, develops, maintained and operates in relation to engaging with art; enjoying the role of our afferent/efferent functionalities and capacities; analysing what is embodied in the artefact's materials, structures and gestures; the semiotics and hermeneutic extrapolation of meaning from what is embodied; making what is irreducible somehow reducible to words; moving beyond assumptions about intentionality and its transmission; separating fact from fiction; desire and wishful thinking from objectivity; does the term 'understanding art' mean mastering a comprehension of all of those components simultaneously? I think not. For many, there is another generalised assumption based on personal observation. However, aspects of those components may be understood to a degree. I believe much of the concept of understanding art and music is reduced to an affective equation between like, pleasure, stimulation, desire and understanding. In other words, if it feels comfortable, if I grasp its structures, social conventions, culturally formatted expectations, icons and referent symbology, if it affects me and mainly if it affects me positively, I understand it. And for most, that seems enough. For others, the ubiquitous artist's statement provides sufficient context and explanation of artistic work for a sense of understanding to take root without any necessary further analysis of the work itself.

Though useful, my 'understanding' of art is not contingent upon knowledge of every facet of how it is or was conceived, created, historically and contextually situated or to appreciate the physics of its operation. Understanding an artefact—its meaningfulness—remains a matter of

---

[36] Matthews.
[37] Ibid.

hermeneutics and embodied knowledge, perhaps, as some would have it and expressive and emotional knowingness. In terms of a relationship, engagement with the artefact itself, its appreciation and its making, I understand exactly what I am doing and what is happening through the functionality of my interpretation and hermeneutic plateau, even though I cannot articulate all aspects of that process using words pragmatically. All other categories of information and knowledge serve as additionality and learning that enriches my hermeneutic operation and experience. I accept that understanding art is a combination of embodied knowledge ranging from the intellectual to the experiential, but I also create understanding through motion, forward momentum and experience.

## Memory and Resonance

*gentle, simple, truth*
*therein*
*is often more potent*
*then the conspiracy of intellect*
*to quantify our souls*[38]

Memory, too, is in constant motion. It is never fixed. Every new stimulus creates a memory that builds a layer around and relates to another to develop it within networks of memories. Memories can be modified and even generate new memories from experiences already assimilated. Some may be false memories embedded and perceived as legitimate. Sometimes we can see through an immediate, apparent or surface memory to a much older and deeper one and that realisation changes the perception of memories being viewed, sometimes radically. Memory is in flux. Every time I remember something, I develop it just a little.

Memory is central to my practice. I paint from memory and cultivate its instabilities as a creative method. I use the memory of heard sounds to conceptualise music and use memory to comprehend musical structures when listening. Writing down or documenting thoughts along a timeline fixes those occurrences, but the comprehension of what has been fixed at the time of writing—recording speech, video, music, painting, photographs or whatever—can feel very different from the remembered sense of the original matter when re-examined and compared. This is particularly true away from logging facts and figures or essential information transference and when expressing behavioural, motivational or subjective conditions and actions. Data can be fixed, digitised or materialised in some form, like photographs or videos, for example, to make and record memories. Still, the meaning and significance of those externally recorded artefacts will not be fixed precisely or necessarily correspond to identical significances apparent or remembered from the time of recording. The truth and accuracy of memory are further tested when several people's memories of the same event are compared to each other and found to show differences. The more complex the remembered situation, the more radical the differences will likely be. This shows again that our sense of reality is a matter of perspective and not the acknowledgement of universal truth. For me, the embodiment of the 'lived experience' in artwork fixes that experience semiotically within a specific physical manifestation of sound or paint. Despite that fixing in memory, my reading and rereading of what has been embodied will not necessarily elicit a consistent response, experience, memory or meaning. I live and swim within the flux of meaning. The pre-Socratic Greek philosopher

---

[38] Yeats, 14 Poems (12th November 2005). Forthcoming publication on Vision Edition.

Heraclitus is credited as saying, "*No man ever steps in the same river twice, for it's not the same river and he's not the same man*".[39]

In enacting and reliving a memory, I experience a range of sensations in my body that I describe as a resonance. In science, the term resonance has precise meanings. It is helpful to deal with those first as they are not directly related to the meaning I imply and have appropriated when I use the word resonance about my practice and affective experience. *Meriam Webster* describes the scientifically orientated meaning of resonance as:

*A vibration of large amplitude in a mechanical or electrical system caused by a relatively small periodic stimulus of the same or nearly the same period as the natural vibration period of the system; the state of adjustment that produces resonance in a mechanical or electrical system; the intensification and enriching of a musical tone by supplementary vibration; a quality imparted to voiced sounds by vibration in anatomical resonating chambers or cavities (such as the mouth or the nasal cavity); the sound elicited on percussion of the chest; the conceptual alternation of a chemical species (such as a molecule or ion) between two or more equivalent allowed structural representations differing only in the placement of electrons that aids in understanding the actual state of the species as an amalgamation of its possible structures and the usually higher-than-expected stability of the species; the enhancement of an atomic, nuclear, or particle reaction or a scattering event by excitation of internal motion in the system; an extremely short-lived elementary particle; a synchronous gravitational relationship of two celestial bodies (such as moons) that orbit a third (such as a planet) which can be expressed as a simple ratio of their orbital periods.*[40]

The dictionary definitions of resonance I allude to include "*a quality of richness or variety*" and "*a quality of evoking response*".[41] I use resonance to describe the nature and level of affect a given place, experience or artefact triggers within me. In a characterised way, I visualise my bodily mass vibrating sympathetically with place, experience and artefact. In this regard, there is a correlation between my physical experience of resonance as a somatic phenomenon and the scientific definitions of sympathetic vibration between bodies above. In short, I become excited by my surroundings or my work. I detect or imagine on some level of consciousness that this excitement is physical energy where my body sympathetically resonates through vibration at what I assume is a similar frequency to the environment I find myself in, other people or the work I engage with. This resonation may continue for some time. At some point, I need to discharge that energy. I do this through making work. The creation of paintings and compositions restores equilibrium.

This is my concept of resonance in relation to experiencing the landscape and making work about the landscape. It is more metaphor than science, but vibration sensation is real. I discuss my experiences concerning resonance in more detail in later chapters.

Memory and resonance are connected. As described previously, place-specific resonance is a bodily vibration I perceive as resonating with specific places, either in situ, through image and

---

[39] The scarcity of direct quotes from Heraclitus stems from the loss of much of his original works and the reliance on later authors who referenced or interpreted his teachings. Notably, Plato's *Cratylus* references Heraclitus, but the nature of these passages—whether direct quotes, paraphrases, or interpretations—remains ambiguous. <https://latin.stackexchange.com/questions/9471/looking-for-a-direct-quote-from-heraclitus-expressing-that-everything-changes> [accessed 18 January 2024].

[40] 'Resonance', in Merriam-Webster.com Dictionary, *Merriam Webster*, <https://www.merriam-webster.com/dictionary/resonance> [accessed 12 September 2022].

[41] Ibid.

sound or triggered through the memory of place. Those resonances can be generic or specific. For example, I can identify resonance in paintings and music in the most general sense, as a sense of region, season, weather, light, geology, topography, landscape, horizons, vegetation, and colour associations, down to specific locations and their 'sense of place'.

Ideally, this resonance is built through complete corporal contact and hermeneutical immersion within a location or with images of various places. Total physical immersion is best, as in a residency involving high degrees of contact and onsite experience, but other means of exploration through photographs, maps and writings, for example, also work. Resonance embodies a 'sense of place' through my body and all its senses and thought capacities. It is triggered somatically through sensory inputs ranging from sight, sound and smell. It is also triggered through the memory of those somatic inputs.

Resonance is amplified through reliving the original immersive and situated experience within memory. As memory recalls experiences, it develops them gradually until a personalised 'mapping' of a place has been created. This 'mapping' is no mere tracery. It makes something new based on what was experienced previously. It deterritorialises the original remembered mapped experience (that particular experience) through the act of remembering to create a new conceptual territory that is now the interior resonance. It has reterritorialised the initially experienced 'data' into something different; a new yet connected territory. This 'mapping' characterises, condenses and enriches a 'sense of place' as an internally constructed topography, with its resonance and affect upon recall. This inner landscape resonance chimes with any newly encountered external stimuli that it recognises (resonates sympathetically with). This recognition response combines a 'sense of place' in my work with physical locations through mark-making, sound, textures, colour and form. When this recognition is triggered, to any degree, it amplifies and draws together the now internalised resonance with resonance generating content and signification within an artefact and thereby unites the inner 'sense of place' and its progenitor landscape with a 'sense of place' embodied in the artefact. When my internally constructed landscape resonates in sympathy in this way, I feel fully alive as an artist.

I understand that resonance is a product of hermeneutics, of interpreting the landscape and of interpreting and responding to my inner landscapes as an act of interpretation to bring meaning to those sensations. I understand, too, that those vibrations and concepts of resonance are as much rooted, present, experienced and thought-through in my body as they are in my mind. Each time I experience resonance, new memories are formed and those memories become embedded along with other memories associated with similar experiences. Over time, those memories become highly complex, multi-dimensional interconnected entities. They become part of a vast network of memories housed in an equally extensive network of connected nervous tissue.

Resonance, as I perceive it, is a dynamic symbol recognition and memory trigger action combined. It is impossible to separate memory and resonance from any associated affect elicited upon remembering when affect and resonance are immanent to what is remembered. Is resonance a type of affect? When affect becomes embedded with memory as a remembered condition, an interconnected loop of affect, memory, immanence and subjectivity becomes bound together and difficult to separate experientially. Does, then, affect trigger associated memories or does memory trigger associated affects? Does A trigger B trigger A? To answer this question, looking more closely at affect is useful.

# Affect

*permanence*
*is the shadow*
*cast by*
*the edifice of time*[42]

The term 'affect' crops up repeatedly throughout this book. I use it to articulate concepts ranging from emotions to physical sensations in relation to my experiences of the landscape, creating work, engaging with the art of others and the impact of living life. According to affect theorists, describing affect is a tough question to answer concisely and straightforwardly—to wrestle into language—as Professor Gregory Seigworth explains in a YouTube video interview called *What is Affect Theory?* owing to the phenomena's condition being an ongoingness rather than a process.[43] Seigworth explains that any description of affect is also conditioned by the particular discipline of which the question was asked, making a singular and neat definition challenging to formulate. According to Seigworth and Melissa Gregg writing in *The Affect Theory Reader*, the authors ask:

*How to begin [in describing affect] when, after all, there is no pure or somehow originary state for affect? Affect arises in the midst of inbetween-ness: in the capacities to act and be acted upon. Affect is an impingement or extrusion of a momentary or sometimes more sustained state of relation as well as the passage (and the duration of passage) of forces or intensities. That is, affect is found in those intensities that pass body to body (human, nonhuman, part-body and otherwise), in those resonances that circulate about, between and sometimes stick to bodies and worlds and in the very passages or variations between these intensities and resonances themselves. Affect, at its most anthropomorphic, is the name we give to those forces—visceral forces beneath, alongside, or generally other than conscious knowing, vital forces insisting beyond emotion—that can serve to drive us towards movement, towards thought and extension, that can likewise suspend us (as if in neutral) across a barely registering accretion of force-relations, or that can even leave us overwhelmed by the world's apparent intractability. Indeed, affect is persistent proof of a body's never less than ongoing immersion in and among the world's obstinacies and rhythms, its refusals as much as its invitations.*[44]

Such a description of affect is useful, perhaps in artistic contexts, but remains challenging to grasp. Dictionary definitions, for example, in *Meriam Webster*, are more pragmatic and state that affect means: "*to produce an effect upon (someone or something), to act on and cause a change in (someone or something), to cause illness, symptoms, etc., in (someone or something), to produce an emotional response in (someone), or to influence (someone or something)*".[45] The primary difference between the dictionary definitions and those given by affect theorists is the absence of ongoingness. The dictionary definition implies that actions operate within a closed system as isolated events instead of along a continuum of experience. Returning to the *What is Affect Theory?* video, transcribed and much paraphrased here, Seigworth says of this ongoingness that:

---

[42] Yeats, 14 Poems (12th November 2005). Forthcoming publication on Vision Edition.
[43] Seigworth, Gregory, *What is Affect Theory?* in *Let's Talk About Art and Culture*, YouTube Video <https://www.youtube.com/watch?v=PuKIqF72Bwo&ab_channel=Let%27sTalkaboutArtandCulture> [accessed 22 August 2022].
[44] Gregg, Melissa and Seigworth, Gregory J., 2010, p. 1.
[45] 'Affect', in Merriam-Webster.com Dictionary, <https://www.merriam-webster.com/dictionary/affect> [Accessed August 2022].

*It's at once that encounter or impingement; that point of contact in which some kind of intensity or some feeling shifts in the nature of your own understanding of the world or reciprocally, in the thing that you're encountering within this moment of contact out of which arrives this intensity in the midst of an ongoingness of everything. I mean, it's not as if the world just arrived in that moment of intensity or contact, [the world is] something that's already happening [and continues to happen so that the encounter point locates itself into] a gradient of positive or negative intensities. This is what Spinoza and Deleuze refer to as 'a continuous line of variation'.*[46]

Difficulty in articulating descriptions of 'ongoingness', 'becomingness', immanence and unfolding, as opposed to describing the process in clear and straightforward—objective, if you like—terms, is a frequent challenge I encounter when attempting to come to grips with aspects of affect theory primarily because of the descriptive language used and abundance of neologisms on every page. I appreciate the difficulties in making ongoingness or any condition constantly becoming expressible in words as my attempts to articulate similar concepts remain highly challenging. It is all too easy when without appropriate language, it sounds like one is spinning gas and air, whether this is the case or not. Because of the opacity of many of its concepts, I shall limit my description of affect to terms of emotional valency, intensity and duration.

*threadbare map*
*I know so well*
*every crevice*
*fingered*
*intricately travelled but still lost*
*on a journey to*
*nowhere in particular*
*seeing backwards, we move forwards*
*our pasts colour future*
*and trip us to fall*[47]

Affect is an immanent consequence of signification and vice versa as there can never be a point where signification ceases to signify or elicit an affect. For instance, regarding my painting, there cannot be a brush stroke too far that renders mark-making meaningless or moves what I paint from landscape signification to non-landscape signification, for example, no matter the extent of abstraction, if my hermeneutics determines that meaning category as 'landscape' or 'artwork'. Interpretation is all. It is impossible to think about anything beyond or outside signification and symbolic constructs because it is impossible to imagine, project or think beyond thought, which also is a symbolic construct. However, it is possible to think outside of word-based language. Thinking outside of words can produce different ways of 'thinking'; through the body, through sensation, viscerally, through movement, image and sound or perhaps all of those in tandem, that do not use words to transmit significance and where interpretation of those sensations brings about meaning that cannot be easily expressed through words.

Consequently, I employ two ways to communicate interpersonally; one that uses words for description and another that uses non-word-based languages (I use the word languages flexibly here), such as music, painting, sculpture or dance, for example, to describe sensation and

---

[46] Seigworth, *What is Affect Theory?* Timepoint 2:08-3:02.
[47] Yeats, 27 Poems (9th November 2005). Forthcoming publication on Vision Edition.

emotion I feel are irreducible to words or where the use of words would cascade into yet more opportunities for interpretation not necessarily related to my communicative intentions.

Should I have communicative intentions? If I want to order a pizza, word-based transmission of intent is generally useful and its outcome is easily confirmed. But making art isn't the same as ordering a pizza. Art transmits ideas and emotional conditions that may not sit comfortably within word-based communication, such as articulating a 'sense of place' beyond a mere description of physical features. In such instances, I choose the languages of painting or composition to embody my thoughts and I frame my work in particular ways to shape my perceptions and the perceptions of others. Part of this shaping process involves associating titles with artefacts.

## Titles, Intention, Indeterminacy and Superposition

I name works after they are completed and after I have the measure of them in some way. By measure, I imply knowing a work's structure as an actual value of pitches, rhythms and expressive components organised in time as a conceptual entity and, subjectively, how the relational content within that structure affects me. Those factors subjectively guide the choice of title to sit either within my appreciation of the perceived associated affect or to deflect from it entirely to act like a red herring title. I do this either explicitly as a public name or identifier or privately and implicitly as a personal identifier. What this title implies is significant to how I imagine the work is received. In contradiction, particularly with music compositions, I create a textual disclaimer that disassociates any perceived intentionality I may project through the title and its possible association to my work with any programmatic bias the listener may bring to the title and the piece of music. In short, my disclaimer states that the work's title operates solely as an identifier but that this identifier is poetic and elusive in nature.

Conversely, I know many artists, painters and composers who do not begin work until they have a title established and then, in their view, create work that reflects or embodies what they believe is meaningful about that title, I assume, driven by an understanding that such values and affects are transmissible from artist to receiver. But do titles yield more influence than I imagine? Do they help shape concepts of reality?

With perception passing through so many preconditioned filters, what I see and hear has been filtered and shaped, consciously or otherwise, to fit my expectations and perceptual, physiological and neurological pre- and self-programming. What I perceive and think is real may not correspond to the perceived phenomena when viewed or analysed from another perspective by someone else or when using scientific equipment to gather and process data. What I see and hear as an artist can never be truly objective. It is not fact, but it is what I frequently take as fact in my daily life. It is the currency I use to exist, function and communicate. Considering this, should I reassess my throughs around something 'being' what I think it is because I name it so?

The artist-researcher Robert Pepperell worked extensively with neuroscientists to discover more about the relationship between preconditioning viewers to interpret artwork through induction, training and titles and what constitutes visual indeterminacy. Pepperell explains that in his research paper *Connecting Art and the Brain: An Artist's Perspective on Visual Indeterminacy* where he discusses the intersection between art and neuroscience from the perspective of a practising artist. To achieve this, Pepperell has collaborated on several scientific studies into the effects of art on the brain and behaviour, looking particularly at the phenomenon of 'visual indeterminacy'.[48]

Figure 4. *Cranborne Chase No. 1.* Digital print. Marc Yeats (2022).

Although focused predominantly on aspects of visual indeterminacy (visual indeterminacy is a perceptual phenomenon that occurs when a viewer is presented with a seemingly meaningful visual stimulus that denies easy or immediate identification, for example in Figure 4, where the viewer has to interpret whether the brush marks, colours and structural relationships are symbolising landscape objects or arbitrary mark-making), Pepperell's research also saw an investigation into how titles affect the interpretations of paintings. To achieve this, the study used a collection of Cubist paintings by various artists. Pepperell continues:

*Cubist paintings made by the artists Pablo Picasso, Georges Braque and Juan Gris in the period before First World War. Cubist paintings of this period are characterized as being highly indeterminate in so far as they are directly observed depictions of everyday objects—tables, fruit, newspapers, glasses, etc.,—but represented in a fragmented and 'exploded' manner that makes immediate identification very difficult. […]. One part of the study looked at the extent to which descriptive titles presented alongside Cubist paintings affected the viewer's capacity to identify objects in the scene. Crucially, however, half the subjects undergoing the task of detecting familiar objects received a short training session before the trial in which they were instructed on how to 'read' Cubist paintings and find objects in them.*[49]

---

[48] Pepperell, Robert, [accessed 10 august 2022].
[49] Ibid. See Wiesmann, Martin (2010) for further details of the cited research.

Pepperell writes:

*Despite the fact that the subjects were not art experts and received only a relatively brief training sessions (30 min) they were significantly better than the control group in recognizing familiar objects. The study also found that the role of the descriptive titles, which effectively declared what the paintings depicted, has little effect on the control group but a marked effect in helping the trained group to find more familiar objects. To me, as both an artist and art teacher, these results were somewhat counterintuitive inasmuch as: (a) I would have expected the process of learning to read Cubist paintings to be something only acquired over many hours of study rather than the brief period of training undergone by these subjects and (b) that meaningful titles would have had some positive effect on helping those with no training to find familiar objects more often than when looking at the same image only accompanied by the word 'Untitled,' as was the case here. The study also showed enhanced activation in the parahippocampal cortex of the trained subjects, the amplitude of which increased as a function of the number of objects recognized. This suggested that the subjects had used broader contextual associations to identify the objects in the paintings rather than the cognitive resources normally linked more specifically to object recognition.*[50]

Pepperell's experiments into the influence of titles point to viewers with training or familiarity looking at paintings of a more indeterminate nature to conceptualise imagery more easily within those surfaces where no such imagery is present as being increased relative to the inexperienced or general viewer, where titles may not help direct or shape recognition of indeterminate forms in the same manner. As one experienced in conceptualising imagery from the indeterminate, I wonder if this train of thought holds true: I think; therefore, I am = I make; therefore, it is = I title; therefore, I know? And leading from that, I ask again, am I constructing my own reality? Quantum mechanics suggests I am.

There are elements of science that seem entangled with aspects of metaphysics, awareness, being, ontology and the independence of consciousness and the properties of observation alone to effect change in outcomes, particularly in quantum mechanics, along with the speculation around how phenomena operate on the subatomic level as opposed to within classical physics. Some of those theories and projections read like a magic manual, particularly when their condition as a mathematical expression, impenetrable for those other than theoretical mathematicians, is reformatted into words for the layperson.

To emphasise how unsettling this reformatting may be to the uninitiated, a June 2022 article written by Stav Dimitropoulos appeared in the online magazine, *Popular Mechanics*, displaying the intriguing title *Objective Reality May Not Exist at All, Quantum Physicists Say* followed immediately by the sub strap line *Reality might be "in the eye of the observer"*, according to new research.

The article explains that one of the biggest mysteries in quantum mechanics, the branch of science dealing with the behaviour of subatomic particles on the microscopic level, is whether physical reality exists independent of its observer and that new research provides strong evidence there might be mutually exclusive, yet complementary physical realities in the

---

[50] Pepperell, Figure 12 of the article shows a very useful schematic representation of the pictorial 'interpretation space' reproduced from Wallraven, Christian et al., pp. 115-122, representing the 'abstract/representational' and 'unique/ambiguous' parameter dimensions existing of both perceptual and conceptual layers of vision.

quantum realm with further research providing surprising answers to the world's greatest mysteries.[51] Dimitropoulos explains:

*In a field where intriguing, almost mysterious phenomena like 'quantum superposition' prevail—a situation where one particle can be in two or even 'all' possible places at the same time—some experts say reality exists outside of your own awareness and there's nothing you can do to change it. Others insist 'quantum reality' might be some form of Play-Doh you mould into different shapes with your own actions. Now, scientists from the Federal University of ABC (UFABC) in the São Paulo metropolitan area in Brazil are adding fuel to the suggestion that reality might be "in the eye of the observer".*

In their new research, published in the journal *Communications Physics* in April, the scientists in Brazil attempted to verify the 'complementarity principle' the famous Danish physicist Niels Bohr proposed in 1928. It states that objects come with certain pairs of complementary properties, which are impossible to observe or measure at the same time, like energy and duration or position and momentum. For example, no matter how you set up an experiment involving a pair of electrons, there's no way you can study the position of both quantities at the same time: the test will illustrate the position of the first electron, but obscure the position of the second particle (the complementary particle) at the same time [...]. That reality might be in the eye of the observer is a very peculiar aspect of the physical reality in the quantum domain and the mystery itself shows no signs of abating.[52]

The more research into quantum mechanics is revealed, the more the comprehension and implications of that research reinforce the now long-standing adage of American quantum physicist and Nobel laureate Richard Feynman: "*If you think you understand quantum mechanics, you don't understand quantum mechanics*".[53] With the possibility that reality might be 'in the eye of the beholder', my mind turns to the status of knowledge as similarly being in the eye of the beholder, or in this case, the mind of the thinker. Are such concepts postmodernist tropes, or do they hold a possible basis in fact?

Knowledge is embodied. It resides in the minds and bodies of those who hold that knowledge. It is situated physically within the brain's organic fabric as a biochemical material fact. However, thinking about duality and difference in the context of superposition, I ask myself what the opposite of embodied knowledge may be. Is it disembodied knowledge? I don't think such a state can exist because knowledge is always embodied. Even a concept of the unknown is defined and differentiated from notions of what is known. Nevertheless, the concepts of absence and presence, embodiment and disembodiment are mutually interdependent. In relation to what is embodied in an artwork, only what is embodied in the maker of that artwork can be embodied in an artefact. It is impossible to embody something in an artwork not previously embodied in the maker.

This train of thought brings me to notions of superposition and quantum mechanics, where, with a great deal of elasticity, I imagine that a phenomenon, like knowledge, may have two completely different yet simultaneously present conditions—embodied and disembodied—that can only be observed as one condition or the other at any one moment even though they

---

[51] The research referred to here is drawn from Dieguez, Pedro R. et al., [accessed 12 August 2022].
[52] Dimitropoulos, Stav, [accessed 2 August 2022].
[53] Ibid. Further reading around partial superposition can be found in *Can Particles Really Be in Two Places at the Same Time?*, in *NewScientist* (online article) < https://www.newscientist.com/article/2328087-can-particles-really-be-in-two-places-at-the-same-time/> [accessed 8 August 2022].

exist as a unified singular state when not fixed through observation. I conceive of disembodied knowledge as those observations, findings, analyses, experiments, conjectures and conclusions yet to be formulated and formatted as knowledge. The potential for such phenomena and the conclusions their observations elicit when viewed through a theoretical framework exists but are not yet embodied as knowledge. In this scenario, I imagine the superposition's unobserved condition is both embodied and disembodied. Upon observation and realisation, the state resolves to embodied and present as it is now known, or disembodied and absent, as it points to unknown unknowns. Thinking about embodied and disembodied knowledge in this way is speculation of the highest degree, most likely nonsense and with no theoretical basis. Using a crude understanding of superposition, presence and absence, I am projecting, conflating and extending the conditionality of knowledge and embodiment to encompass additional properties that are not readily connected to them. This is a creative leap, an intuition, connecting condition A with condition B as it suits my purposes. It certainly isn't science. It's almost certainly incorrect. But I'm an artist. I make those jumps.

I am still determining where quantum mechanics leaves me. What I am sure of, however, is that whatever reality is, it is a far more complex and paradoxical condition than I can comprehend and science can yet reveal.

*the edge is the place to be*
*from here*
*you can see what is*
*and what is to come*
*knowledge and potential*
*the cost is high*
*when you burn brightly from both ends*[54]

## Composer, Performer, Audience: Intentionality, Interpretation, Transmission, Convention, Deterritorialisation and Meaningfulness

There is a categorical difference in transmission method between music and painting. With music, certainly the music I write, it is necessary for any conceptual manifestation of my compositions as symbolised in notation to be rendered as sound by performers, the mediation of which introduces a range of variables that are not present in the fixed embodiment of thought and action manifested in painting. In other words, a painting brings what it embodies from me to the viewer as an act of direct transmission. In contrast, a composition is realised as sound through third-party mediation as an indirect transmission from me to the listener via performers (this does not hold if I am producing electronic works where I exercise control over all parameters of sound production).

There are several things to consider here about the transmission of music from the composer, via performers to the listener, including the role of the composer, authorship, composer intention and meaning; the nature, scope and limitations of notation and what it signifies; the mediation of notation by the performer, shared authorship, interpreting notation and the ownership of meaning, indeterminacy in performance, the consequences of interpretation that could be seen as a secondary encoding with the addition of sonic artefacts not indicated in notation as part of the performance to produce what is heard; and last, how the listener receives and perceives the rendered sound and what meaningfulness they construct from it. As I shall

---

[54] Yeats, 27 Poems (9th November 2005). Forthcoming publication on Vision Edition.

discuss, several nuanced and sometimes opposing perspectives exist. Still, despite their differences, all agree that the relationship between any of those components of composition, performance and listening is unstable.

Beginning with the composer, the basic premise is organised around the notion that the composer chooses to build a composition by creating relationships between pitch, rhythm, structure, expression and speed that, through performance, play out in time. Those elements are brought together and organised often within the codification of a music notation, in my case, European music notation, that uses a range of more-or-less agreed-upon symbols to convey significance associated with actions necessary to produce sonic outcomes—sounds—situated along a timeline, either for one or many individuals to perform. The relationship between the signs used in notation and the materiality of sounds produced is an arbitrary one. There is nothing inherent within the signs themselves that indicate in any way the signification of specific sound production. The semiotics used here are not mimetic of the outside world, they exist as an independent incommensurate system of graphic traces. Their meaning has been established and assigned over hundreds of years as an artificial construct within a system of signs that have also undergone revision to arrive at a point where their 'signified's are based upon a more-or-less agreed-upon composition and performance convention situated within the context of wider European texts, particularly music text. In other words, music notation and the sound it initiates share no intrinsic relationship outside of any decoding within the convention it has evolved. Without specific interpretation, notation shares the same open signification as any collection of dots and lines on paper and could be interpreted from any number of hermeneutic perspectives. However, interpreted within the parameters of meaning acquired through convention, music notation shows, to a certain extent, at least, the relationships between compositional elements as organised by the composer in graphic or symbolic form. This symbolic information represents the relationships between basic musical elements such as pitch, some aspects of rhythm, structure and speed as metronome markings that can be related to numeric values, proportions and frequencies. For example, where metronome markings are given, precise numeric values may be calculated around how many beats occur within one minute of clock time. Seventy-two beats per minute (BPM), for example, establishes that each beat has a duration of 0.83 seconds. From that tempo, the proportional and numeric values of divisions of the beat can be calculated, meaning that rhythms, too, can be reduced to proportional and numeric values. Pitch also operates at specifically identified frequency values, although there is some variation between countries and larger variations historically.

Aspects of notation such as expression and dynamics have no absolute agreed values between composer and players or players and players. They, therefore, remain largely ambiguous and open to wider interpretation. None of those symbolic elements is sonorous until players render them as sound. That sound production is influenced by a notational context informed by many other factors.

Playing styles, their conventions, received learning and training in conservatoires or through a range of imitative traditions, assumed or researched historic stylistic performance approaches, philosophical orientation and human capacities and even personal taste and preferences are all brought to the rendering of a piece of music through the player's interpretation and hermeneutics; in other words, the baggage each person brings to interpretation. This additional baggage, sonically encoded by the player, is secondary because the composer has already encoded aspects of their compositional thought into the choice and organisation of notional symbols used within a musical score. With much that is potentially encoded by the composer in notation having no absolute and objective assigned value and with meaning belonging to the interpretant, the hermeneutics of each performer generates simultaneous multiple layers of meaning that may be quite distant from particular notions the composer had around the sound outcome of their piece. Even with notational elements such as structural relationships, pitch, rhythmic content and metronome markings holding more-or-less agreed-upon values within the established performance conventions of European classical music, ambiguity will still arise.

With so much that is unclear within this convention, the performer, if inclined, may ask: "*what does the composer intend and what do they mean?*" This raises the question of 'composer intention' and what exactly that implies. Roland Barthes, the French literary theorist, essayist, philosopher, critic and semiotician, in his famous 1967 essay *The Death of the Author* has much to say about the nature of authorship, of text, including by implication musical scores and notation, author originality, the author (again by implication, composer as author) intentionality and the ownership of meaning.[55]

*The Death of the Author* is a landmark for twentieth-century literature, literary theory, poststructuralism and postmodernism. According to an online article by Lamos Ignoramus, Barthes' seven-page essay opposes the established trends "*in ordinary culture […] tyrannically centred on the author, his person, his life*", and abolishes the classical literary criticism that analyses a literary work within the biographical and personal context of the author of the work.[56]

The essay argues that a literary work should not be analysed by the information about the real-life person who created it and rejects the idea of authorial intent, instead developing a reader-response critical theory where "*The reader is the space on which all the quotations that make up a writing are inscribed without any of them being lost; a text's unity lies not in its origin but in its destination*".[57]

Barthes's use of the word 'quotations' expresses that a text cannot be 'created' or 'original'—it is always made up of pre-existing quotations or ideas. Therefore, the 'author' is not an author but a 'scriptor' who compiles pre-existing texts. The idea of scripting is perhaps analogous to a DJ rendering simultaneously complex mixes of extant music to generate a new multi-layered composition. In this regard, the role of a single 'discoverer' or contributor is challenged or denied making the scriptor the one that reorganised and confirms already extant ideas.[58] Barthes writes:

*We know now that a text is not a line of words releasing a single 'theological' meaning (the 'message' of the Author-God), but a multi-dimensional space in which a variety of writings, none of them original, blend and clash. The text is a tissue of quotations drawn from the innumerable centres of culture.*[59]

*In the multiplicity of writing, everything is to be disentangled, nothing deciphered; the structure can be followed, 'run' (like the thread of a stocking) at every point and at every level, but there is nothing beneath: the space of writing is to be ranged over, not Peirced; writing ceaselessly posits*

---

[55] Barthes, pp. 142-149.
[56] Ignoramous, Lamos, *The Death of the Author: Roland Bathes and the Collapse of Meaning* on the website *Films Lie* <http://filmslie.com/death-of-the-author-roland-barthes-meaning/> [assessed 6 August 2022]. This website is no longer available.
[57] Ibid.
[58] Ibid.
[59] Barthes, p. 146.

*meaning ceaselessly to evaporate it, carrying out a systematic exemption of meaning. [...]*[60] *Once the author is removed, the claim to decipher a text becomes quite futile. To give a text an Author is to impose a limit on that text, to furnish it with a final 'signified', to close the writing.*[61]

It is worth stating that as soon as I make a score using notation or graphics, as soon as I create a painting or write words, I have necessarily generated an interpretation, a representation of thought using symbols where that thought is embodied in whatever media I choose to make a material trace. This suggests that beyond conceptually authoring an artwork, creating material artefacts is first and essentially an interpretive act that renders my role as author instantly to the interpreter. Once created, the meaningfulness of the artefact leaves my interpretive field to be interpreted by others. Whatever intentionality those traces may hold must be empirically manifest within what is embodied to be categorised as objectively verifiable intentionality. According to Barthes and Derrida, everything else associated with transmitted intentionality is metaphysics and assumption. As Barthes writes above, "*writing [composing, painting or the creation of any text] ceaselessly posits meaning ceaselessly to evaporate it*". This holds for authorship and interpretation, too.

Many philosophical approaches now question the validity of the author's intention as transmitted through, in the case of a composer, notation per se, particularly those in postmodern thinking. Nevertheless, for those who continue to operate within concepts of intentionality and particularly the replication of compositions through performance (and in my experience, this community comprises the vast majority of musicians and composers I encounter), it is the acknowledgement and implementation of the more-or-less agreed-upon conventions of symbol interpretation present within the received learning, stylistic and historical considerations, philosophical orientation and training that composers and players generally receive that notionally help to support players' hermeneutic approaches to what is 'signified' in notation through a somewhat more cohesive approach to symbolic meaning. Reliance on performance convention is a less-than-perfect interpretive art with the assigned significance of meaning to symbol and much debate around second-guessing what a composer's intention is by examining what lies before the players symbolised in notation alone. Debate continues to rage around all aspects of the many performance conventions, with each claiming slightly more authenticity than the other or claiming access to a particular and often very specific window on the true meaning or intent of this or that codification or intended action. Owing to the non-specific nature of many aspects of the original notational encoding and its inability to hold specific meaning away from indicating pitch as an agreed-upon frequency (although there are well-documented regional and historical differences), rhythm as proportional divisions of duration and tempo given as a specific metronome indication, all of which can be expressed as numeric values (as opposed to a vague textual description of speed such as andante, presto or largo relating to tempo, for example), the debate will continue indefinitely. With this abundance of flux around precisely what is meaningfully conveyed through notation, it is time for me to state my position on composer intention.

But before that, it is useful to consider what the French musical semiotician Jean-Jacques Nattiez writes, particularly as he would be aware of Barthes's 1967 article, *The Death of the Author* and the influence it subsequently yielded within literary theory and beyond. However, in Nattiez's writings, in particular his 1990 book *Music and Discourse: Towards a Semiology of Music*, he acknowledges composer intention as an active consideration in the writing and

---

[60] Ibid. p. 147.
[61] Barthes. p. 147.

interpretation of music through notation.[62] Rather than totally challenge and ultimately disregard notions of authorship and intentionality, Nattiez recognises those conditions as present yet unstable components of the relationship between composer, performer and listener. As Nattiez writes:

*What defines the identity of a particular musical work? Ingarden shows that this being cannot be reduced to any of the following: a given performance (since the score determines different potential performances); the here-and-now perception of a work (since each listener hears it differently); the acoustic reality (since the work's temporal profile and formal configuration are not, strictly speaking, sonorous elements); or the score (since the work will always and everywhere transcend that score).*[63]

As Nattiez explains: "*notation is indeed the trace that renders the work's identity possible. In this case, we need to realize that, from the analytical standpoint, notation is an image—imperfect but indispensable—of the notation's sonorous equivalent*".[64] From this image-imperfect, the performer renders the score as a sonorous fact: "*The work's physical mode of existence is, then, divided between the score and performance. The work's ontological mode of existence is situated in the realm of pure intentionality, beyond the score, yet guaranteed, rendered possible by the score*".[65] The nature of this tripartite relationship between composer, performer and listener is an unstable one and demonstrates that owing to the shared nature of authorship inherent in the relationship, any elements of composer control or direct authorship being 'transmitted' as a cogent message or instruction via the score between all three parties, are tenuous at best: "*For the musical event, there are three points of view: the author's, the performer's and the listener's. Their relation to one another varies in the extreme, sometimes contradictory, sometimes confused*".[66] Considering the positions laid out here, what are my views concerning authorship, composer intentionality and the transmission of meaning?

I see the composer intention as what is symbolised architecturally in notation, where that architecture reflects what the composer has intended to build as a composition through actual relationships of musical elements (as mentioned, pitch, rhythm, structure, expression and tempo) 'signified' through the symbolic conventions of traditional European music notation (aleatoric and graphics notations will have different, new, or perhaps no conventions associated with them). It is the combinations of those relationships, particularly pitch, rhythm and tempo, that can be assigned more-or-less agreed-upon values that, when organised in particular ways, for example, through idiomatic harmony, gesture and structure, become the building blocks capable of reflecting a composer's style, aesthetics and organisational choices.

When musicians interpret a musical score they are not generally making conscious numeric calculations for rhythmic subdivision (though an element of this may be necessary during practice to work out certain notational configurations for performers working within those interpretive conventions) but operate within a different concept of time called musical time which, through a more-or-less agreed value for the beat, enables them to 'feel' those divisions and as necessary, assign pitches to them. If compared to their actual frequencies, the accuracy of pitches produced during the performance is a more variable affair, not least because of the changing materiality of instruments, performance environments and factors relating to a

---

[62] Nattiez, Jean-Jaques, p. 16.
[63] Ibid, p. 69, paraphrasing Ingarden, Roman, 1990, p. 90.
[64] Ibid, pp. 72-73.
[65] Ibid, p. 82.
[66] Ibid, p. 31, paraphrasing Souris andré, 1976, p. 47.

player's capacities in a particular moment on a particular day. Those considerations introduce various indeterminacies to what is commonly called 'playing in tune'. Similarly, throughout a performance, there may be variations around what the players or a conductor feel is the beat within musical time.

When I begin composing a piece, my actions are full of intentionality. The act of composition itself; conceptualisation; generating materials; processes and transformations; choices and consequences; embracing serendipity; discarding materials or their combinations I do not like and keeping those that please me; instrumental choices; constructing structures and architectures, durations and tempi; recursive and assimilative actions, technical performance and instrumental considerations, choices around harmony and gesture and the relationships between all materials through to the finest detail and nuance that I perceive and assemble along with the motivations that drive those choices conditioned psychologically and emotionally by the affect, significance and meaningfulness I associate with those materials and their combinations, concepts and relationships at that moment in time. In other words, the conceptualised sound my actions generate as part of building that composition is all bound into composer intentionality, with those values and conditions acting as the foundation to the choices, decisions and notational traces I leave behind on paper (or in my electronic music notation software) as what is symbolised to signify those structures and relationships as compositional intentionality.

What is in question is how much of that intentionality, if any, is effectively (or affectively) transmitted to the performer through notation, where the meaningfulness of what is notated is shared as an equivalent value between the composer and performer. As mentioned above, what remains of this intentionality—the trace—is now embedded into the meaningfulness of notation symbols and the relationships between those symbols representing pitch, rhythm, tempo, structure and expression as triggered hermeneutically within performers decoding the meaningfulness of that notation as a personal act of interpretation. My intentionality is, I believe, transmitted to the performer regarding the relationships between the building blocks of pitch, rhythm, tempo and structure mentioned above, crucially when both composer and performer operate within an agreed convention of codification and interpretation through, for example, the more-or-less agreed on meaningfulness of those 'signified' elements as implemented through the European notation system.

What cannot be 'signified' through the term composer intention is any potentially metaphysical transmission of precise meaning on an affective, psychological, emotional, programmatic or messaging level through what is intrinsically 'signified' in notation alone. In transforming my compositional ideas and directions into symbolic representation as part of the initial act of notating a composition, such motivations and their affective intentionality at the moment of composition are fundamentally lost, leaving only something of their consequence embedded as the choice of symbolic representation and whatever meaningfulness that symbol or relationship of symbols may trigger in others. Although there will be those composers and performers that happily accept a metaphysics of transmission of meaning through authorship and performance, as far as I'm concerned, what a composer 'means' as an exact value transmissible through notation remains an unlikely concept and as such, is viewed as irrelevant. What the composer intends architecturally through the relational organisation of sonic and temporal symbolic elements in notation is far clearer to ascertain and realise through performance as a sonic reality owing to such meaning being able to survive the secondary encoding of each player's hermeneutics if those musicians are performing within a system of agreed composer/performer conventions, owing to those symbolised elements having mutually understood values within that particular composition and performance framework.

The transmission of those notational values from composer to performer to the listener (Nattiez's tripartite relationship) though flexible and open to degrees of interpretation and instability, ensures a potentially broadly consistent compositional identity through the performance and particularly the reproducibility of performances, providing the performer operates within the given convention. This understanding gives rise to the phenomena of multiple performances of Beethoven's *Fifth Symphony*, for example, by different conductors and orchestras, to remain recognisable to the listening public despite the somewhat indeterminate range of differences that arise as part of the process of individual performance deterritorialisation. By deterritorialisation, I refer to the concept created by Deleuze and Guattari in their book, *Anti-Oedipus* and later in *A Thousand Plateaus*. However, associated with a range of uses, particularly associated with taking order or control away from a place or territory that was previously established as a consequence of war, invasion, colonisation, appropriation, misinformation or propaganda, for example and replacing it—to reterritorialise it—with ideas, population, religion, ideologies, politics and information chosen by those who reterritorialise. In a more general sense and appropriate to musical performance is the use of deterritorialisation to describe any process that decontextualises established relations ready for recontextualisation as another set of relations. In my thesis, *Control, Flexibility, Flux and Complexity: A Timecode-Supported Approach to Polytemporal Orchestral Composition*, I state:

*[The identity of a piece of music] is constantly subject to different kinds of change brought about through player mediation of notation during performance. In [my own compositions] deterritorialisation is seen as the distance travelled or approximate measure of difference between the fixed (territorialized) audio generated through computer playback of a compositional model and the audio recording of its concomitant flexible, player-mediated live performance when both are compared. It is this deterritorialised imminent instantiation that is heard by the audience as the sounding music.*[67]

Performance training and execution within a given convention also enables the replication and recognisability of a piece of piano music rendered by several pianists of similar experience, capacity and training to sight-read identical materials for the first time and produce broadly similar results between all renditions despite the effects of deterritorialisation. Despite this homogeneity, the relationship of all aspects of composer intention as transmitted through notation to performers remains unstable. Nothing survives the hermeneutic process without a degree of modification.

If a composer performs or renders their own work in some way, perhaps through an instrument they play or an electronic rendition and notwithstanding any limitations to capacity, they can create a sonic fact that reflects their compositional intentions exactly, in principle at least. When performers interpret notation within the European classical music conventions and away from the basic elements established as indicating pitch and rhythm, players will be making many assumptions around the implied meaning of what is symbolised if their point of reference is a notion of being true to composer intentionality using what is intrinsically embedded as meaning within the notation itself. In such an event, the player must ask, "*What is intentionally?*" "*What is the composer's intentionality?*" "*Where is it located?*" "*How is this intentionality 'signified'?*" and "*How will I know if I've got this intentionality right?*"

---

[67] Yeats, Marc Kenneth, 2021, p. 22.

Although there may be an external textual source of information indicating intentionalities, such as a programme note, previous work, writings on or about that composer to reference, or even recordings of the work, those external information sources do not alter what is symbolically embedded within the notation itself. They only bring another layer of third-party encoding that filters and shapes perceptions about composer intentionality. It is also worth remembering that composers writing about their intentionality are likely myopic (my writings being a case in point), as are other commentators writing through their own bias and perspectives, yet another hermeneutic layer of interpretation to consider. There is no guarantee that those perspectives are either the right or the only perspectives possible. In short, ascertaining the composer's intention regarding meaning through external reference or examining the notation itself is a challenging, if not impossible, task. Add to this that nothing intrinsically within the notation itself suggests the composer's concept of the perfect performance, if they hold such a concept, or if the composer is present, that their perception of performance is the only realisation possible.

As meaning resides independently with the composer and players, there is no way of ascertaining which of those meanings, away from any notions that the composer knows best because of the intimate knowledge of the music their authorship brings, or the players in some way being privy to the composer's compositional intention, are correct or perfect. Decisions remain a matter of taste, aesthetics or even expectation contextualised within social and historical convention. Some of those positions may be more fully developed objectively or experientially. For many composers, a premiere performance is all that is available, with that performance possibly being less than optimal. In such circumstances, decisions about a perfect performance are even more confined. For each of us, the best performances often resonate or stimulate us or demonstrate the greatest technical, expressive or dramatic approaches in our opinions. For some, such qualitative values may arise from studying the music, its composer and historical, social and technical considerations and as such, opinion may be shaped by what is considered objective information. For many others, the best performances or pieces of music are often just the performances they like and enjoy. Among listeners, concepts such as 'the best performance' rarely signify the same agreed-upon phenomena. Any such conclusions ultimately reside within each critic's subjective domain.

Whether the player is using notions of composer intentionality or a desire to be 'authentic to the score' or an independent or non-traditional hermeneutic approach as a point from which to proceed in performance, notation interpretation brings with it, stimulates, if you like, sonic elements added by the player that are not indicated in the notation itself. Those include a whole range of indeterminate actions (discussed later) to do with how the player feels and their capacity for performance on any particular day; stylistic approaches or habits transmitted from and appropriated into one experience of performance to another; hermeneutic processes that shift from day to day, responses to the performance environment including ambience, conductor and colleagues; responses to a changing sense of the materiality of their instrument; familiarity and assumptions around the composition itself; different performance approaches and enthusiasms to music they like and don't like; the degree or extreme to which the notation is imbued with expressive elements; their own take on composer intentionality; if composer intentionality is a consideration; technical issues with their instruments or realising what is notated to a level they feel comfortable with; their own perceptions of the piece; even the use and context for vibrato; the list of additions, enhancements and overlays to notation at this level are abundant. Those indeterminate additions to the sonic fact, not indicated in notation, are always a component of performance and sound production. Amplify those hermeneutic additions through the performance of around one hundred orchestral players and the layers of interpretation manifested as sound become great. So, what prevents a hermeneutic free for all from unfolding and what would be the problem if it did?

Crucially, within standard European classical music notational practice, what results from interpretation is shared authorship of what is heard owing to the combination of assumed realised composer instruction as semiotically embodied in the score and how such indications stimulate mediation of that notation by the players themselves. In orchestras, the conductor provides beats for the players to follow as one body. It offers an overarching interpretive perspective that the players themselves will largely fall behind. This involves players often surrendering their hermeneutic possibilities to those of the conductor. Describing the relationship between conductor and orchestra in this way is a caricature and oversimplification. It is worth pointing out that many players, far from seeing themselves as subservient automatons, thrive and derive great satisfaction and pleasure from performing within orchestras, not least because of the synchronised action of rendering the music as a largely unified entity across all musical spectra. This phenomenon is similarly transmitted to the delight of audiences across a wide range of musical genres. Nevertheless, there is a significant difference in how hermeneutics are realised as sound between the interpretive freedoms of individual players, soloists and those working under a leader, artistic director or conductor and the concomitant expressive freedoms and choices each can make independently.

But in all cases, solo or orchestral, within this tradition, what is heard as music is a combination of assumptions realised as sound: assumptions around what players feel the composer is intending the composition to sound like as implied through their understanding of what is notated as well as its style and wider historical and musical context, assumptions around the meaningfulness of every aspect of notational signification and assumptions around the appropriateness of their interpretations to realise that perceived intention and just how much consideration this regard for assumed intentionality need receive. Where a conductor is involved, similar consideration is given to their hermeneutics and the directions and intentionality resulting from it as another interpretive overlay. Those assumptions are bounded by further considerations around how free a player or conductor can be regarding expressive elements such as dynamic, phrasing, tempo, rubato, vibrato and many others. This describes the most common, traditionally embedded approach to performance through notions of replication, simulacra and 'authenticity to the score' I encounter. As discussed shortly, other performance approaches are adopted by performers that take a different road.

Approaches to the mediation of notation vary greatly among players and orchestras, with many seeking to produce what they would consider an accurate or faithful reproduction of a piece of music within somewhat agreed contexts and often received knowledge concerning composer intentionality, history and playing techniques of the time in a fashion not dissimilar to the proliferation of an aural tradition as if there is a perfect a priori performance to emulate. In this instance, how a piece of music sounds and how that sound is achieved is duplicated, often with some differentiation, to broadly replicate what has been heard. Similar behaviours occur where performers consult the recordings of others, where such exist, to reference their interpretations. The attractiveness and relevance of such performance approaches will depend upon an individual's philosophical, educational and social situatedness. Still, regarding the comments of many players, critics and audiences I have encountered, I believe it is fair to say that such beliefs and approaches dominate European classical music making and its appreciation. The belief in a perfect, God-like rendition of given compositions is a preoccupation and goal for many, even though the existence of such a performance identity or object is difficult to locate or justify beyond cultural, aesthetic and taste considerations. In my view, those beliefs and practices continue to fill concert halls with audiences expecting to hear Schubert that sound like Schubert and delight in the recognisable and more-or-less repeatable listening experience. This includes most of the classical repertoire and perhaps all popular music. Within this field of realisation, the player attempts to interpret and render music with a degree of flexibility within the conventions accepted as existing between composer, notation and performer, conventions laid down and reinforced in conservatoires, schools, by music tutors and even when we hum, whistle, sing or play along to familiar music, we too are engaged in the reinforcement of sonic repetition. Such an approach leads to the familiarity of what we hear and the recognisability of our genres, artists, composers and even the sound of national identities or historical periods of composition. Any disruption to this system of composition, performance and listening to extant works would not, I suspect, be received warmly. People know what they like and want to hear and, with an established repertoire, know exactly what they are expecting to hear. Even new music performances are gauged within this lens of convention, with the more radical works often eliciting the greatest rejection. This is the established order of things.

It is a convention that supports the vast economic model of the music industry, including its artists, concerts, festivals and recordings that frequently vie with themselves to produce the most authentic, affecting and profound renditions of familiar repertoire through the production of simulacra. There is frequently more than a little metaphysics behind claims made by record labels and their artists in their justification for and pursuit of the perfect performance and recording. But in all those performances, the indeterminate elements resulting from each player's interpretation and rendition bring variety, novelty and new insight to performance and recording. Deterritorialisation exists even in those circumstances—it brings performance to life and music off the page—but the appropriateness of deterritorialisation is always a matter of degree that stretches reproducibility just far enough to create a variety of experience but never an entirely new territory. This confined deterritorialisation does not overwrite what may, through convention, be implied concerning how the piece will sound to the extent it creates a completely new identity for a piece of music.

However, not all performers or composers are drawn to the conventions of reproduction and its nuanced reinterpretations to create and render music. Within the performance conventions so far discussed, there is an acceptable elasticity in player mediation. This flexibility will vary depending on performance style and taste, but in all cases, will be considered to have its limits. If that elasticity is stretched to breaking point or beyond, what results ceases to be a reproduction of a composition, it instead becomes a new composition realised through a hermeneutic plateau that is no longer confined by the aforementioned conventions of reproduction and what is assumed around the transmission of composer intention through notation, or, where such exist, even the notational signification of values such as pitch, rhythm and tempo and their relationships to one another. In the most extreme application of deterritorialisation, I call this action 'total deterritorialisation', all compositions and their notational signification are interpreted in whatever manner the performer sees fit, bypassing any given or anticipated assumptions around composition and performance/interpretive conventions. Deterritorialisation will situate renditions on a spectrum ranging from varied, coloured reproductions through to original performances that still possess an audible connection to anticipated performance outcomes associated with what is notationally 'signified' when interpreted through European classical music conventions to at the other end of the spectrum, renditions that have little or no sonic connection to notation as interpreted through European classical music conventions. In this scenario, the composer's contribution serves only as a starting point or stimulation for the performer's unique interpretive journey.

Here, intentionality as sound resides entirely with the performer. Simulacra, through performance, is dead, as is the traditional role of the composer as the instigator of the sonic fact as interpreted by the performer.

This philosophical approach to performance sits comfortably within ideas expressed through Barthes's *The Death of the Author* but is also at home in post-structuralist and postmodernist thought and the writings of Derrida. I am thinking of this text from Derrida's *Signature, Event, Context* that says:

*Deconstruction cannot limit itself or proceed immediately to neutralisation: it must, by means of a double gesture, a double science, a double writing, practise an overturning of the classical opposition and a general displacement of the system. It is on that condition alone that deconstruction will provide the means of intervening in the field of oppositions it criticises.*[68]

Derrida's text is an invitation to overturn "*the classical opposition [of those dualities and binaries]*" and the assumptions around the hierarchies they support. It does this by proposing there is nothing of fixed meaning 'signified' in any word, text or symbol (including music notation) and where such meaning as is implied constitutes a veneer of inherited and learned convention based in a metaphysical hierarchy of presence and an a priori 'right way' conceptualised only through and in relation to an understanding of a 'wrong way' of interpreting that is by its nature considered inferior, misguided or unnatural. To requote from Derrida as cited earlier in The List, this metaphysics shows "*the enterprise of returning 'strategically', 'ideally', to an origin or an a priori thought to be simple, intact, normal, pure, standard, self-identical, in order then to think in terms of derivation, complication, deterioration, accident, etc*".[69] According to Derrida and greatly simplified through my description, such metaphysics is inherent in the language we use that itself supports notions of natural and unnatural aspects of duality including notions around correct and incorrect meaning generated through interpretation concerning what is present in a text or anything at all that is 'signified' in some way. Derrida asserts that to a greater or lesser extent, meaning is opaque and ultimately exists within the individual and that dualities that emphasise what is considered through convention a correct meaning or correct interpretation over what is thought incorrect in both cases serves only to reinforce the metaphysics of presence, thereby limiting interpretive potential and an understanding of the rich multivalent possibilities of meaning construction, in this case, meaning construction generated through multiple possible interpretive perspectives 'signified' within music notation. From this position, a player may legitimately consider their meaning, their truth and their interpretation—their decoding and recording— to be as valuable and legitimate as any other when it comes to producing sound from notational or graphic signification and, as such, with what is 'signified' having no fixed meaning, their rendering of notation valid no matter how distant from any known or assumed reiterative performance outcome that rendition may take them.

Similarly, such a position renders notions of composer intentionality as a transmissible concept 'signified' in notation as null and void. In considering this position and as Barthes asserts, there is a conflict between compositional authorship, how this is shared between composer and performer and if composer intentionality, not in the sense of a metaphysical transmission of meaning but regarding the relational properties of a piece as set out conceptually within the

---

[68] Derrida, 1988, p. 21.
[69] Ibid, p. 93.

semiotics of traditional European notation, remaining a consideration at all. Faced with such a performance philosophy, the role of the composer as the author becomes questionable, even redundant.

Lucia D'Errico is an exponent of new performer-centred performance practices of European notated art music. I have cited the preface to her book, *Divergence: An Experimental Approach to Music Performance*, in full, as it eloquently explains her position and reasoning:

*This book is an integral part of the five-year research programme Experimentation versus Interpretation: Exploring New Paths in Music Performance in the Twenty-First Century or MusicExperiment21, funded by the European Research Council, hosted at the Orpheus Institute, Ghent, Belgium and led by Paulo de Assis. The programme has explored and developed notions of "experimentation" in order to propose new performance practices of Western notated art music.*

*The research project of which this book is the outcome proposes a move beyond commonly accepted codes and conventions of musical interpretation. Crucially, the project is founded on a strong creative and practical component, presenting a new approach to the performance of Western notated art music. In this new approach, corresponding to an artistic practice supported by reflections and research, the performance of past musical works is not regarded in its reiterative, reconstructive, or reproductive function. This new practice instead insists on performance as a locus of experimentation, where 'what we know' about a given musical work is problematised. The performative moment becomes both a creative and a critical act, through which new epistemic and aesthetic properties of the musical work emerge.*

*This new practice insists on the unbridgeable divergence between codification (score) and materiality (sounds, gestures). Rather than being minimised, this divergence is amplified, so that performance happens through sounds and gestures unrecognisable as belonging to the original work as an interpreter would approach it. Instead of relying on the culturally constructed system through which symbolic categories are biunivocally connected to material events, this practice exposes the arbitrariness of such a system, together with the boundaries of its epistemic implications.*

*The activity of interpreters and executants focuses on the balance between objectivity (the instructions contained in the score, the 'facts' accumulated around the musical work, etc.) and subjectivity (the performer's freedom, his or her expressivity, etc.). This new practice goes beyond both objectivity and subjectivity, embracing an experimental approach to music performance that challenges traditional notions of interpretation. Whereas execution and interpretation relate to an ideal and aprioristic sonic image of the musical work (as Platonic copies), the performance practice proposed here posits itself as a production of simulacra: thus, performance becomes a sonic 'image' that relates to what is different from it (the score) by means of difference and not by attempting to construct a (supposed) identity. In this process, internal resemblance is negated, together with the idea of composition as origin and performance as its telos.*[70]

Though an entirely legitimate philosophical approach to performance that uses notation as an interpretive stimulus necessary to produce what is heard, the resultant totally deterritorialised rendition, as D'Errico explains, has little or nothing to do with the composer's authorship, the pitch, rhythmic, structural, expressive or other relational qualities of the work 'signified' within the conventions of notation. For the composer who wishes to build reproducible sonic

---

[70] D'Errico, Lucia.

structures through the mediation of players, 'total deterritorialisation' offers little in the way of collaboration or shared authorship and has no relationship with composer intentionality. Similarly, for the audience wanting to hear a particular Schubert symphony, a totally deterritorialised rendition would not, I suspect, prove satisfactory for those listening beyond the novelty of an experimental outcome. I assume those attending a concert expecting to receive a 'Platonic image' performance would feel short-changed. In this performance scenario, what the composer has built conceptually within a performance expectation of simulacra, the performer has, to a very large extent or entirely, recomposed in favour of their hermeneutic plateau. The performer has become the composer by overwriting or perhaps even creating something completely new upon the foundations of what has been mediated. The original has been destroyed or radically transformed and replaced.

The potential disappointment of an audience to this reconstruction, creation of an original or destruction and replacement isn't the issue here and neither is moving beyond any regard for composer intention if such exists. The point is the experiment. It will ruffle feathers and cause composers and performers to question what they are doing and how they are doing it. It destabilises tropes concerning interpretation, its limitations and appropriateness and any consensus around what music or any composer 'means'. It abolishes the dualities between what is the right and wrong way to perform music. It dissolves and re-establishes the hegemony, relationship and roles of composer and performer. It replaces notions of certainty with the dynamism of contingency. In permitting the individual to interpret and assign meaning to any sign or symbol as a hermeneutic act outside any convention and with complete freedom, it brings to the fore outcomes associated with the interpretation of conventional European notation that was hitherto inconceivable. The alternative approach to the performance of Western notated art music documented in D'Errico's book demonstrates that a new approach to performance has been established and this choice is open to performers (and listeners and composers) to embrace should they wish.

For this approach to performance to be classed as experimental in the manner D'Errico lays out, both performers and listeners must be familiar with European musical conventions, tropes and genres. In this regard, D'Errico's alternative renderings of extant compositions rely on structuralist-like assumptions around performers and listeners being embedded in and aware of wider social texts and meanings—their meta-narratives—associated with musical composition and performance practices that themselves contextualise D'Errico's renditions. One cannot appreciate what is experimental or alternative about any approach unless one is embedded within the convention it moves against to ascertain the difference between them. This context provides the established conceptual framework against which D'Errico's research can claim to be experimental. In this regard, I see D'Errico's philosophical foundation as situated in opposition to, rather than independence from the performance conventions it offers an alternative to and that the edifice of convention D'Errico seeks to deconstruct is an essential component of her project's identity since D'Errico's work—the sonic fact of it—is present and in opposition to (a duality with) conventional European music notation interpretation that has through her interpretation become what is absent. I see this as a contradiction between the need to tear down structuralist tropes and conventions while simultaneously depending upon them to contextualise the premise of the research. There is also the contradiction that over time and wider implementation, challenging and destroying tropes succeeds only in replacing an old trope with a newer, different trope. I believe this research offers performers and composers a mind-opening choice concerned with asking and answering questions about the why, how and what they render from notation.

Situated within the thinking of Barthes and the philosophical implications of *The Death of the Author*, D'Errico's approach to performance falls more widely into postmodernist thought that sees notions around agreed meaning, narratives and shared myths replaced by an interpretation which, if taken to its philosophical endgame, see the death of the author as an authority and holder of intention and transmissible meaning replaced by the rise of the individual reader, performer, listener, viewer or anyone who engages with a text of any kind as a critic, as the new God-like creator and author of all they encounter, offering unbridled individual conceptual and interpretive freedom. Regardless of 'the authors' fate, it certainly implies the death of the composer as we know it. As the writer Lamos Ignoramous points out in his online article *The Death of the Author: Roland Bathes and the Collapse of Meaning*:

*The philosophical implications of The Death of the Author transcend literature and are closely related to the postmodern trends of collapse of meaning, inability of originality, the death of God and multiple discovery. It is the freedom from the shackles of meaning and Author's intention. The death of the Author is also the inability to create, invent, or be original. It is the spinning out of control into the abyss of multiple meanings and inevitable meaninglessness.*[71]

In the possible dystopian future cited above, all that remains are free creator-God individuals with everything around and within them, as if through a process of social entropy, reduced to no meaning and equal value and to no value at all, without order or context outside of the self. If, as Barthes suggests in his later writings, there is only layer upon layer of myth or mask with no face beneath, no matter how deep within or without one looks, an ultimately nihilistic point is reached that challenges any notions of an external, verifiable reality, questioning any projection of the self beyond the Cartesian condition 'cogito, ergo sum'.

I am not associating D'Errico's project with this nihilistic, solipsistic focus or possible every man or woman for themselves type outcome. Still, in anyone adopting such deconstructionist thinking, even in part, I cannot help but wonder where its conclusion leads philosophically when those principles are applied and played out more widely across all social texts and our lives in general. Perhaps we choose to stop thinking about the consequences of such philosophical directionality long before we reach a nihilistic brick wall but carry on regardless as if such outcomes are not inevitable. In our postmodernist, post-truth age, such thinking is already influencing our lives locally and globally.

In concluding that we process and author meaning as individuals, I believe there to be an interaction, a covalent influence, in authoring our own meaning through the interpretation of interior and exterior stimuli where meaning is shaped by the communal communicated interpretations of others through books, film, education, law and ethics, science, philosophy, celebrity, religion, society, culture and one to one communication, for example. We are both influenced and influencers moving between interior and exterior space networks, time and experience, processing and interpreting as we journey. This is the hermeneutics of our lives. All meaning formation has implications for how we may live our lives as individuals and collectively as societies, but I suspect that as we do still communicate through language, through semiotics more widely and through what is embedded in and transmitted through artefacts as meaning, embedded knowledge and understanding and importantly concerning this section of The List, still perform music following shared, organised communicative

---

[71] Ignoramous.

operations as a communal activity. I believe, too, that as we author and move seamlessly between our own meanings in multiple scenarios, the way we integrate incommensurate semiotic systems into our lives to fathom truth and meaning is a multivalent and, as such, a highly complex and evolved system of its own full of flux and contradiction. Perhaps this constant mixing, matching and adaption of extant and generated experience, knowledge and meaning are commensurate with Barthes's scripting, where the elements are no longer original in and of themselves but become newly potent and generative in their combination, amalgamation or hybrid state, but whether conscious or subconscious, through hermeneutics, become the ultimate regenerative creative act we all engage in where a postmodern future doesn't inevitably signify doom, gloom and the violent deconstruction of everything good, bad or indifferent that is inherited from the Enlightenment to the present day?

Returning to music performance and composition, D'Errico's project is situated entirely within past and present compositions written and conceived within musical conventions already discussed. Alternatively, within forms of notation that do not determine any or all elements such as pitch, rhythm, structure, expression or tempo that invite indeterminate, contingent and open responses from performers such as text scores, mixed scores (standard notation and graphics/images/text combinations) drawn scores, found object scores, transduction of another art form to sound and indeed the reading of any artefact or object as a score, total or any degree of deterritorialisation performance approaches can be very productive with both player hermeneutics and if a composer is involved in creating such a score where composer intention is similarly open, being as one.

To emphasise this point, I cite Markus Wenninger's, comment to me on playability:

*There's no such thing as an 'unplayable' piece: If it's recognisable as an arte factum, it's playable per definition. The fundamental mistake is to assume a score has to provide the performer with everything to be played. It is not so—you just practice to self-sufficiency.*[72]

Away from 'total deterritorialisation', there are many degrees of deterritorialisation possible, including those that are very much mindful of and stimulated by what is symbolised in a score, including values such as pitch, rhythm and expressive elements but where the hermeneutic approach applied takes all phenomena to degrees of expressive overload and density. This is hermeneutics that renders sound and instrumental capacities to extremes. It has no interest in histrionic politeness, mannerisms, conventions around taste and behaviours or other stylistic moderators. It operates as a direct and visceral relationship between what a composer has notated, how it has been notated and the hermeneutic response such stimuli initiate within the performer. This form of deterritorialisation can be practised, too, until such a point that its interpretive fabric becomes physically and emotionally embedded in the performer to create a consistent yet still reactionary response to the music in performance.

Within this interpretive context, though the player seeks to approach each composition from a fresh contextual perspective, the embodiment of sound as a physical property will likely condition them to generate a repertoire of sound production and accompanying somatic, physical and neuroplastic responses that develop into a personal repertoire of actions, both physical and sonic, associated entirely with them and the uniqueness of their hermeneutic milieu. Their style of playing will become their identifier as well as an aspect of their sonic

---

[72] Quoted from a Twitter conversation between Marc Yeats and Markus Wenninger on the 31st. March 2021 <https://twitter.com/MarkusWenninger/status/1377211321830277123> [accessed 29 August 2022].

authorship when rendering music composed by others. Such hermeneutics enables those players to become the most intrepid and surprising of interpreters within the sphere of shared authorship.

'total deterritorialisation' operates at an extreme. Deterritorialization, in general, is, as mentioned, built into all forms of human performance as a matter of hermeneutics and inherent human indeterminacy and many exciting and fruitful collaborations between composer and performer are possible along the spectrum of deterritorialisation from the production of simulacra to 'total deterritorialisation'. Along this spectrum, authorship is shared between composer and performer to differing degrees, weighted either more towards composer or performer from moment to moment and piece to piece. Sometimes, those relationships will exist in flux. Away from the extremes of simulacra or 'total deterritorialisation', it will be difficult to ascertain exactly where divisions of authorship lie and where what stimulus equals which action.

Such is the nature of collaboration between composer and performer. At the most basic level, the composer can be seen as a provider of stimuli that the performer uses as a starting point for their hermeneutic journey. In most senses, a performance based on a third-party notation can be reduced to this description. However, at its most sophisticated, the collaboration between composer and performer, as the relationship between stimuli and hermeneutics, can share an intimate, nuanced and evolving communication and transmission—a shared authorship—within a novel, bespoke or generic convention relating to signification, meaning and action. At its most confined, deterritorialisation brings novelty, interpretation, colour and new insights to simulacra. At its most extreme, deterritorialisation creates something completely new from something pre-existing. Between those two points lies a continuum of expressive, interpretive and hermeneutic possibility that renders the sonic fact through cognition, artistry and imagination to generate collaboration between composer and performer. Markus Wenninger again:

*Let me add here: It's not a separation (of stages) per se (ontology is far away from here, it's hermeneutics, basically), but a de-coupling, an action, the result perhaps even, of the différance-gesture. Hermeneutical categories, yes, in heterogeneity of total hermeneutic situativity. Writing music is categorically different from performing it and again totally (not only gradually, as tradition has it) different from painting. Both decoupling + interconnections are made, violently so.*

*Although re. the point about ontology, are we? I often think performance and composition, for instance, are as different 'worlds' as can be imagined...with their own incompatible strategies, desires...let alone the subjects that inhabit them.*[73]

In laying out my experiences within the realm of performance, it becomes pertinent to define my position and the context of my work in relation to performers. My focus is distinctly on how the intentions embedded within my structural framework are conveyed to audiences, stemming from my role as a composer. This perspective, however, is not fixed; rather, it dynamically shifts with the specific musicians I collaborate with and the nature of the composition itself. Thus, my expectations surrounding elements such as reproducibility, recognisability and the transmission

---

[73] Quoted from a Twitter conversation between Marc Yeats and Markus Wenninger on the 1st. April 2021 <https://twitter.com/MarkusWenninger/status/1377579436095250437> [accessed 29 August 2022].

of structural intent undergo a continuous evolution. The performances I've encountered span a spectrum: from those deeply entrenched in structuralism, drawing upon wide-ranging cultural touchpoints encompassing genres, forms and communicative codes—what I have been referring to as European notation and performance convention—as is the case with many orchestras and ensembles I have worked with, to post-structural. The latter revolves around an intricate interplay between performers' interpretations, their hermeneutic processes and the foundational notation provided by the composer. This dichotomy has led me to recalibrate my anticipations regarding performance outcomes. What has struck me profoundly is witnessing the same composition mediated in vastly distinct manners along this continuum. This variance engenders radically different sonic realities, owing to the involved performers' diverse philosophical and hermeneutic orientations. In my experience and as a broad generalisation, the larger the group of players, including orchestras, the more structuralist their performance orientation (and my performance expectations) will be.

So far, my experience of post-structuralist and deconstructionist performance approaches has gravitated around individual performers often, though not exclusively working alone. Although my notation and compositional approach does not alter when working with musicians from either extreme or any point along the continuum between structuralist and post-structuralist ideologies (it doesn't need to as it is the hermeneutics of the performer that interprets the notation from their situatedness and therefore shapes what is rendered whether simulacra or totally deterritorialised), I only need to adjust my expectation around possible performance outcomes as I will never know exactly what will be rendered in both scenarios until I hear it. However, my conceptual guesswork is more likely to be close to the mark with orchestras and ensembles, especially in my synchronous works, but even in my polytemporal compositions to a lesser extent, than my expectations around more deterritorialised performances where it is challenging to form an expectation other than the expectation that I cannot form an expectation.

If I were a different kind of composer, I could operate without expectation or any sense of intentionality within or without convention and banish all notions of and filtering through subjectivity (assuming here that 'total deterritorialisation', if it isn't already, will eventually become a convention with its tropes and established behaviours). Even so, I do not believe any of those performance approaches or outcomes is correct or superior to the other, as all hermeneutic responses are legitimate. Still, from a psychological and emotional level—from my subjective positioning—I find some outcomes more to my liking and closer to my conceptual model or expectations than others. This is my performance reality. I am not disposed to like everything equally. My work—the identical notation—is rendered using approaches frequently situated within commonplace performance conventions and those ranging into degrees of deterritorialisation. I need to be flexible. I can also add that from a personal perspective, performances within more structuralist conventions and simulacra are not guaranteed to be great performances per se. This is true of any performance approach, as some performances will resonate more affectively than others. Those may not always be the performances I anticipate as important to me. But what I think of any performance is not the only perspective worthy of consideration. There will be many opinions.

Throughout my composing life, I have learned a considerable lesson from the hermeneutic responses of players to my notation and this learning has and continues to inform my notational practice. All my music composition is expressed using the European notational tradition enhanced using a few idiosyncratic additions to signify concepts of performance and sound generation not adequately supported within standard notational expressions. Those additions are designed to suggest my intention through an assumed psychology and meaning of the line, graphic, gesture and symbol so that their embedded kinetic condition suggests a direct symbolic relationship to the implied action, preferably without recourse to a legend to establish meaning. As with all my notation, I attempt to achieve a clear and direct form of visual symbolic communication and transmission. This clarity may or may not ensure the effectiveness of predictable outcomes from my perspective, depending upon the hermeneutics of the interpretant and the degree of shared conventions around assumed symbolic meaning held between us. Still, in either event, it will elicit a hermeneutic response.

When working with orchestras, ensembles and most soloists, there is a shared understanding, a collaboration within the conventions of European classical notation and performance. Within conducted or uncounted synchronised compositions particularly, this shared convention results in a broad alignment between the realisation of my conceptual score as sound, especially on the structural level, but also including expressive elements that correspond to my expectations taking into consideration hermeneutic sonic overlays and the range of indeterminate responses already mentioned that form part of the sonic fact within this convention. My structural codification in notation is generally interpreted within the context of a similar shared meaning I used when composing and choosing the symbols and the relationships between them to represent my thought as embodied through pitch, rhythm and structural relationships. This performance scenario parallels my concept of a piece and its sonic instantiation. As previously discussed, I make no claims over my notational codification transmitting meaning as an affective or emotional/messaging value.

In recent years, with the proliferation of my timecode-supported polytemporal approach to composition, I have introduced greater degrees of structural flexibility as part of the performance convention established in my work. I write that I developed this approach to:

*Expand independent simultaneous polytemporal activity [where more than two and up to any number of players perform at simultaneously independent speeds to one another] to every instrumental voice in the orchestra using self-borrowed temporally unrelated heterogeneous materials while preserving the highest possible levels of structural integrity in performance. [...] Although timecode-supported polytemporal orchestral music fully determines structure, rhythm, pitch and expression through notation, it does not use conductors, click-tracks or scores for performance organisation. Instead, players and their materials are decoupled from each other and their actions coordinated by reading [fully notated parts containing] part-embedded timecode continually referenced to the rolling timecode found on orchestra-wide loosely synchronised mobile phone stopwatches with players adjusting their tempos as required throughout performance so that both align. This approach to performance introduces player-generated temporal indeterminacy where many players interpreting their respective tempos simultaneously creates cumulative degrees of misalignment between their materials when compared to concomitant material relationships fixed within computer-generated composition models. Temporal indeterminacy along with the uncertainties it generates is an anticipated and welcomed outcome of this methodology.*[74]

Although temporal indeterminacy is anticipated as a necessary part of this methodology and as such, the vertical alignment of structural elements such as pitch and rhythm displaced from any fixed vertical relationships as represented conceptually in any computer modelling, the flexibilities that ensue are confined, in theory at least, by the mediation of notation materials within rolling timecode frameworks. This confinement restricts temporal indeterminacies to

---

[74] Yeats, 2021, p. i.

local fluctuations rather than global structural anomalies. In other words, it provides degrees of wiggle room without changing the overall architectural relationships of the piece. Performances of this type with the BBC Scottish Symphony Orchestra in 2021 revealed a close resemblance to and structural coherence with my computer modelling, enabling me to take the subjective view that timecode-supported polytemporal music, when approached within the umbrella of performance conventions associated with European classical music and despite its greater performance flexibilities, produced a sense of recognisability and structural integrity I was more than satisfied with on a personal level. The same recognisability has been true in the performance of ensemble and chamber music performed through this methodology by a range of performers internationally, suggesting that my intentions for performance and structural outcome have been transmitted. It is still early days concerning orchestral rendition using this methodology and a range of more divergent hermeneutic outcomes may result. Once again, all renditions are legitimate hermeneutic responses, but some will resonate with me more than others. I also remain continually open to the unexpected within the instantiated sonic fact and how it is rendered. This is how I learn. The unexpected is always particularly informative.

Figure 5. *Near the River Blyth, Blythburgh, Suffolk.* Pencil drawing. Marc Yeats (2018).

On several occasions, performers have rendered sound from my paintings and drawings (Figure 5 shows a drawing that has been interpreted this way). Players have read the surface of those works as a score and rendered significance and meaning as sound through hermeneutic approaches to an image's line, gesture, structure, colour and texture. I always find this treatment exciting and interesting. I have no sonic expectation for my artwork when it is rendered as sound by another. I completely surrender myself to the sonic outcomes brought about through their hermeneutics. As the performer is 'reading' my artwork and what I have embodied within as a score, their rendition acknowledges my authorship as part of a collaboration between artist and performer. Still, unlike a music collaboration, I have relinquished all desire to contribute anything other than a visual/symbolic stimulus for the performance to take place. I experience no shared ownership or responsibility for the sound produced and understand that what is instantiated is entirely the product of the performer's hermeneutics that, unlike a musical composition, is without any intentioned or conceptual direction towards elements of sound production from me. In this scenario, I do not consider myself a composer as much as a provider of stimuli that, as I wrote earlier, provides the starting point for the interpretant's hermeneutic journey. I am always fascinated by the dual use of a painting or drawing as a musical score. Such embedded versatility appeals to my sense of economy and utility.

To sum up, as a composer, I am interested in notions of structural (not structuralist) transmissibility through performers to audiences. I realise that such ambition is tempered by the hermeneutics of both performers and, ultimately, listeners, with whom the final meaningfulness of my work resides. I take great care in making musical structures and nurture those constructions in every detail, nuance and relationship to generate a composition. I thrive in collaborative relationships with mutual respect and regard for what each party brings to the sonic fact. Any performance that enhances and transmits those concerns to some degree and within the scope of what is hermeneutically feasible brings me great satisfaction. Having said that, the surprise that unanticipated interpretive outcomes bring continues to be a source of learning, pleasure and wonder. Although I enjoy unpredictable performance outcomes that explore differences and travel some distance from my conceptual modelling and expectation, I feel most at home with renditions where I can retain some degree of recognition of the sounding music. Generally, the closer performance and expectation align, the more satisfaction I gain as a co-author. From an egoistic perspective and despite all that Barthes asserts about authorship and originality, I like to recognise my works in performance. I am similarly pleased when listeners also identify my work as authored by me.

## Polyphony for the Eye, Polyphony for the Ear

As well as working with and encouraging degrees of flux in my practice, I work with entanglement—entangled ideas, materials and making processes. Within my compositional practice, for example, I add layers of musical material to create vertical stacks of sonic strata that become increasingly dense. Similarly, I add layers of paint, one over the other, to make the optical and surface detail I require. In both cases, they are material entanglements. The entanglement of those layers gives the work its structural, sonorous or colouristic and textural qualities. Together as one, those strata form part of what is embodied. In many instances, substrata are hidden from view or not audible as they have been corrected, adapted, irradicated or over-written. Still, their influence remains significant, whether through their absence or the actions their making instigated to subordinate or eradicate all physical traces of them in the finished work. Those elements operate as a whole. Their function is greater than the sum of their parts.

Within this interwoven visual condition, but particularly musically, I consider such entanglements a polyphony and the perception of those entanglements an interpretation of polyphony but, more particularly, a polyphony through complexity. I shall elucidate this idea.

In *Control, Flexibility, Flux and Complexity*, I explain:

*According to writers on the subject, polyphony is 'music in more than one part, music in many parts and the style in which all or several of the musical parts move to some extent independently'.*

*Although this definition would appear to embrace almost any combination of independent materials under the umbrella of polyphony, '[m]any authors take the function of harmony as a criterion [within polyphony] so seriously' that they exclude works that do not conform to that criterion 'or consider its harmonies the product of the part-writing.*[75]

By contrast, polyphony through complexity, as defined by the composer and conductor Simeon Pironkoff, moves beyond a description where "*all of the musical parts move to some extent independently*" to a condition:

*[Where] polyphony is [...] based on a multiplicity of superimposed lines [but where in polyphony through complexity] the dimension of complexity develops from the intensity of the dynamic interplay between the separate structural levels underlying a single line. Accordingly, it is mediation that constitutes one of the most important characteristics of complexity rather than superimposition, the latter leading to the subsumption of already existent qualities, as opposed to their differentiation. We should therefore recognize the fashioning of linear contours as one of complexity's foremost tasks, which will necessitate a new definition of the term 'polyphony'.*[76]

To further clarify his point, Pironkoff illustrates the operation of polyphony through complexity using the example of how British-born composer Brian Ferneyhough constructs polyphony through the interlocking of various simultaneous time structures, saying:

*Ferneyhough, for example, has rigorously thematicized the temporality of music through the interlocking of several time-structures, thus achieving a heightened linear intensity (where this linear realm is loaded with countless relationships and ambiguities) and a resulting shift from the level of the individual co-ordinates to the issue of their mutual interpenetration. If complexity is to be defined primarily as the stipulation of relationships, it has thus raised polyphony to the level of a new language; one could, therefore, currently speak of 'polyphony through complexity,' in this manner updating the definition of polyphony.*[77]

In music, polyphony through complexity is described as the subsumption of layers of musical material and the parametric diversity they hold when mediated through the performer's hermeneutic processes. This action generates a sense of polyphony through performance and listening, whether for personal or public-facing purposes. I consider this analogous to the processes and outcomes a viewer undertakes when interpreting a painting through looking, particularly where sensory data is densely constructed, thematised and consistently symbolised, for example, where the subsumption of multiple interlocking structures, lines, focal points, perspectives, textures, transparencies, mark-making, colour densities and the relationships between all of those comprise the parametric strata of a whole, is an interpretive act similar in nature to a musical performance, where the act of looking establishes visual priorities and meaningfulness through interpretation. Polyphony for the eye, then, may be thought of as the act of seeing a multiplicity of stimuli at once and navigating a somatic labyrinth to perceive the many parts forming that whole. This comparison to sonic polyphony is also applicable to an exhibition comprising many paintings or an installation where one is surrounded by an assemblage of phenomena operating in different fields of experience. This perceptual complexity may be experienced through engagement with any heterogeneous or arbitrary collection of objects or phenomena where the mind will seek to pattern connectivity. There is

---

[75] Yeats, pp. 118-119. The citation is from Frobenius, Wolf and others [accessed 9 June 2021] pp. 1-5.
[76] Pironkoff, Simeon, (2002) p. 1.
[77] Ibid, p. 1.

also a likely correlation between the perceptual experience of spatialised music performance and the spatial element of an exhibition or installation, where the listener or viewer must draw those spatialised threads together to generate a sense of the whole experience. I believe this subsumption of multiple sensory data and parametric layers of experience, if you like, is equivalent to polyphony through complexity in music.

In 2004, I curated an installation of my paintings and music titled *stillness in movement* at An Turieann Art Centre on the Isle of Skye.[78] I designed the installation to link paintings and music together through shared processes of making and transduction of themes. I wonder if, when heterogeneous objects are placed together, as in this exhibition, the viewer/listener's perception fashions relationships between the two purely because of the context of their presentation regardless of any associative intentions I may have indicated. The installation was built on the assumption that it is a human creative function, inherent in our neural makeups, to see relationships and meaningfulness between objects, space and time. I believe we do this constantly; it is our way of creating relationships and developing the fabric of our realities. This is hermeneutics in operation.

## Polyphony, Assemblage and a 'Sense of Place'

I associate the term assemblage with an installation like *stillness in movement* but also with sonic polyphony arising from the experience of multiple components operating simultaneously in time to generate material and perceptual complexity. To clarify this relationship, I shall explain my use of assemblage as used in *Music, Painting, Landscape and Me*, as separate from the concept of the assemblage as the 'general logic' at work in Deleuze and Guattari's *A Thousand Plateaus*.

In my compositional practice but particularly timecode-supported polytemporal composition, an assemblage is seen as a musical entity generated when heterogeneous materials, often in the form of complete pieces or strands of music, are brought together in various combinations to make new pieces of music that, through player mediation in performance, create iterative, immanent instantiations. This description of an assemblage is in broad alignment with the *Oxford Dictionary* definitions of an assemblage that states it is: "*1.) A collection or gathering of things or people. 1.1) A machine or object made of pieces fitted together. 1.2) A work of art made by grouping together found or unrelated objects. 1.3) The action of gathering or fitting things together*".[79]

Compositionally, I describe larger polytemporal pieces, such as ensemble and orchestral works, as assemblages. They are made up of a collection of self-borrowed smaller compositional works or assemblages that form the components of the work. A process of recontextualising self-borrowed materials through combination and re-combination—plugging in and unplugging—into various compositional assemblages where those materials in and of themselves do not change their identities (unless aspects of identity are altered through various transformational operations) but where the combination and mediation of those materials together produce new identities and immanent outcomes where the whole (the assemblage) is greater than the sum of its parts (the self-borrowed materials). Compositionally, I refer to those constructions as nested

---

[78] More information about the *stillness in movement* installation can be accessed from Marc Yeats's website at <http://www.marc-yeats.com/blog/stillness-in-movement/> [accessed 10.12.2021].
[79] 'Assemblage', Oxford University Press, in *English Oxford Living Dictionaries* (2018)
<https://en.oxforddictionaries.com/definition/transformation> [accessed 25 April 2019].

assemblages and the processes of assembling them as 'recontextualising materials' and 'temporal realignment'.[80] Once constructed, the identity of those assemblages is constantly subject to different kinds of change brought about through player mediation of notation during the performance. Other changes involve how the sounding music's affective qualities will alter as different materials and musical assemblages are combined to create new works.

In this transformative and assemblage-building context, what happens to a perceived 'sense of place' associated with a composition when it is integrated with another to form a multiple heterogenous or homogenous assemblage of compositions? Does such action a) destroy those independent and distinctive senses of place, b) unify them as a completely new combinatory 'sense of place', or c) enable the continued perception of a separate 'sense of place' for each component as complexity and polytemporal density increase? I imagine that the entire assemblage of sound is interpreted as something new and significance is generated from that interpretation hermeneutically, no matter how complex new relationships or rendered sounds become. Are there, then, similar possibilities affecting a 'sense of place' in visual work that is combined in an assemblage of imagery: a montage, collage or bricolage, or perhaps partial overpainting or the creation of a palimpsest or where, in video, the transparency of various images is compromised so that several moving images show simultaneously?

## Flux, Jelly, Indeterminacy and Fuzzy Sets

Much of my practice involves multilayering events and phenomena to achieve a state of perceptual and material complexity. From my perspective, I construct surfaces in paint or sound that trigger a 'sense of place' through those operations. To manage the performance of temporal complexity in music and surface construction in painting, I utilise processes that generate indeterminate outcomes, meaning results cannot be predicted precisely. I also develop strategies to confine indeterminacy so that I can, in part, shape and confine those possibilities. I'm happiest making work in managed chaos—confined flux and ambiguity. But for ambiguity to function, it must exist between the familiar and unfamiliar. It must simultaneously exhibit open and closed relational possibilities to the viewer or listener and me as the maker. It must obfuscate.

Returning to Pepperell and his research into the creation and perception of indeterminate paintings, he writes:

*The challenge in making artworks that are genuinely indeterminate, then, was to achieve a delicate balance between recognizability and abstraction in order to excite the inquisitiveness of the viewer's visual system while frustrating its capacity for recognition at the same time. After many years of experimentation, I gradually developed a method of drawing and then painting, which seemed to produce this effect quite reliably. I discovered that by using a classical pictorial architecture, of the kind frequently found in European paintings made between the 1500s and early 1900s, I could create an image that incited strong expectations of recognizable objects and scenes. (This classical period was the epoch in figurative art that many people associate with recognizable depiction of forms, in contrast to later Modernism where artists turned increasingly to distortion and abstraction.) By using this overall pictorial structure but omitting, or otherwise manipulating those features of the image that would be readily recognized I was able to achieve a consistently*

---

[80] Yeats, 2021, pp. 21-22.

*indeterminate image.*[81]

I'd go as far as to say that nurturing ambiguity and indeterminacy through manipulating physical properties and their perception is at the heart of what I do as a composer and painter. I particularly like the idea of simultaneously exhibiting open and closed relational possibilities. This chimes with much of my compositional ethos, too, particularly regarding polytemporal composition, where musical activity is managed across a range of strata operating together yet individually using simultaneously different speeds but, in any case, as a general principle concerning the perceptual obfuscation of materials often through complex and dense relational conditions. In this state, a range of relationships between materials and their structural presentation in time exhibit open and closed relational possibilities simultaneously. However, ambiguity and obfuscation affect what can be transmitted from work to viewer or listener. This potential for flexible relational outcomes increases the range of possible goals and iterations of the work and, at the same time, exponentially increases the capacity for multiple and unpredictable affective responses from listeners. When considering ambiguity and indeterminacy in composition, I think of my concept of 'jelly' in timecode-supported polytemporal composition.

Imagine a jelly moulded in the shape of a castle, along with its towers and castellations, that sits on a plate unmoving. When the jelly is on the plate in its neutral state, it is still and one can observe its architecture from all perspectives. The jelly is structurally constant and remains the same, with all its angles and shapes in a fixed relationship to one another. This fixed, neutral state of the jelly represents, for example, any of my computer software conceptual composition models in their stable version of the compositional form. When the jelly is wobbled, either delicately or with greater degrees of force, the structure of the jelly, though remaining intact, becomes somewhat distorted and extended as it moves rapidly back and forth, vibrating and quivering at great speed. Those slight and localised distortions of the jelly (The Model) represent the effect of live performance on the neutral form with a slight wobble signifying the vertical alignment of musical elements such as a rhythm and their associated pitches being in a small degree of relational flux. By inducing a greater degree of wobble, relational flux is increased proportionally. The intensity of jelly-wobble, in theory, could be so rapid that it would be hard to ascertain the original form of the jelly as a castle because its structure would be blurred by the speed and distorted by the violence of the action, so much so that it could break apart and disintegrate. Alternatively, the degree of jelly-wobble may be so slight that the original structure remains easy to discern within and despite its wobble. The ambition for any performance of timecode-supported polytemporal works is for them to manifest somewhere on the continuum between correspondence with the graphics source and appropriate performance convention (slight to moderate jelly-wobble) and to fall just short of no correspondence between the graphics source and performance (disintegration of the form owing to violent jelly-wobble), but in either case, where the original structure of The Model will be discernible in performance by me as the composer, to some extent at least. As discussed earlier, this analogy of jelly wobble concerning image or structural recognisability in performance holds for degrees of territorialisation and deterritorialisation.

The American experimental composer John Cage uses a similar analogy to describe the flexible relation between instruments. He writes:

*There won't be a score that connects all of the parts. There won't be a fixed relation between those*

---

[81] Pepperell.

*instruments, but rather a flexible one. It resembles, perhaps, that aspect of architecture in, say, San Francisco where, because of the fault in the earth, the architecture has to be flexible and to be able to move, so when there is an earthquake, the building will shake instead of falling down.*[82]

From flexibility to indeterminacy, writing about music composition and performance, the British composer Brian Eno stated:

*An experimental composition aims to set in motion a system or organism that will generate unique (that is, not necessarily repeatable) outputs, but that, at the same time, seeks to limit the range of these outputs. This is a tendency towards a 'class of goals' rather than a particular goal and it is distinct from the 'goalless behaviour' (indeterminacy) idea that gained currency in the 1960s.*[83]

Eno's mention of classes of goals within indeterminate but not goalless outcomes makes me think again of 'Fuzzy Logic' and 'Fuzzy Sets' and if those are comparable with classes of goals in some way.

To understand the quote, how it concerns my work and what possibilities it holds for 'Fuzzy Logic' analysis, terms such as determinacy and indeterminacy need to be fully described and unpacked in relation to my music and painting practice. To achieve this, I shall first create an overview of the types of indeterminate techniques, some of which I use in my composition, then draw some broad analogies between those and techniques I employ in painting and finally examine the practicality of determining and analysing those conditions within 'Fuzzy Logic'.

In her 2016 thesis, *Determinacy, Indeterminacy and Collaboration in Contemporary Music-Making*, Emma Jane Lloyd produced a very useful taxonomy of terms regarding types of indeterminacy that may occur in music composition as processes of composer creation, player creation and player interpretation. I have heavily summarised those below. Although this information does not answer the questions around any potential similarity between Fuzzy Sets and indeterminate practices in composition and performance, certainly not regarding data collection and human behaviour, nor does it help ascertain if Eno's 'class of goals' is indeed a Fuzzy Set, it does help to describe the fuzziness of certain practices in music. Lloyd points out that indeterminacy,

*Which is to say that which has not yet been determined [...] is a term that can be used to describe a range of different attributes, rather than being a musical term in itself. Broadly, there are two categories—indeterminacy as a result of incorporating chance elements and indeterminacy that invites conscious interpretive decision-making.*[84]

Inverting Lloyd's definition points to the meaning of 'determinate' being that which has been determined or decided, something with fixed limits or something definite. She goes on to explain that:

**Aleatory**

Is that which employs elements of chance such as the throw of dice, but may also include aspects of random choice, sometimes using statistical or computer techniques during composition,

---

[82] Kostelanetz, Richard, 2005, e-book, p. 122.
[83] Eno, Brian, p. 316.
[84] Lloyd, Emma Jane, p. 18.

production or performance. Aleatory is also used to describe performance choice elements indicated in a score.[85]

## Ad libitum

In Latin, ad libitum means 'at the pleasure'. In most compositional contexts, ad libitum is an instruction directed towards the performer applied to various musical features, including instrumentation, ornamentation, cadenza or time. In some compositions, the term is used for various temporal freedoms, including how specific material is organised and performed, often accompanied by additional instructions regarding speed, rhythm, repeats and variations, for example. *"[Ad libitum] may be used to contrast with aleatory methods of determining musical factors. The term may also be used as a familiar way of describing improvisation [in a speech, for example]. Whether an improvisatory approach is taken or whether it is pre-planned, 'ad lib' implies choice as opposed to chance"*.[86]

## Notational hierarchy

Figure 6. *William Mumler's Spirit Photography* (2019), bars 1-6. Marc Yeats (2019).

Lloyd identifies indeterminism in various forms of notation, where a musical score contains multiple layers of information as shown in Figure 6, with each layer of information giving instructions on the feature it describes.

---

[85] Lloyd, p. 18.
[86] Ibid, p. 18.

Lloyd writes:

> *In a typical and relatively simple example, the position of the note heads will indicate pitch, other details of the symbol will show the length of the note, which, along with other information and other notes will show a rhythm. Usually, a dynamic scheme is notated under the stave and various diacritics and lines indicate the articulations and phrasing. […] While all notation on the page is generally considered important to the performance of the music there is a hierarchy […] centred around pitch and rhythm. […] Earlier music may have no more than [pitch and rhythm] indicated, the rest being decided or inferred by the performer.*[87]

Increasing complexity and extended notations mean that traditionally anticipated hierarchies may no longer apply, leading to multiple individual expressions of pitch, rhythmic and expressive component relationships, as shown in Figure 7, where graphics approximations indicate pitch ranges, rhythmic activity and the textural interplay of both.

## Graphic notation

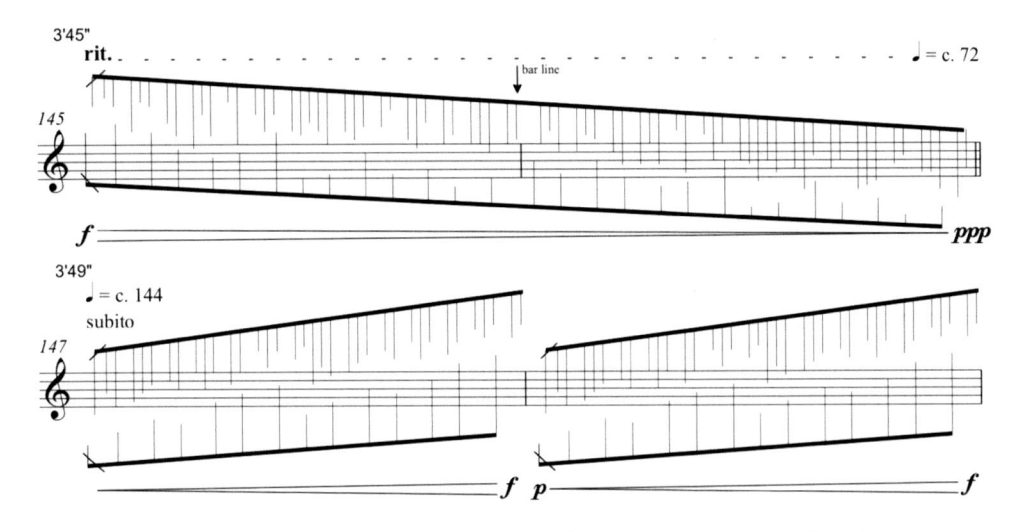

Figure 7. *Vulgar Gorgon*, electric guitar part bars 145-148. Marc Yeats (2014).

In graphic notation, as illustrated in Figure 7 and Figure 8, the symbols used can imply pitch, rhythm, dynamic and texture, but do so using a selection of other symbols that can range from text to drawing and painting (with similar techniques of interpretation applied to the 'reading' of various found objects, either incidentally occurring or artificial).

Graphic notations may also be combined with standard notational formats. However, the composer may provide some guidance around interpreting those symbols. The symbols may have no agreed-upon meaning within performance conventions. Where this is the case, the player will react to the symbols they encounter to produce a sonic fact as a matter of hermeneutics. Player interpretation will establish meaningfulness (for the performer), with results being impossible to determine in advance. Lloyd writes:

---

[87] Lloyd, p. 20.

*Let's consider 'standard' notation to include the collection of symbols commonly used to notate Western classical music which have more or less direct meanings, for example, time signatures, clefs, notes which indicate pitch and rhythm, dynamic symbols. This is another large category of pictorial notation that sits outside this.*[88]

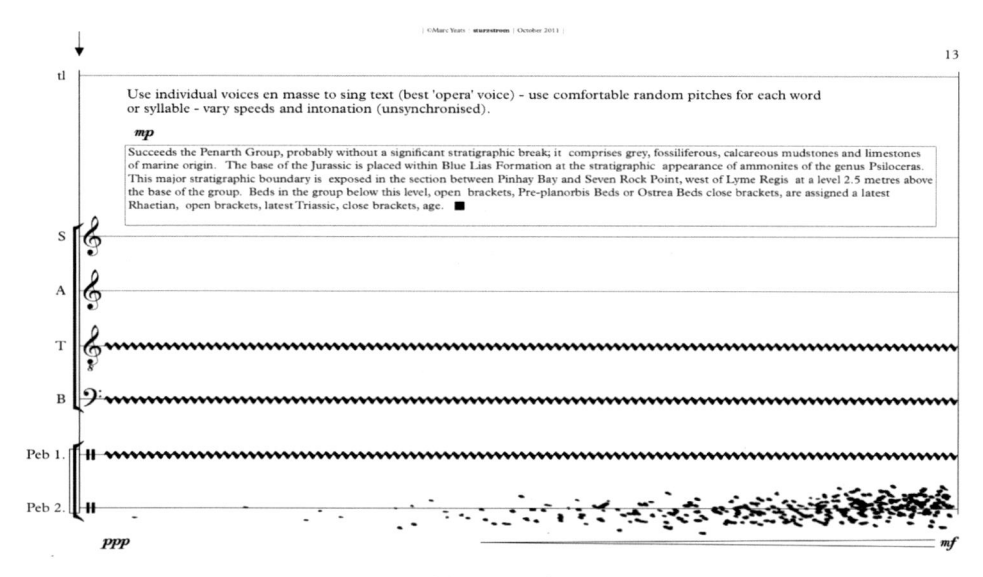

Figure 8. *sturzstrom* (a landslide event for voices). Marc Yeats (2012).

**Temporal indeterminacy**

Temporal indeterminacy is the term used to express forms of indeterminacy of musical factors that rest on time:

*The fermata is a common example of this. Spatial notation, where space rather than rhythmic values represent rests between notes may also present some temporal indeterminacy. Rubato is a form of temporal indeterminacy commonly assumed in notated music.*[89]

In timecode-supported polytemporal music, I describe sonic flux as:

*Player-produced temporal indeterminacy specifically related to tempo interpretation has implications for how elements I have determined in notation as the composer, such as structure, pitch, rhythm and expression, are instantiated as sound in relation to one another along the timeline of a piece by the performer. Sonic flux occurs within timecode-supported polytemporal music owing to the absence of a conductor or conductors, click tracks, or any sense of unifying or referential pulse between players and where those performers approximate a certain degree, the speed of performance their tempo indications specify. Owing to the action of players responding to timecode frameworks, levels of temporal indeterminacy should be confined to and affect only local (bar to bar) detail rather than global structural elements. Nevertheless, such actions and their inherent indeterminacy would result in the exact vertical alignments of pitches and their associated rhythms organised, fixed and determined in my compositional computer models being impossible*

---

[88] Lloyd, p. 21.
[89] Ibid, pp. 22-23.

*to reproduce precisely in performance. As such, each rendition would be iterative in its detail and the confined differences between these outcomes brought about through player actions render performances with similar identities but never exactly fixed identities.*[90]

Figure 9. Illustrative example of score-based polytemporal notation.

Figure 9 shows three polytemporal streams as they appear notated in a score, illustrating the temporal relationship of the materials through vertical alignment. In timecode-supported polytemporal composition, there is no score or visual indication of temporal relationships. Notated materials exist only as individual parts loosely synchronised using timecode.

**Pitch indeterminacy**

Pitch indeterminacy is a type of notation where the pitch is not determined precisely or at all. For example, as illustrated in Figure 10, the upper stave shows an indeterminate pitch indicated by graphics. Alternatively, on the lower stave, the indeterminate pitch is produced by finger positions represented by alternative note-heads. "*Such indeterminacies may also occur where various tunings and temperaments are used as in historically informed performance and the choice of exact tuning relies upon performer choice and musicianship*".[91]

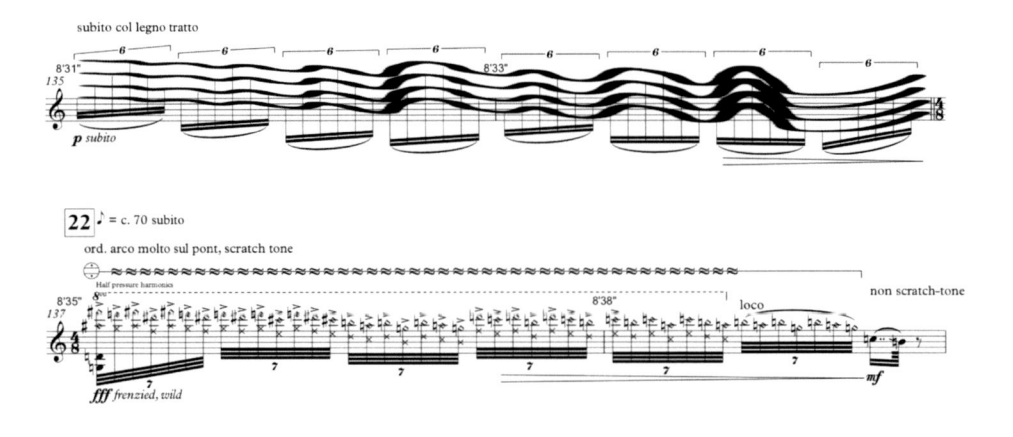

Figure 10. *obscure sorrows*, violin part bars 135-138. Marc Yeats (2019).

---

[90] Yeats, 2021, p. 14. As should be apparent from the definition I give of 'sonic flux' in my thesis, I do not mean to evoke the use of the exact phrase found in his book of the same name, which, as its subtitle indicates, is more concerned with sound, art and metaphysics. See Cox, Christopher, 2018.
[91] Lloyd, p. 23.

## Structural indeterminacy/indeterminacy of form

Performers may order, include or omit various compositional components to generate a varied overall shape and expressive components unique to that configuration, making the piece's overall structure or forms indeterminate within specified parameters.[92]

Within timecode-supported polytemporal performance, degrees of structural flexibility are generated through player mediation of notation materials, including tempi, part-based timecode indications and the loose synchronisation of those elements with each player's again, loosely synchronised mobile phone stopwatch rolling time display. Those timecode-confined flexibilities permit degrees of temporal flux to effect the alignment of performance events with timecode frameworks, resulting in localised fluctuations of structural integrity. However, timecode meditation prevents localised structural fluctuations from effecting global structural integrity.

## Timbral indeterminacy

*"Timbral indeterminacy occurs when a prescribed action (notated or otherwise) results in an indeterminate sonic response".*[93] Such responses may be an unintentional consequence of playing an instrument or a quality that is privileged for attention by the composer but where the sonic result is contingent upon the player's performative, technical and interpretive actions. To this end, a composer may instruct the player to use their instrument so that sonic results will be contingent upon several factors outside the player's control.

## Instrumental indeterminacy

*"[A] piece that does not determine the instruments to be used will produce sounds not specifically determined by the composer".*[94] This outcome is a form of timbral indeterminacy. The sonic results will be contingent upon the notational or graphic component of the score and how that is realised on any given instrument. Even where instrumentation is specified by the composer and the composition written within the technical and physical capacities of the instrument, a player may choose to perform the composition on a different instrument than that specified, transducing one notational or graphic meaning or significance to another considered of equal or comparative value.

## Human indeterminacy

Lloyd explains:

*The human element of performance yields its own indeterminacies which are perceived in different ways. On one end of the spectrum, we have what is commonly perceived as 'human error' and on the other end we have the musical nuances that give each performance its individuality. Roughly speaking, these are positive and negative ways of looking at the same thing. Both depend to a large extent on a subconscious response to the environment on other performers and the variation in their playing and one's own mood and state of well-being.*[95]

---

[92] Lloyd, p. 23.
[93] Ibid, p. 23.
[94] Ibid, pp. 24-25.
[95] Ibid, p. 25.

**Painting Techniques and Indeterminate Outcomes**

There are also indeterminate aspects to the act of painting within my practice and I concur with Pepperell that: "*The challenge in making artworks that are genuinely indeterminate, then, [is] to achieve a delicate balance between recognisability and abstraction in order to excite the inquisitiveness of the viewer's visual system while frustrating its capacity for recognition at the same time*".[96] Rather than attempting to correspond and thereby ascribe meaningfulness values to indeterminate elements of composition and performance as listed above with techniques of painting, a task as previously discussed, I consider flawed, I will broadly categorise my indeterminate actions into two categories: chance and unexpected outcomes as a wilful act of making and chance and unexpected outcomes as a by-product of making.

I see chance and unexpected outcomes as a wilful act of making premeditated to produce indeterminate outcomes to a degree at least, as outlined by Pepperell, for example, when I have used a blindfold or closed my eyes so I cannot coordinate my actions as effectively in space as I would by looking. This approach transfers control away from hand-eye coordination to other sensory and proprioceptor feedback that will produce results only apparent to me upon removing the blindfold or opening my eyes. Those actions are not generated through chance and probability in the same way as, for instance, throwing dice to determine steps. They are confined to my physical movements, materials and external conditions. Still, the lack of visual control does produce unpredictable results that, regarding artist intentionality, are indeterminate or abstracted to some degree. However, the decision to paint in that fashion is predetermined by me, hence the production of indeterminate results through a wilful act. Similarly, throwing or splashing paint across a surface, away from the calculable outcomes of classical physics regarding velocity, direction, viscosity and other factors where the results of such action may be plotted in advance are, from the artist's perspective, chance and incidental operations that play out in the moment of execution.

I also use scraping techniques a great deal. Once a particular surface has dried, I may paint over it again and scrap away the wet or dry paint to reveal strata that show through from underneath, creating a palimpsest-like surface. The process could also be considered like erosion, where outer layers of soil or rock are removed to expose deeper layers. The outcomes of those scraping activities are not known precisely in advance as they depend upon the indeterminacies of the scraping action; pressure, speed, the sharpness of the tool used for scraping and the physical activity itself as well as the relationship between the various revealed layers themselves. I cannot calculate precisely what will be shown in advance or my reaction to it, which in and of itself will stimulate a decision to continue with the scraping or stop. This process may be repeated several times and, although a wilful act, produces uncertain or indeterminate results. Again, those outcomes become what I determine as an act of embodiment in the work once I acknowledge the process and, therefore, the work as finished.

On a finer scale, mixing paint on the palette while in a cycle of recursive action and rapid movement between paints-brush-palette and paint-loaded brush and surface produce indeterminate outcomes regarding the actual mixture and application of paint as it appears upon the surface. Unlike mixing a specific colour precisely before its application, those actions are mixing on the hoof, governed by estimations and approximations of amounts and force or speed of mixing, the amounts and number of paints involved and the type of brush or palette knife used to mix and apply the paint. Once applied, the mixture is either accepted or further

---

[96] Pepperell.

adjusted, over-painted, blended in or wiped away until the desired result is reached. This process assimilates indeterminate colour mixtures until their condition and relationship to other components of the painting are satisfactorily achieved, rendering indeterminate actions as embedded determinate outcomes. The result says: *"This is what I meant because it is here"*. Unlike music performed and reinterpreted, the painting is fixed in its relational and semiotic properties.

**Indeterminacy and Fuzzy Sets**

Considering the information presented here around indeterminacy in composition, performance and painting, I am now better positioned to discuss the relationship between those indeterminate parameters as classes of goals with Fuzzy Sets. As described earlier in The List, Fuzzy Sets incorporate elements that possess degrees of membership; in other words, they can be partly in or partly out of a set where values are indicated as any value between 1 and 0. These are truth values. If one were to consider a range of indeterminate outcomes in music or painting as values between 1, let's say, as fully determinate outcomes as defined by x criteria and 0 as entirely indeterminate outcomes categorised as y criteria, the set of goals identified between those two positions could, I suspect, be considered as a Fuzzy Set.

The challenge arises in ascribing meaningful numeric values to all degrees of possible indeterminacy within any set, each requiring assigned values anticipating all possible outcomes. Whether those possibilities represent an infinity, I do not know, but, in any case, the variables will encompass enormous numbers. How those values could be aggregated and processed to represent truth values that demonstrate the occurrence and degree of indeterminacy in various performance scenarios is beyond my capacity for logic. Working with very large numbers or infinity is always difficult to comprehend. I imagine that the usefulness of this exercise in 'Fuzzy Logic', should it be anything other than theoretical, would prove limited as values between 0 and 1, being so vast, would only point to results that would correspond to a possibility range like that of a lottery, therefore being a challenge to interpret meaningfully as part of artistic practice. This thought experiment highlights the difficulties of bringing truth values to art and artistic practice where interpretive thought, action and outcome operate within massive fields of possibility or perhaps values of n+1. Such a vast array of possible outcomes results from, for example, my practice as I generate multiple possible responses to multiple possible stimuli through the operation of many layers of neurological activity within or outside my awareness. My conscious and subconscious minds interact with each other constantly. Motivations, fears, hopes, anxieties, joy, projection, analysis, reaction, calculation, spontaneity, humour, anger, jealousy—the list is endless, all conditions generated through layers of my neural network, through this neurone entanglement of connections producing sensations, thoughts feelings and responses could be described in terms of Fuzzy Sets. Certainly, 'Fuzzy Logic' is already applied to a range of human behaviours that cannot be explained simply in black-and-white terms. The biochemistry of our processes, reactions and their neural pathways can be mapped and analysed in detail; they can be viewed effectively through the scientific lens, with electrical impulses following given routes and engaging specific chemical agents proven and verified, but what the actual thoughts and feelings associated with those neural activities are and mean to the individual and what that 'lived experience' is from moment to moment, remains unclear. For example, the state of happiness cannot be verified using current scientific methodologies, yet to the individual experiencing joy, the sensation is as objective as material reality. Some scientists diminish the role and impact of subjectivity because it cannot be verified and measured even though it occupies most of our lives, thoughts, feelings and actions.

In a 2022 article titled *Neuroscience Research Triggers Revision of a Leading Theory of Consciousness* published in the multimedia portal *Big Think*, Moheb Costandi, a science writer and contributor to *Scientific America* and *New Scientist*, explains that *"[a] new finding that unconsciously processed images are distributed to higher-order brain networks requires the revision of a popular theory of consciousness"*. The theory in question is called the global workspace theory of consciousness, which states:

*Conscious awareness arises when a large-scale central network hub of brain structures in the frontal and parietal lobes 'broadcasts' information to make it available to other neural systems involved in cognitive processes such as attention, language and working memory. Thus, different types of information are processed in their relevant local domains and only enter conscious awareness if they are first received and then shared by, the central hub.*[97]

According to the article:

*Modern neuroscience tells us that we are completely unaware of most brain activity, but that unconscious processing influences behaviour. A recent brain scanning study published in Nature Human Behaviour shows that unconsciously processed visual information is distributed to a wider network of brain regions involved in higher-order cognitive tasks. This may require a revision to [...] the global workspace theory.*[98]

There has always been a question about how and how much unconscious information processing influences behaviour. Freud suggested that our behaviours are driven by thoughts and feelings deep within the subconscious mind, an idea that became increasingly suspect as it was viewed as unscientific. Some modern neuroscientists say that we are completely unaware of most brain activity, but unconscious processing influences behaviour. Costandi explains:

*A recent brain scanning study now shows that unconsciously processed visual information is distributed to a wider network of brain regions involved in higher-order cognitive tasks. The results contribute to the debate over the extent to which unconscious information processing influence the brain and behaviour.*[99]

The author's findings, published in the journal *Nature Human Behavior*, "suggest that mental representations of conscious and unconscious information overlap in some regions of the visual pathway and they suggest global workspace theories of consciousness need to be revised".[100]

Unpicking the conscious and unconscious layers of operation behind the biochemical nature of brain function may provide insights into the mechanisms involved that support consciousness but do not come close to explaining the experience of self-awareness other than speculating that it arises through the culmination of multiple functionalities of the brain and its highly complex and interwoven neurological impulses. Science has understandably bypassed such ontological concerns in favour of materialism, objectivity and the verification of material objectivity to create theoretical frameworks. Nevertheless, as mentioned, the role of the observer and consciousness effecting outcomes at the quantum level, particularly regarding superposition, indicate more to discover concerning our concepts of reality and how our

---

[97] Costandi, Moheb, [accessed 11 August 2022].
[98] Ibid.
[99] Ibid.
[100] Ibid. Additional information from Mei, Ning et al., [accessed 11 August 2022].

observation and consciousness may unfold it than are currently available through scientific modelling and theorising. Some quantum physicists state that a paradigm shift from the traditional scientific method is necessary to fully explain the unresolved questions, enigmas and paradoxes quantum mechanics continually throws up.

## Observation and Quantum Mechanics

In July 2021, Professor of Physics and Director of the Center for Excellence in Quantum Studies at Chapman University, California, Jeff Tollaksen, talking in a video interview for *Closer to Truth*, an online portal describing itself as *"the definitive source for cosmos, consciousness and meaning"* discusses his research and thoughts regarding quantum mechanics.[101] In particular, Tollaksen is asked: *"Does the concept of observation have deep relevance in fundamental physics? What about in quantum physics, where some observation seems to be needed to transform 'wave function' probabilities into actual events? What's an 'observation' anyway? What does it take to be an 'observer'? Must it have some sentience?"*[102]

This is a thought-provoking interview from which I have extracted and transcribed (with limited grammatical tidying) a few aspects that illustrate my thinking around the scope of current scientific models to explain quantum phenomena meaningfully and the importance of the interior human world in interpreting this data. Tollaksen says:

*I feel the deep thing about observers we haven't even begun to hit the beginning of is that we must start talking about what it means to, for example, look inside. What does it mean for us to observe ourselves without making a division between a measuring device and a system, so it's the issue of the observer as one category of several things? I believe that we're still waiting for a major revolution in science.*[103]

The questioner asks: *"why is it important to look inside of ourselves if we're just observing external events in the quantum world [and] what's the meaning of looking inside ourselves to assess what an observer is internally?"*

*Well first, if we think about our most successful theory of all time, quantum theory, what happens in our personal experience—in our internal experience—couldn't be more dramatically different from how we understand what's happening in the external world. I can't emphasize that enough. It's spectacularly different in every aspect and there are still very deep unsolved problems. For example, we can understand—consider—the idea we both observe something red. Obviously, we're both seeing the same frequency of photons and those kinds of things and we can understand that very well in terms of our theories but we have no idea if what I'm experiencing internally as red has anything to do with what you're experiencing internally as red and in my view, the inner laboratory (we do experiments on our inner laboratory all the time) is just as important to understand in terms of physics as the external laboratory. [However], there are some major gaps; huge glaring, you know, guerrilla in the room type gaps, in terms of our inner experience. The three big examples I would say are awareness and what it means for a system to look at itself without being mediated, without being divided into two pieces [where] it's just self-reflexive. It's aware.*

---

[101] *Closer to Truth* YouTube channel at <https://www.youtube.com/c/CloserToTruthTV>
[102] Tollaksen, Jeff, *The Physics of the Observer* transcribed from a video interview for *Closer to Truth* <https://www.youtube.com/watch?v=opInpBIKtXw&ab_channel=CloserToTruth> [accessed 12 August 2022].
[103] Tollaksen interview, time points: 1:01-1:32.

*That's one; a second big one that our physics has no idea of how to deal with in my opinion is how to talk about meaningful free will and the third one is our human experience of the flow of time, so in all these areas, I predict that we'll have a major revolution in physics yet to come. […] You know, it may be five-hundred years of development in the neurosciences before we can get the right kind of experimental devices to figure these things out conceptually.*[104]

Tollaksen continues:

*I do believe that very significant progress can be made in these questions by using the very same methodology that theoretical physics in the past have used very well […] called the Gedankenexperiment or thought experiment.[105] [For example], Einstein made some of his big discoveries [this way]. A nice example is the case of relativity. […] We had these two […] pedestals of physics; Newtonian physics and Maxwell equations of electromagnetism [as] very well-established theories. Nothing wrong with them, but as soon as Einstein started to combine them, he saw that there was huge tension between them. For example, Newton says that if I […] throw a baseball, I know I can measure the velocity between me and the baseball. If I get in my Ferrari or whatever and then throw it, […] I must add the velocities [together]. […] Einstein was able to look at combining the Newtonian physics of adding velocities with [Maxwell's theories that] light is always [moving at] the same velocity. [Einstein] was able to find where those theories were in great tension and do it in [such] a way that he was able to embody—bring deeply into his personal experience—what it would look like if you could do an experiment to look at the tension between the two theories. That's where he discovered Special Relativity and I do believe that even though there's so much we do not know about the mind and the brain; I do believe we can apply the same methodology to these great questions and find some insights into these biggest of mysteries.*[106]

Is it possible, then, that, like superposition, some ideas exist in a state of flux and are not fixed until they are embedded and embodied into notation or the surface of a painting, where the act of embodiment has an analogous relation to the observer's role in fixing particle states and even then, how the viewer or listener interprets those ideas, or performer introduces yet more variables? The entire process of embodying and transmitting meaningfulness involves strings of flux.

Having read many articles from various disciplines dealing with the question 'what is consciousness?', there are clearly no definitive answers. Different schools of thought defend

---

[104] Tollaksen interview, time points: 1:50-4:09.
[105] "*Gedankenexperiment (German: 'thought experiment') term used by German-born physicist Albert Einstein to describe his unique approach of using conceptual rather than actual experiments in creating the theory of relativity. For example, Einstein described how at age 16 he watched himself in his mind's eye as he rode on a light wave and gazed at another light wave moving parallel to his. According to classical physics, Einstein should have seen the second light wave moving at a relative speed of zero. However, Einstein knew that Scottish physicist James Clerk Maxwell's electromangnetic equations absolutely require that light always move at $3 \times 10^8$ metres (186,000 miles) per second in a vacuum. Nothing in the theory allows a light wave to have a speed of zero. Another problem arose as well: if a fixed observer sees light as having a speed of $3 \times 10^8$ metres per second, whereas an observer moving at the speed of light sees light as having a speed of zero, it would mean that the laws of electromagnetism depend on the observer. But in classical mechanics the same laws apply for all observers and Einstein saw no reason why the electromagnetic laws should not be equally universal. The constancy of the speed of light and the universality of the laws of physics for all observers are cornerstones of special relativity*". This citation is taken from Perkowitz, Sidney, 'Gedankenexperiment' found in *Encyclopedia Britannica*, 12 Feb. 2010,
<https://www.britannica.com/science/Gedankenexperiment> [Accessed 12 August 2022].
[106] Tollaksen interview, time points: 4:10-6:11.

their intellectual territory fiercely depending on bias, experience, knowledge and inclination; physics, neuroscience, philosophy, metaphysics and religion all attempt to answer the question from their perspectives. I'm drawn to quantum mechanics as the eventual route to a solution, but my bias may not prove my inclinations correct.

## Writing for Answers: Hermeneutics and the Perpetual Symbol

*a local map in a foreign land*
*will free your hand*
*to forge a new route*
*and seek from outside*
*what you have lost within*[107]

I am writing this book in the hope that the writing process—of using words—will help me articulate areas of my practice that I find challenging to describe. I appreciate that this is a contradiction. How can I understand more about what I find difficult to express using words when using words to write a book attempting to express those ideas? I hope new vistas of thought and understanding will open unexpectedly in writing this book when describing and analysing the phenomena and territories surrounding those much harder-to-define areas. This is like describing the shape of an object by identifying its borders and intersections with more easily identified phenomena, but where those defining phenomena may also be vague or obscured. Is this a description of 'the missing middle' or a product of my editorial actions that includes the working upon and eventual deletion of objects that nevertheless shape content, reasoning and determining what is present in the finalised text? They now leave only a trace of their presence through what is fixed and present as words (though not fixed hermeneutically as meaning).

Such editorial actions, as well as the power of what is absent, similarly shape what is present within my music composition and paintings, activities that abound with deletion, over-writing, over-painting and over-composing where the finished work is the manifestation of a multiplicity of actions concerning presence and absence worked up together in an iterative cycle towards completion. As all knowledge and realisation within the autoethnographic writing process will become part of my conceptual reality and lenses and filters, it is inevitable that writing *Music, Painting, Landscape and Me* will influence my artistic practice generally.

Although paintings and music, like words, have no fixed meaning, I continue to use words assuming they have something akin to a fixed meaning. If I didn't believe in this tendency towards somewhat stable meaningfulness, I wouldn't trouble myself about the words I use and the meaning and intent I'm trying to transmit when speaking or writing. I think in words. I also rationalise my pictorial and sonic thoughts and memories in words. I build concepts with words. I appreciate the difficulties and contradictions inherent in verbal and textual communication, but what are the alternatives? We communicate. We use word-based language as the foundation for that communication. The resolution of what we say and what we receive depends on the resolution of the words used, the user's associated meaning and the receiver's associated meanings of those words. Those two things may not be the same.

Words are symbols. They represent what is not present. They symbolise the idea of a thing, action or condition. They are a substitute, a stand-in. Pictures and sounds or music

---

[107] Yeats, 14 Poems (12th November 2005). Forthcoming publication on Vision Edition.

compositions are also symbolic and operate as such. They can function as substitutes for things that are absent (the image of a lion, house or tree, for example, or music familiarly representing water; a cartoon character running up and down stairs; a siren for danger or alarm sound for robbery or fire) but may also express their condition without reference to words or objects. This is particularly true of abstract, non-representational music or painting that originated without cliché. Those works can symbolise themselves as self-contained, self-referential sonic or physical fact. An artefact with a meaning inherent to that condition and referenced only through that condition. Its meaning is not fixed and cannot be adequately reduced to words, although its meaningfulness may be transduced, reinterpreted and transmitted through another artform, for example. This is its embodied condition. Word-based language is not necessary to define it.

All verbal and written communication is based on assumptions about what is transmitted and received and around premises of what terms we think we've agreed upon. We test those assumptions using more words in exchange for clarification. Ultimately, there is little evidence to know when transmission equals precisely what is received or when a message is understood as intended within more complex messaging that moves beyond simple instructions and describing objects. This is particularly so when representing mental states, conditions, subjectivity, relationships and behaviours.

As discussed earlier, I believe that despite our meaning conventions, word-based communication is the art of approximation, assumption and trust: approximation for the reasons stated; assumption because of the ongoing belief that communication is succeeding sufficiently and like building a house of cards, the assumption that the foundational cards are adequately robust to support the intricate and perhaps precarious construction above it; and trust that what has been communicated will result in the desired understanding in the receiver as an effective modus operandi for human communication.

*we travel on each other's love*
*strange, wild adventures*
*territories unknown*
*sometimes, lost*
*blind alleys*
*or mazes*
*bewildered*
*searching always*
*for home*[108]

What lies beyond hermeneutics? Is it like peeling away the skins from an infinitely structured onion, revealing layer upon layer of symbolic interpretation no matter how deep down I look? Thoughts such as those open a new plethora of questions, including: Is this how my realities are constructed, where, at my ultimate core, I encounter an infinitely unfolding symbolic panorama? Is there an ultimate, foundational, a priori symbol upon which all else is constructed? Is this symbolic entity solely the evolutionary consequence of my genetics and neural network, foundational to external material reality or merely the perception of that reality?

---

[108] Yeats, 14 Poems (12th November 2005). Forthcoming publication on Vision Edition.

I don't know the answers and as far as I am aware, neither does anyone else. But even in realising this, like a moth inexorably drawn to the flame, I'm compelled to log my thoughts using words—to write this book—in the vague hope I may understand something more through the process of writing than I would by not writing.

Away from an a priori symbolic condition, I know that hermeneutics pervades and governs all comprehension, action and response aspects. Hermeneutics is to think. I interpret symbols at all levels of consciousness. Each successively deeper layer gives way to more symbols, interpretations and symbols. Symbols beget symbols. Like words, they are generative. Meaning is derived from the relationships and context between symbols. This places us inside the frame, trying to look at the picture. I build an inner world of symbols encompassing everything about my experience and interaction with the world as an individual and as part of wider communities and networks. This symbolic world, including language and the mechanisms of thought, time, mathematics, painting, music, architecture, drama, dress and fashion, design and living, the natural world, the strange world, dreams and fantasies, politics and what is present and what is absent, everything around us, are constructed from our earliest moments of life and further built upon and developed after that. Everything I think and experience is coloured—filtered—through this inner symbolic world. Those symbols become my tools of interpretation. They also become my filters and lenses for viewing the world, its components, processes and 'becoming'.

My neural network is constructed from a lifetime of connections, relations and networks. My work is programmed through experiences, calculations, deductions, assumptions and conclusions to construct and project my reality. Again, is this constructed reality real as an objective, independently observed reality or as in experiential, projected and subjective?' Is it both simultaneously? I cannot vouch for all that is considered fact, but I can say that *my* reality is real to me and I assume that another person's reality, though equally real to them as mine is to me, will be different, perhaps very distant from, my reality. Which of those is the reality?

I have a working hypothesis—assumption, of course—that landscape exploration and experience, reconnaissance and similar activities are central to everything I do in some aspect as preparatory-making behaviours. Are my physical experience of landscape and the work I produce, including writing about landscape, connected with landscape conceptualisation to format the brain to receive information and are those 'reception formats' merely lenses that reinforce and organise those conceptual assumptions further? In short, do I view the world through landscape-orientated spectacles?

## Hallucination

Neuro and cognitive science show us that our brains make sense of vast amounts of information received every moment, day by day and year by year. As this information is obtained, primarily through the somatic system and subsequently accumulated, the brain learns how to predict outcomes of various stimuli before sensory inputs are fully received, most likely to conserve, streamline and prioritise processing power. In other words, based on multiple probabilities, the brain projects a best-guess scenario for what exactly it is we are perceiving based on minimal or initial stimuli to create a type of controlled simulation; some refer to it as a controlled hallucination of reality that is only modified by contradictory sensory data that challenges the prevailing model.

*we march through time*
*motionless*
*to the ends of the world*
*and beyond*
*blind, deaf and dumb*
*impotent*
*to find order, sense and definition*
*to know*
*without wisdom*
*and control and suppress*
*the dance of creation*
*in a box so small*
*even our limitations*
*cannot define it*
*the moment cannot be suspended*
*from past and future*
*for it lies in the void between them*[109]

In a 2019 article in *Current Biology* titled *Perceptual Prediction: Rapidly Making Sense of a Noisy World*, the authors, Clare Press and Daniel Yan, tell us:

*Our brains have to make sense of the vast quantities of information constantly bombarding our senses. The information reaching our eyes, ears and other receptors changes rapidly across space and time and the signals are imperfect: for example, when we listen to a friend on the metro the sound of their voice is masked by the noise of the train. Our brains must rapidly generate a best guess about what we heard to guide our behaviour effectively—we will be a poor conversation partner if it takes us several seconds to work out what they said.*

*Work from the cognitive sciences across the last few decades has demonstrated that we likely use our expectations to help shape what we perceive. There are many statistical regularities within our environment and we can combine these with the sensory input to represent the likely state of the world. [...] Biased perceptual decisions have been shown across a number of disciplines and with a number of methods. For example, we are faster to identify everyday household objects (for example, loaves of bread), when they are preceded by observation of contexts in which they are typically seen (kitchen counters) and we are more likely to report the presence of stimuli that are expected on the basis of arbitrary, probabilistically-paired cues. Such biasing is also demonstrated through perceptual errors that occur when typical regularities are disrupted. For example, we report concave faces to have the more typical convex structure when shading cues are ambiguous and that sensations last for a similar length of time to concurrently performed actions—likely because they typically last for comparable durations.*[110]

As an associated thought and in response to notions of building my reality through predictive perceptual and cognitive processes, it is possible that semiotic and hermeneutic processes are equally comprehended as part of my hallucinatory construct of reality. How can I tell if I experience a genuine material reality or a constructed hallucination?

---

[109] Yeats, 14 Poems (12th November 2005). Forthcoming publication on Vision Edition.
[110] Press, Clare, pp. 751-753.

Such thoughts about the interior or exterior nature of reality, or both simultaneously, drive me to wonder why ontological instability and flux are so challenging to come to terms with. Is it because I am inadequately equipped to externalise such thoughts verbally as a state or lived condition? Perhaps the clue is in the word 'inadequately'. Even though certain states are difficult to express in words beyond a description of their physical properties or conditionality, for instance, the sensory and affective experience of listening to music or being emersed in a colour field without form, I (we) still try to describe those states using word combinations we consider closest in meaning to the original experience. In that process, the meaningfulness we attempt to communicate expands and multiplies possible interpretations. The hermeneutics of the artist, performer, viewer and listener always expands meaningfulness through interpretation regardless of the artform or media. I am comfortable with this kind of meaning-expanding flux in making my work. However, I ultimately seek to confine and focus its potential into a finished artefact. But in contradiction, my pleasure in and acceptance of flux does not preclude my thirst for fact.

*a network of moving objects*
*minds pattern random*
*uncomfortable with chaos*
*we stop*
*hold*
*make solid*
*and crush wonder*[111]

Contrary to the expansive nature of hermeneutics, my understanding of how the brain works indicate that comprehension and perception are reductions—the filtering out of the unnecessary; clarifying the signal against the noise; losing the background in favour of the foreground; privileging safety and survival above all else owing to primordial programming; saving our processing capacity for what is predetermined as necessary. Reduction of sensory input is essential and an inbuilt capacity of humankind.

If this is so and there is much scientific evidence to suggest it is, our reduction and construction of reality reveal to us just a fragment of the input we receive. Consequently, our grasp of ourselves, the world around us and how we operate within it will be similarly limited. No wonder embracing the enormity of chaos, instability and our physiological and emotional selves make us uncomfortable. Fixed states with their narrow and known parameters, permutations and possibilities take much less neural processing to manage. They break the world into knowable, sometimes predictable and useable chunks. If I were exposed to the entire afferent avalanche of neural data, unfiltered and unedited, it would most likely crush me. But I am not crushed by art even though its implications and embodiments are expansive.

Considering the scientific evidence, how would I know what is reality or truth as I cannot step outside of my construction to see back into it or see it objectively and in context to anything else outside of it? Even the scientific method operates through the human condition and the limitations of its situated frame of reference. How would I know? Thinking back to Plato's questioning mind and how his thought was contextualised within the knowledge of his time, the Swiss/Israeli psychologist, psychiatrist and existential psychoanalyst Carlo Strenger wrote:

---

[111] Yeats, 14 Poems (12th November 2005). Forthcoming publication on Vision Edition.

*Plato (like any one of us) could not be fully aware of the horizons of intelligibility, the pre-understanding of the world that made his world and his life meaningful. Human beings are never completely transparent to themselves, as we are embedded in historical contexts that are not fully understood.*[112]

My technical and perceptual capacities and the wiring of my neural network limit my thinking. How I experience reality is a self-limiting, self-programming act that frames and generates my style or voice. This style then reflects that format. I am not recreating the world as simulacra. I am not replacing a real world that exists externally through my artwork. I do not in any way deny the presence of an external world. I am creating a symbolic representation of it, or rather, a symbolic representation of how I perceive and present my expressions of that world as a visual and sonic phenomenon.

> *though we mark it*
> *cut it*
> *count it*
> *are never fixed*
> *in the continuum of experience*
> *lies infinite space*
> *without line, dimension or division*
> *save our mutilations*
> *to stop this riot*
> *and hang on*
> *for dear life*
> *is measured*
> *by fear of passage*
> *to the other side of time*[113]

Do I become a self-fulfilling artistic prophecy in this regard, seeing only what I want to see? Yes. And am I defined by my limitations? Yes. Within my 'lived experience', all perceptual limitations are so well embodied and programmed into my being that I barely notice their filtration and influence. I live in a prison surrounded by invisible bars. Most of the time, I operate entirely unaware of their confinement. But creatively, like all humans, my ability to interpret and generate meaningful relationships between phenomena offers a limitless capacity for interpretation and, thereby, for creating artefacts.

Even though I perceive and comprehend through limitations, as a painter, I act as an amplifier, an exaggerator, of what I think I see and, perhaps more critically, what I sense somatically and the emotional responses such stimuli trigger. This distinction is important. What I see are the physical shapes that I will encode as lines, form, structure, colour and texture to represent the physical structures of the place in paint. What I sense in the landscape, its ambience or atmosphere and its emotional affect on me is considerably more difficult to describe using words or justify pragmatically through the physicality of paint when embodied within an artwork. Nevertheless, to achieve a sense of that place, it is crucial that I signify physical structures and ambience to my satisfaction through the marks that I lay down. This is true regardless of the 'realism' or abstraction of a painting I make.

---

[112] Strenger, Carlo, [accessed 8 August 2022].
[113] Yeats, 14 Poems (12th November 2005). Forthcoming publication on Vision Edition.

My paintings are not intended to be duplicates of my seen world; how could they be? They are categorically different things. The landscape is a materially real place. The painting is a materially real artefact. To achieve a semblance of visually perceived landscape duplication, I would need to use an array of optical trickery and techniques to render the illusion using symbols as icons to represent what wasn't present on the canvas. This attempt at likeness could only ever succeed through a complicit agreement within a socially situated and developed framework between artist and viewer where the terms of encoding and decoding visual imagery were established in advance through a convention. I began painting using this representational or photorealistic approach between the ages of fifteen and my late twenties. I aimed to create the illusion of a perceived, mutually agreed-upon reality on canvas, as illustrated in Figure 11.

Figure 11. *Wastwater.* Oil on canvas, 30 x 20 inches. Marc Yeats (1999).

Now, I ramp up the signification of all perceptual elements, shapes, structures, colours, light and ambience, sometimes enormously so (see Figure 12). In symbolising an alternative embodiment of meaningfulness in paint, I deterritorialise what I see as an iconic reflection of material reality through degrees of abstraction but not to the point where the imagery I create is wholly independent of that reality or arbitrary to it. I do not entirely break but 'stretch' the symbolic referent relationship between what I perceive as material landscape and what I perceive as conceptual landscape. To quote Pepperell again: *"[…] to achieve a delicate balance between recognisability and abstraction to excite the inquisitiveness of the viewer's visual system while frustrating its capacity for recognition at the same time"*. This 'stretching' is not a contrivance. It is a symbolic expression language that has evolved and developed over decades of artistic practice through observation, immanent action and reflection. If I were successful in my terms, I would have created an artefact that triggers emotional states like those experienced exploring physical or remembered landscapes. As stated, my aim as a painter and composer is not to imitate reality nor to limit, reduce, project or confine it in some way; I aim to create a new material artefact through a personal semiotic encoding that itself enables a hermeneutic expansion of the subject that resonates in me and potentially within the viewer. I believe this expansion is possible because the viewer has shared in the work's authorship through their interpretive engagement, using what is embodied as the springboard to meaning construction. Those 'ramping-up' actions are undertaken because, as a painter, I want to show the viewer something additional to seeing and experiencing landscape other than what is possible through art as perceived replication. Although I have no hard evidence to support the transmission of the sensations and emotions I encounter as a 'lived experience' of engaging with landscape art, I continue making art as if what is embodied has the commonality and potential to transmit those conditions and values. This knowingly false assumption brings a sense of purpose to communicate, in part at least, what I find meaningful in the landscape. As discussed throughout The List, I am fully aware that whatever my intentions at the time of painting or composing, the exact transmissibility of such actions and their embodied meaningfulness remains speculative.

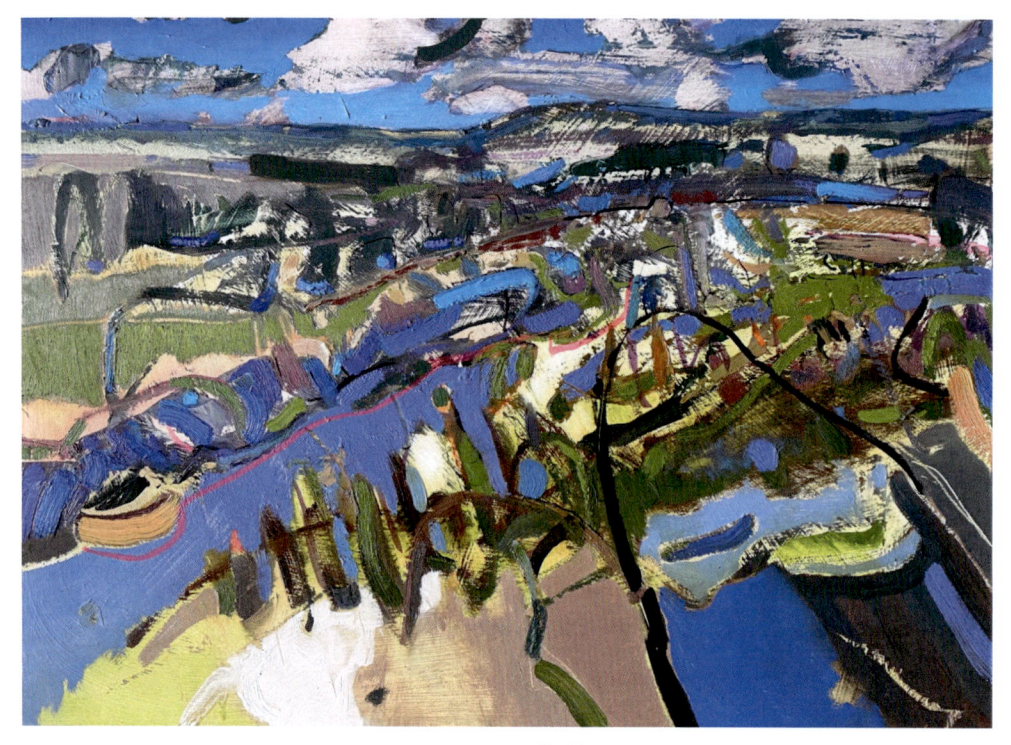

Figure 12. *Letcombe Bassett, Oxfordshire.* Oil on cradled board, 420 x 594 mm. Marc Yeats (2022).

Regarding a lack of hard evidence, it is similarly difficult for me to separate what I have assimilated from encountering the learning of others from learning I have generated or even originated. Perhaps like Barthes's 'author', I am just a scriptor assembling the bits and pieces of thinking I have assimilated, convincing myself that much of it is 'my work?' The boundaries have been absorbed and blurred into my awareness and practice. I have held some concepts for many years. Their origins, assimilated or otherwise, are unknown. Still, through more comprehensive reading and research in recent years, I have associated those concepts with the established philosophical work of others, in part or whole. This assimilation has implications for terms like written 'in my own words', as I suspect any words or ideas used are not entirely my own. I want to be the originator of all I think, but I realise this to be unlikely. However, I concede that my take on any received concepts will be conditioned through my 'lived experiences' and thereby hold some scope for original thought or, if not thought, original perspective, not least through thought embodied in painting and music.

Although we share much owing to our human condition, how we think and feel, as well as our common physiology, the particulars of our neural setups and how those operate with everyone's unique life experiences and internal symbolic landscape results in multiple interpretations of the same stimuli when that stimulus is part of an artwork (and probably anything else). This understanding reminds me that the notion of musical semiotics as a shared language with inherent transmissible fixed meaning throughout all its signification is untenable.

With meaning held by the interpretant, The List and *Music, Painting and Me*, only expands its meaningfulness through self-guided revealing rather than enframing processes and pronouncement. Such revealing is true of all interpretations. Tangentially, it amuses me how a book is a tangible, physical object that embodies thought—nonsolid phenomena—physically represented through the symbolism of words as verifiable printed matter that signify meaningfulness when interpreted by a reader. The book is real and material. Its hermeneutic content is implied and conceptual. I enjoy this paradox of condition. It is a duality where the parts mutually depend on one another for their coexistence, presence and absence. The actuality of what a book *is*, its ontological state, moves beyond notions of material and conceptual duality to become a unified third condition that comprises both aspects.

This conditionality reminds me of a painting or piece of music where thought is embodied in physical form, be that paint on canvas or in sound, but where that thought—constituting just about everything else in an artwork relating to its qualities away from its material properties, are 'signified'. Meaningfulness is in a constant state of flux. Flux, in turn, reminds me of superposition in quantum mechanics, leading me to a final question with potentially huge implications.

Where is thought once it is thought? Does it leave the thinker to affect or effect other phenomena? Is this what happens in the observer effect in quantum mechanics, or does that sound too metaphysical to be plausible? I have no answers, but my favourite phrase from all science, taken from quantum mechanics, is 'spooky action at a distance', a term coined by Einstein to dismiss theories of quantum entanglement. Quantum entanglement, the phenomena by which one particle can effectively 'know' something about another particle instantaneously, even if a great distance separates those two particles, has been proven to occur repeatedly.[114]

The question concerning where thought is once it has been thought could be the foundational question of this project. The question encompasses the nature of thought and the nature of consciousness itself and, stemming from that, intentionality, directionality, transmission, flux and meaning and specifically in this writing, between music, painting, landscape and me and then, between those and the receiver within whom all aspects find context and meaningfulness. Could quantum mechanics finally describe consciousness in the future? Could consciousness be found to be part of the observer effect and quantum entanglement?

---

[114] Popkin, Gabriel, [accessed 29 August 2022].

Writing in a recently published online article in *BBC Science Focus Magazine* about the evidence for Dark Matter and the work of physicists generally, Dr Katie Mack, a theoretical astrophysicist, tells us:

*A physicist's task is to constantly create equations that keep up with our observations of physical phenomena [...]. While the vast majority of physicists find the evidence for dark matter's existence convincing, some continue to examine alternatives and the views in the press and the public are significantly more divided. The most common response I get when I talk about dark matter is: 'isn't this just something physicists made up to make the math work out?' The answer to that might surprise you: yes! In fact, everything in physics is made up to make the math work out.*[115]

That physicists make up everything to support their observations gives me some comfort as in my tongue-in-cheek, limited way, *Music, Painting, Landscape and Me*, similarly seek to explain my observations of experiential and immanent phenomena through 'making it up'.

*"We've made a map of Dark Matter and still don't know what it is. And that's OK"*, is another phrase I have appropriated from Dr Mack.[116] I appreciate this comment as it chimes with my thoughts around what I have termed throughout The List, 'the missing middle,' and how to locate or map it despite not knowing what it is. It also brings context to my thoughts around trying to answer challenging questions about my processes, being and 'the missing middle' by mapping the territories surrounding those conditions through what can be more easily described. Even though I cannot say what everything in this book is in pragmatic terms, *Music, Painting, Landscape and Me*, is that 'Dark Matter' map and it's OK!

---

[115] Mack, Katie, *Yes, Everything in Physics is Completely Made Up–That's the Whole Point* in the online magazine *BBC Science Focus* (published March 2023) < https://www.sciencefocus.com/news/everything-physics-made-up/> [accessed 13 March 2023].

[116] Ibid, *We've Made a Map of Dark Matter but Still Don't Know What It Is and That's Okay* in the online magazine *BBC Science Focus* (published September 2022) <https://www.sciencefocus.com/news/weve-made-a-map-of-dark-matter-but-still-dont-know-what-it-is-and-thats-okay/> [accessed 13 March 2023].

# CHAPTER TWO

# 'MAPPING'

## Introduction

I have rituals—a great many—that are becoming increasingly apparent the more I think about the processes I undertake before beginning a body of work. I say a 'body of work' as if it were a grand and visionary undertaking. It is not. I use the term to differentiate between ongoing work and new work created following a thorough exploration of a landscape area that I have purposely visited in the expectation that my time there would stimulate and inform the creation of new paintings and music. This chapter lays out, as far as I can articulate and with the degree of insight available to me, the processes I initiate in preparation for such a visit (I think of those visits as research trips) and how those actions shape what follows.

I call this undertaking 'mapping'. It is, first and foremost, an act of interpretation, hermeneutic situatedness and total immersion, the experience of being in the landscape and reading and responding to it as an immanent condition of that situatedness. It is also how I would describe the interpretation and reinterpretation of my inner constructed conceptual landscapes, their relationship to each other and their material counterparts. With landscape at the heart of this field of experience, the term 'mapping', with its cartographical implications, feels appropriate for discussing my interpretive relationships to the conceptual and physical landscapes I encounter as distinct from the interpretation of all other phenomena.

'Mapping' is at least a two-phase process that involves remote preparatory and onsite investigation. To illustrate what 'mapping' is, I shall describe three research events, the most recent to the Berkshire Downs in May 2021, the second, an immersive two-week artist residency shared between the South Downs National Park near Winchester and Lymington Marshes, both in Hampshire during 2015 and finally, an ongoing relationship across several years with East Suffolk and its fragile coastline.

When 'mapping' in phase one, I construct new mental territory corresponding to locations through a research process that, in its first phase, involves investigating maps, photographs, literature, videos and the artwork of others. Then, after interpreting the materials, I commit them to memory as I construct a unique, internally visualised three-dimensional landscape of the area. It is this construction that becomes my remembered landscape. I appreciate that my capacity to remember information precisely is limited and that memorised data will be inaccurate and incomplete. Additionally, those memories will be subject to further transformation with each act of remembering and reinterpretation. But the point here is not an attempt to build the perfectly remembered simulacrum of a particular site. That is an impossible task as memory is not materiality; a remembered landscape and material landscape are categorically different as one exists independently from me and the other because of my interpretations—but instead, construct a caricature—a symbolic counterpart—that signifies the actual site conceptually. The 'mapping' data helps me mentally realise specific locations by populating them with discovered content. Once constructed, I can explore and manipulate this conceptual landscape in my imagination.

I undertake those 'mapping' actions for several reasons. First, because I don't paint from life (or compose on location), only from remembered matter where constructing a robust remembered landscape is essential to my practice as a painter and composer. Second, to examine the materials I have assembled when constructing a remembered landscape to establish which landscape features are likely to yield the topographical configurations that hold the potential to initiate affective responses and are, therefore, most attractive to me before any visit to the physical location takes place. I call the results of this calibration of affect affective or 'emotional weighting'. Those affects trigger emotional responses I can approximately describe as mild or intense or on a scale from momentary to sustained. I assume that the level of affect or 'emotional weighting' perceived through experiencing the research materials will translate to similar or increased responses when present in the physical location itself. This is the assumption I operate within, which can only be confirmed or countered after a site visit. Unfortunately, such emotional sensations are difficult to describe beyond the broadest terms, making objective quantifications of their qualities and origin impossible. As such, any attempt to analyse affect or emotional responses further results in no greater clarity. Nevertheless, the impact those affects initiate is profound and requires acknowledgement as an essential component and driving force behind work-making. Despite its subjective nature, the effect of those emotional responses *is* objectively demonstrated in my need to create work—paintings and compositions—where the phenomena are represented materially through what is embodied in the work.

Experiences of 'emotional weighting' are (as I perceive them) immanent to engaging with landscape phenomena, conceptual and material, almost certainly as part of hermeneutics. Interpretation occurs automatically when I have contact with any phenomena, including those related to physical or conceptual landscapes. Such interpretive functionality is genetically programmed into my neural makeup. This makeup, plus a range of historical and experiential antecedents, similarly generates my emotional responses to phenomena, again determined through interpretation. I do not doubt that the operation of the brain and central nervous system (CNS) and how it packages the information it receives as inbound and outbound (afferent and efferent) activity and the connections it makes between the two determines a great deal of the relationship concerning sensory input and how the body and mind respond dynamically to this through automated or responsive and dynamic but often out of awareness processes. This relationship lies at the foundation of association between my being in and sensing the landscape, between feeling and bodily action, how I respond to the landscape and build a symbolic representation of those experiences and how I respond to those constructions emotionally. A detour into proprioception is helpful to delve further into why connectivity between what I feel when in the landscape and how that is embodied to eventually make work can be described in neurological terms.

The online article *Kinaesthesia and Proprioception* delineates between proprioception and the often associated term 'kinaesthesia', highlighting their distinct roles in sensory perception. The article explains that proprioception involves sensing the relative positioning of body parts and the effort required for movement, while kinaesthesia focuses on awareness of body position and movement using proprioceptors in joints and muscles. Despite often being used interchangeably, they have differing components; for instance, kinaesthesia excludes the sense of balance. Proprioception is more cognitive, emphasising awareness of movement, while kinaesthesia is viewed as more behavioural, concentrating on bodily motion.[117]

A 2021 hypothesis and theory paper *Proprioception in Action: A Matter of Ecological and Social*

---

[117] 24 *Kinaesthesia and Proprioception* from *Proprioception: Balance and Phantom Limbs* in *Introduction to Sensation and Perception* <https://pressbooks.umn.edu/sensationandperception/chapter/kinesthesia-and-prorioception/#:~:text=Another%20difference%20in%20proprioception%20and,and%20proprioception%20is%20more%20cognitive> [accessed 27 January 2024].

*Interaction* by González-Grandón Ximena andrea Falcón-Cortés and Gabriel Ramos-Fernández describes how the relationship between the proprioceptive and kinaesthetic system learns about body position and movement options during ongoing action (such as walking, painting or playing an instrument, for example) as part of an active, organised system in continuous and dynamic interaction with the environment including social environments, they term strong embodiment. The paper proposes that some dynamical self-oriented and relational features of the phenomenology of Proprioception-Kinaesthetic (PK), resulting from the coupling of perception and action, called PK coupling, constitute the PK perceptual experience. The different degrees to which this experience happens during a typical episode of being present, bodily aware and prepared to act specifically manifest this in at least three different dimensions: first, PK-sensorimotor contingencies-self (PK-SMCs), which are related to the individual's own spatio-temporal self-orientation, in relation to other parts of their body and possibilities for action in present time; second, PK-self-ecological, which are those that arise from the individual's own embodied activity; and third PK-self-other interactions, which result from the individual's own behaviour when engaging with others. This strong embodiment approach to explaining proprioception in action is rooted in the idea that we must move in order to perceive but also perceive in order to move.[118]

Weak embodiment approaches or B-format representation (where B-format refers to "*muscular sensations as a physiological condition of the body that becomes crucial when they are centrally represented in the brain and instantiated in internal models*") differ from strong embodiment theories in as much as they do not incorporate dynamic interaction of the body with the environment to couple perception with action, instead asserting that motor instruction defines an exact value for a location, speed or other parameters, through a matching unique value at the sensor level, with any fluctuations being completely determined.[119] Weak embodiment highlights the existence of a perfect pairing relation between action and sensation in the case of proprioception, a position the authors find problematic owing to the "*mysterious*" subsequent inferences primed by the brain within internal models, which appear to be formed at random. They ask: "*Where do those commands come from? Why do they take the form that they do? Are they generated by a 'program'?*"[120]

The purpose of their study is to address this issue by "*arguing that the PK perceptual experience is composed of an [individual's] set of abilities to act during the ongoing process of establishing meaningful relationships with one's body and the environment rather than being solely caused by some internal process in the brain, such as a B-format representation or a [specific] somatosensorial cortex correlate*" that acts as a pre-formatted model governing proprioception and its relation to movement.[121] The distinction between weak and strong embodiment is significant because the enactive sensorimotor theory of perception (ESMT), a concept at the heart of PK coupling, is an action-oriented perspective that relies on enaction—putting into practice through action—where perceptual contingencies are inherently linked to movements interconnected with our sensorimotor abilities, emerges from strong embodiment rather than B-format representative ideas. "*Here, perception is a bodily experience closely related to skilful and effective embodied options for action*".[122] The term skilful is used as the researchers believe there is a strong argument that PK perceptual experience is the practice of an exploratory bodily talent that is honed through experience and expertise. "*Whenever the [individual] is effecting an*

---

[118] Ximena, González-Grandón et al., pp. 1-2.
[119] Ibid, p. 2.
[120] Ibid, p. 4.
[121] Ibid, p. 2.
[122] Ibid, p. 2.

*actual change by self-movement, it has the effect of improving the veracity of attentive and sensible perceptual experience by confirming the anticipated sensorimotor regularities*".[123] Additionally, the authors assert that in strong embodiment accounts, "*proprioception is better understood coupled with kinaesthesia (as the proprioceptive-kinaesthetic coupling mentioned), a perceptual system that results from an active and ongoing coupling between feeling and performing*".[124]

As an artist, the take-home from this condensed overview of PK coupling resides in the words "*an active and ongoing coupling between feeling and performing*". Although the conclusions of this research remain speculative, the implications of its findings for me as the author of this book, concerning the connectivity between landscape, painting and music, a 'sense of place' and embodiment, where I am at the centre of origin and outcome of any couplings between feeling and performing manifested in my work, is now possible to describe in relation to PK coupling, to a certain extent at least.

The paper's authors assert that "*PK perceptual experience is inseparable from sensorimotor expectations*" and go on to describe those PK contingencies as "*depending on the awareness of the self's potential actions and interactions, abilities that an [individual] may acquire over a particular history of learning within a specific ecological and self-other environment*".[125] However, how much can be unpicked concerning the coupling of feeling and performing as neurological correlates remains to be seen. The authors write that to distinguish itself from mainstream theories of perception that claim "*perceiving is about giving rise to internal mental representations from the external world*', ESMT has taken on the much more difficult mission of elucidating the felt component of phenomenal consciousness in addition to being an account of the legitimate links between sensorimotor abilities involved in perception*".[126] "*It assumes that experience is not caused only by some internal correlate, such as a B representation [and their internal models]*" but where "*phenomenality [...] is constituted by the different capacities that feeling involves*".[127]

That there is a CNS relationship between the felt and motor aspects of ESMT and the potential PK coupling of feeling and performing is strongly indicated in this paper. In embracing this indication as a useful hypothesis, my practices, such as walking, painting and composing, are situated within the domain of PK coupling and (potentially) involve direct relationships between what is sensed and experienced as an immanent consequence of moving to perceive and perceiving in order to move. Walking is, therefore, an embodied performance—a manifestation of PK coupling in action. Phase two of my 'mapping' process is contingent upon walking in a physical location. 'Mapping' and walking, along with the actions necessary to paint, compose and be in one's body during those activities, are all embodiments of PK coupling. What's more and perhaps of greater significance, is that the performance resulting from PK coupling does not solely rely on an internal model or preformatted organisation for its actions. The performance is determined as an immanent consequence of those dynamic interactions between feeling and movement, embodied in painting, composing, walking or any activity involving proprioception and kinaesthetic action as an adaptive, immanent response to that environment. PK coupling is "*a perceptual experience of spatiotemporal self-orientation in present action and interaction*".[128] As Ximena et al. write of their paper:

---

[123] Ximena, p. 6.
[124] Ibid, p. 2.
[125] Ibid, p. 6.
[126] Ibid, pp. 5-6.
[127] Ibid, p. 6.
[128] Ibid, p. 2.

*The perspective that we have defended here is a stronger notion of embodiment. We suggest that it is the PK system, with its coupling history of interacting and by the individual's personal experiences, that enables specific perception-action loops, learning to interact and to respond to the world rather than representing it. Specifically, skilled proprioceptive and kinesthetic coupling plays an important role in the felt perceptual experience of spatio-temporal self-orientation in present action and interaction in ways that are irreducible to B-formatted representations.*[129]

Reacting and responding to the world as a performance rather than representing it as a fixed internal, brain-based model is crucial to ESMT and PK coupling. It is also central to my practice as a painter and composer, particularly where I open myself up to serendipitous or spontaneous-like practices that involve immanent physical responsiveness in relation to particular environments, the feelings engendered when experiencing environments, the performance in spatio-temporal self-orientation in present action and interactive terms as an outcome of PK coupling and my recursive and assimilative dynamic responses to those outcomes, physical and emotional, perhaps all sensed simultaneously, where my actions correspond to PK-sensorimotor contingencies-self, PK-self-ecological and PK-self-other, as the functionality behind making work.

It is also likely that I have associated activities with and been drawn to locations where I have perceived the feeling and performative aspects of significant PK coupling as a form of embodied stimulation which has resulted in the necessity to create a performance in situ or in the studio without being cognisant of all the processes undertaken (away from the intention to engage in the activity in the first place) that require no preconception—no brain-based model—of what I'm doing or what I'm going to produce as a performance owing to the immanent and responsive nature of the work's production. The additional levels of PK coupling and the physical outcomes engendered through my body as the gestalt of being in the moment continue to attract me to such locations and conditions. This leads me to ask four questions: Is the work I produce as performance entirely the consequence of ESMT functionality and PK coupling? Do levels of PK coupling excitation contribute to my sense of affective weighting in the landscape and artworks more generally? Can the consequences of ESMT and PK coupling be re-experienced as dynamic and interactive forces enacted through some notion of connectivity between PK-coupled responses experienced on location that is then transferred to the studio through memory? And the final question is, suppose one inhabits a body possessing exploratory bodily talent honed and embedded through experience and expertise. Is it possible to conceptually invoke PK coupling as a physically perceived experience through imagination alone?

Embodiment and performance through PK coupling operate continually, whether or not such performance is engaged, conceptualised or described as artwork. I am mindful of its performative aspect when walking in landscapes that stimulate me visually and when writing music or painting. I am particularly mindful that when making a remembered landscape, I am purposefully exposing myself to conditions necessary to initiate landscape-focused neurological and emotional responses of a certain kind. Before I had any knowledge of PK coupling, I was drawn to locations that held strong emotional and, in PK coupling terms, compelling performative expressions. This is because activities, such as walking, painting and composing, are mediated through my body and are automatically embodied within it, where that process of strong embodiment inevitably involves PK coupling and the physical actions that coupling elicits. In undertaking those activities and perhaps because of them, I am drawn to landscape phenomena I identify as associated with strong emotional or affective triggers. Those triggers

---

[129] Ximena, p. 19.

are encountered through walking or the varied processes of making or the artwork of others, particularly if I can connect that landscape experience to my conceptual constructions and, ultimately, the artefacts I produce as another embodiment of those experiences.

I hypothesise that alongside PK coupling, the symbolic significance of phenomena encountered and interpreted in the landscape becomes associated with symbolic phenomena I happen upon in the production of my work, be that in material and conceptual form or visual or sonic manifestations that trigger similar emotional responses to each other. Through this association, I interpret personal responses between my artwork and landscapes as a 'sense of place' particular to specific locations. And when I perceive such symbolic configurations in my work, I also assume that a 'sense of place' has, through my actions as an artist, transmitted from a material landscape to what is embodied in an artwork, where I respond similarly to the symbolic configurations it presents. There is no evidence to support the transmission of this specific 'sense of place' to others. Such notions remain interpersonal and subjective. However, the transmission of what is embodied in the artwork, its meaningfulness and significance, will take place through the hermeneutics of any receiver that engages with it as an artwork. What cannot be identified are the specific components of that transmission. I am also drawn to ask if PK coupling and the recognition and creation of symbols as part of interpretation function as another coupling. I am not suggesting that PK coupling and hermeneutics are categorically the same things, but I do wonder if my concept of reality and the conceptual world as an artist and the means through which such is embedded are dependent upon the functionalities of both to develop the fullest interpretation, feeling and performance of my internal and external environments and ultimately, their embodiment in my work.

As mentioned, my concept of affective weighting relies upon my sense of significance, that is, the strength of emotion that is generated within me when I examine third-party materials—maps, videos and photos—collected in phase one to ascertain what extent that material triggers emotional responses either as independent phenomena or relationally when contextualised within my manufactured conceptual map, the remembered landscape. Maps, photographs and videos are already symbolic representations of materiality that, through their specific material form (the digital or paper body of a photo, the digital and electronic component of film, the paper and ink of maps) and the framing and contextualising decisions of others that shape and present those symbols, have been previously encoded and distanced from the original material through that encoding process.

To illustrate this, look at a cartographer's map. Here, the landscape is rendered to a particular range of coloured two-dimensional symbols that signify contour, topography, roads, rock faces, forest, rivers, field boundaries, conurbation and settlement as well as trackways and footpaths, in detail and various resolutions using lines and drawings distributed onto a surface. A third party has decided what symbols would be designed to represent specific features and designated how they would operate together. The third party, in this case, the mapmaker, has also provided a key or legend to the map so that others can unlock the meaning behind the map's symbols. Using this decoding, the meaning of the map can be deciphered. When I use a map, my hermeneutical experience with such codifications enables me to conceptualise the landscape being symbolised by translating the symbol to what is being 'signified' and comprehending a great deal of information about the landscape. But reading this map is nothing like experiencing the landscape through one's body, where what has been symbolised on paper cannot incorporate, anticipate or recreate the full expression of the 'lived experience' of being situated in the place itself. When experiencing the landscape in situ, all previously encountered third-party filters and encoding are bypassed and replaced—overwritten—by the first-hand direct experience of perceiving the location itself. Inevitably, exploration will yield many surprises on the ground not encoded into or possible to decode from the map.

The map is not the territory. The map is never the territory.

In engaging with those already encoded symbolic forms, such as maps and photographs, I generate another layer of encoding through further acts of interpretation. This encoding generates yet more symbols and symbolic networks further distanced from the original phenomena that build my conceptual understanding of the phenomena. In doing this, the significance of the originally encountered third-party phenomena has doubled many times over as it has passed through the hermeneutics of each interpretant. When I produce an artwork, my conceptual, symbolic representations generate yet more symbols, this time embedded into the artwork's materiality, which I and any receivers will further interpret hermeneutically through our symbolic makeups.

The more intensely I experience landscape-associated emotion, the more I am drawn to the landscape configurations I identify as stimulating those emotions. I have also observed that the more I engage with affective conditions through practising visualisation that situates my focus within a conceptual landscape construction, the stronger the initiated attraction and emotional response becomes. In effect, I feed the intensity of my reactions through practising visualisation. Over time, levels of affect become quite intoxicating and, like a drug, somewhat addictive. Is this form of visualisation practice similar in its bodily embeddedness to the learning and expertise acquired through living, engagement and exploring different environments through feeling and movement implied in PK coupling's experience-honed bodies? In those scenarios, does practice make perfect?

As mentioned, correlates between exact feelings and actions found in PK coupling remain largely unidentified. Making further comments about those relationships is challenging and can easily verge into the subjective or even metaphysical. What I can say objectively is that within this concept of 'mapping', I experience emotional sensations stimulated through bodily and conceptual connectivity to an external condition, in this context, real material conditions found in the landscape environment such as trees, hills and clouds or my symbolic concepts of them, or a piece of art or music, in what is materially present as paint or sound formats, that correspond to the theory of PK coupling regarding feeling and performance or action. Whatever I perceive and conceive, my CNS and brain play an essential role in its organisation and presentation, facts that can, to a greater or lesser extent, be quantified and described scientifically.

Phase two of the 'mapping' process takes place in situ at the location. The 'mapping' (interpretive) process reignites as I explore a site physically. I re-map the territory in this situated bodily context, engaging my range of sensorimotor abilities. Away from sight, sound, smell, touch, taste and temperature, many other physical sensations are hard to situate as embodied experiential locations even though they are felt through and within my body. The sometimes-disparate nature of those bodily impressions makes them difficult to describe. As such, their origin and function remain unknown even though their emotional and sometimes physical impacts are considerable. They are no doubt linked to PK couplings. Somatic inputs and their related efferent couplings, along with hermeneutics and the building of concepts, enable an ongoing process of 'mapping' through and with my body because of immanent and total immersion in the landscape. This is not a subjective condition; it is a neurological fact. As well as afferent/efferent relationships, I am hermeneutically immersed in the landscape, reading, creating and interacting with what is symbolically recognised and represented there through my perceptions of its physicality and ambience, a quality I assume is related to my construction of a 'sense of place' forged between bodily sensation and experience, interpretation and the mind. This interpretation is a performance. Through hermeneutics and unfolding interpretation, as an immanent consequence of that situatedness and interpretation generated through reflection, I am also building new symbol and sign networks to interpret what I experience, constructing layer upon layer of significance. This is where affect and ambience are generated and located. It is an immersive physical experience. It is the starting point of composing and painting if such a starting point can be definitively located.

I map through walking the landscape. What I experience is not a projection. The landscape exists external to me and independently from me. I experience phenomena as it happens, not as a subjective response to that phenomenon. I experience it immanently because of my situatedness in that environment, but the materiality of that environment exists whether I experience it or not. I 'perform' my walk in a particular way and interpret all incoming somatic data through my various senses, filters and concepts to build a 'picture' or symbolic construct of that place determined by my interpretive factors; by the performative action my walk is. Therefore, what I experience isn't a projection. However, what I perceive somatically is organised through the activities of my neural network and those processes present me with a version of reality that is already designed by and filtered through that neurological system. It has been formatted—packaged—in a particular way to make cognition possible. What I perceive is an unstable and sometimes unpredictable experience. My walking does not produce a factual registration of material reality nor construct a fantasy projection. What I am simultaneously presented with are two irreconcilable facts: the fact of the material landscape and the fact of my neurological formatting of that landscape. In other words, I walk the landscape and perceive that walk as a particular immanent experience, yet that experience and the concepts it generates are not the landscape itself. Those two conditions, though related, are categorically different from one another. My walk is formatted in my body to become the source of memories (of that walk) that populate and build my remembered landscapes. My remembered landscapes remain central to the artefacts I produce as stimulated by those remembered places. Those artefacts, too, are categorically different from the material landscape and the walk itself.

Although I experience great stimulation, I do not call 'mapping' processes, sensations and interactions inspiration. I have some difficulties with the word, imagining that many consider the concept of inspiration to operate through an independent and external metaphysical force that is visited upon them as a gift to induce abundant creativity, thereby setting the 'gifted' apart from others. As the definition given in Merriam-Webster explains:

*Inspiration has an unusual history in that its figurative sense appears to predate its literal one. It comes from the Latin inspiratus (the past participle of inspirare, 'to breathe into, inspire') and in English has had the meaning 'the drawing of air into the lungs' since the middle of the 16th century. This breathing sense is still in common use among doctors, as is expiration ('the act or process of releasing air from the lungs'). However, before inspiration was used to refer to breath it had a distinctly theological meaning in English, referring to a divine influence upon a person, from a divine entity; this sense dates back to the early 14th century. The sense of inspiration often found today ('someone or something that inspires') is considerably newer than either of those two senses, dating from the 19th century.*[130]

I take a pragmatic approach, considering my creative excitation as the consequence of neurological rather than metaphysical activity in the context described. This position does not limit the degree of passion or commitment I feel for the work I produce or its processes of making.

Not using the word inspiration requires another term to describe my intended state. I have not settled upon this term yet, but I shall write creative excitation here. I experience creative excitation, an automatic, self-generated interpretive state, through the interaction of body, mind and environment. It is an afferent/efferent excitation. It is a PK coupling. It is a dynamic and responsive cycle of immanent interpretation, significance, meaningfulness, action and reaction. It is a biological, biochemical response to life, consciousness, phenomena and stimulation. In the context of my creative practices and rituals, it is a situation I have prepared for and engineered to engage with new creative possibilities and materials. I appreciate how such a flow and strength of stimulation and cognition can feel as if it is pouring into me from outside or generated externally by some other force, mainly when such sensations and thoughts are immanent and concern no forethought. Still, all such sensations and realisations are self-generated within the body and mind, driven by external or internal stimuli. I am not an empty vessel waiting to be filled. I fill myself continually full during every moment. I am biologically designed to interpret every sensation, experience and thought. This is how I construct my reality.

On location, even though the physicality of the moment can be exciting and somewhat overwhelming, all the information being received is processed within the body through my CNS and within my mind through perception and cognition. Much of this nervous data escape my awareness and as discussed, is automatically filtered out and prioritised by the operation of my brain, but what data does get through begins to adapt, enhance or overwrite my mapped territory, the initially constructed remembered landscape. New experiences create new memories; some are in direct contention with those previously formatted. This is unsurprising as the evidence used to construct my original remembered landscape—I also quite like the idea of thinking of it as my affective or emotional landscape—was acquired using a third party, recorded, edited, framed, translated and adapted evidence materials that had already been filtered through the choices of others and symbolically encoded, often through digital media.

The sensation of conflict between my remembered landscape and the 'lived experience' of 'mapping' a physical location causes cognitive dissonance. This state excites me because I know a new conceptual map is being forged between those two location concepts. My new experiences are deterritorialising my older map to reterritorialise a new one. This results in my interior 'mapping' being in a state of flux, a process that I register as highly creative and one that I anticipate from experience will generate all manner of affective connections that will be useful when I come to make work. Furthermore, each time I revisit this newly constructed mapped landscape, the act of remembering and exploring transforms it again. This is what I describe as cognitive dissonance. It is a battle between conceptual and material territories necessary for forming a stable concept of place. The struggle is ongoing and stability is unobtainable. The memory—this remembered landscape—is environment influenced, self-generating and self-referential. Although hugely condensed here to illustrate more generalised aspects of memory

---

[130] 'Inspiration', in Merriam-Webster.com Dictionary, *Merriam-Webster*, <https://www.merriam-webster.com/dictionary/inspiration> [Accessed 15 Jan. 2023].

formation, a 2023 article in the online news and science magazine *Neuroscience* titled *Zone of Uncertainty Enables the Brain to Rapidly Form New Memories* explains that for memories to form, the brain must create connections between sensory signals that are received 'top-down' (or internally generated) and 'bottom-up' (or externally generated) from the environment. Those top-down (or inside-out) signals remain mysterious. It is the combination of top-down and bottom-up signals that encode memories. Interestingly, this research shows that a stimulus with learned relevance in those systems elicits a stronger response, suggesting that this positive potentiation is one piece of the memory trace puzzle.[131] Perhaps it is this *"stimulus with learned relevance"* that accounts for my sense of practiced visualisations of remembered landscapes increasing their conceptual agency, clarity and intensity?

Whatever the particulars of memory formation, the memories themselves have created an embedded 'sense of place' within my mind, nervous system, body and imagination. From a practical perspective, I experience remembered landscapes more frequently than material locations. Ultimately, the remembered landscapes dominate and shape my concept of place. Although my remembered landscapes are informed by and constructed from symbolic representations (photos and maps, for example) and experiences drawn from the physical landscape, remembered and perceived physical landscapes are categorically different and distinct from one another and both are categorically different to whatever realities they signify as representing external materiality.

Owing to the different phases of the 'mapping' process, I now have two related concepts of place: material and objective and conceptual and subjective. As a symbolic being, it would only be possible to experience, comprehend and conceptualise one with an awareness of the other. Both are inextricably linked. Both constitute aspects of my reality. Both will be re-accessed when I make work. The boundaries between what I consider real and imagined, between materiality, perceived physical landscapes and remembered landscapes, remain permeable. The line is moveable and the boundaries are liminal. This reminds me that my concept of reality is fluid.

I am also reminded of an additional challenge. Unlike the cartographer's map, which comes with a key to unlock the symbolic significance of its content to provide a shared, meaningful interpretation, the 'mapping' undertaken to generate a remembered landscape comes with no legend or key. Specific meaning and significance are not readily associated with symbols outside social conventions, sign networks or specific icons or referent status. Often, A = B remains a distant and unlikely aspiration to link signs with phenomena and meaningfulness. A = A is the likely outcome, where A = A in that way at that moment.

## The Berkshire Downs

I can't remember precisely what drew me to the Berkshire Downs as an area of landscape interest. Still, I remember basing a mid-1990s pencil drawing on a black and white photograph labelled *The Berkshire Downs*, found in a 1936 book I owned titled *English Downland* by H. J. Massingham. At that time, I was painting and drawing representational work (see Figure 13). The photograph strongly affected me even though I had never visited the area. The landscape configurations, typical of chalk escarpment scenery, as represented in the somewhat grainy black and white photograph, appealed to me. However, it wasn't until nearly thirty years later

---

[131] From the Press Office, Max Planck Institute, *Zone of Uncertainty Enables the Brain to Rapidly Form New Memories* in *Neuroscience* <https://neurosciencenews.com/zona-incerta-memory-formation-22202/> January 2023. Original research cited from Schroeder, Anna M. et al., (2023).

that I excitedly planned a trip to explore the area in person.

Figure 13. *The Berkshire Downs*, 56 x 76 cm. Marc Yeats (1995).

The Berkshire Downs cover a significant area of chalk upland in the south of England. I had set aside four days to explore the area and was eager to maximise my onsite time. To ascertain in advance where the best locations and routes would be, I began phase one of the 'mapping' process described above. My first port of call was to investigate Ordinance Survey maps of the area meticulously, searching out, as far as I could tell, the most suitable landscape configurations that I knew would appeal to me. My challenge with reading maps for this purpose was to attempt the conversion of contour lines into mental three-dimensional relief imagery in such a way that I could project in my mind's eye a whole topographical panorama from any position I would place myself into as observed from the ground, situated anywhere on the map, thereby being able to 'view' the landscape and make an informed judgement about its qualities. This operation took much mental projection and was prone to misinterpretation. It amounted to educated guesswork but proved a useful exercise, nevertheless.

To assist and validate this visualisation, I would also look at aerial satellite photographs of terrain that can be exchanged as an overlay to the maps in digital form. Though landscape features are flattened in those satellite images (or through algorithms, artificially and inaccurately given some degree of relief), they provide another stream of topographical information to analyse. In addition, and perhaps most valuable of all the online map features, are the geolocated photographs taken by walkers pinned to the locations they were taken in. Those, along with the photographic mapping of all UK roads on Google Maps, enabled me to view various points in the landscape. Though often limited to locations or routes I was unlikely to take, the photographic images did act as helpful descriptors of local landscape conditions more broadly.

Another valuable source of visual information came from videos posted by bikers and drivers, who toured or traversed the area using byways in their vehicles and made videos of their journeys. However, unsophisticated and frequently overlong, many videos did create a compelling impression of the varied landscapes and features found across different areas of the downs. Also helpful was a collection of drone footage that provided birds' eye views and aerial photographs of whole areas of the downs.

Over several weeks, and armed with this information, I absorbed everything I could to help construct a mental map of the entire area, focusing on the locations where I had amassed the most information or found the most compelling landscapes. Sometimes, those areas were mutually exclusive and I had to make assumptions about identifying the most suitable landscapes based on map evidence alone. Such actions were a leap of faith and an indication of my self-confidence in reading what was for me, the implied affective weight of a particular landscape configuration transmitted through the symbolic surface of the map itself. Self-deluded projection? Possibly. I'm mindful that the map is not the territory and whatever I read from it or assume it implies may be radically different to my experience of the location. That's part of the fun of exploring—finding out for oneself. There were blind spots to my knowledge and my investigation of such a large geographical area was by no means exhaustive. Still, following the initial 'mapping' period, I assembled an itinerary of locations and routes to explore. Some months later, as prepared as I could be, I visited the area. This was my opportunity to compare my remembered landscape with the physical territory.

My first impression of being in the landscape was related to my perception of its scale. Everything was much bigger than I had imagined in my remembered landscape or implied from examining the 'mapping' materials. I felt dwarfed by the distances between points of reference; the size of the fields; the scale of the sky and horizon; the time it took to walk from A to B; my sense of perspective across large vistas; my perception of height, sky and cumulus cloud formations; my aesthetic appreciation of landscape contours and undulations; how stands of trees, like the tumuli, of which there were many, had a visual presence more significant than anything indicated on a map and were conspicuous for miles; my constant visceral sense of being on a vast plateau; the tonal colour reductions apparent in distant hills due to the optical effect of aerial perspective and my open, expansive, three-dimensional sense of space. All preconceptions associated with those originally formatted concepts were to expand in scope massively.

Away from landscape scale, the following impression of difference was driven by the weather's effect and affect. My visit occurred meteorologically at a particularly turbulent time, with an unstable showery air stream that generated localised but very violent thunderstorms and heavy rain. The cloudscapes were significant and magnificent. Their structures and progress affected how the light was distributed across the landscape and what was visually privileged or obscured. This illuminated interplay of shadow and light scuttled across the land's surface at speed, animating every aspect of relief, every shade of green, brown, white and more. It was pronounced across the large field systems where the travelling rays of light would change my affective relationship to the land moment by moment. Things far away appeared near; things dark appeared suddenly light. The transition was everywhere. The dynamic aspect of the weather and how the landscape was lit brought this topography to life in ways I had not anticipated when 'mapping' my remembered landscape. It changed everything.

Perhaps most significantly, my sense of the landscape's affective weighting increased dramatically, with the greatest dramatic effects of lighting—those producing highly significant contrasts between light and dark—being the most compelling. The sky was an integral and influential aspect of my landscape perception. However, when constructing my remembered landscape, I paid no particular attention to the sky or weather. It may have been sunny or overcast. I can only recall neutral weather. I did not notice. This does not mean that an impression of sky or weather was wilfully absent, just that it was not sufficiently characterised to register in or influence the remembered landscape. I took its presence for granted. Although an obvious conclusion to reach, reflecting on the difference between my remembered landscape and experience of the physical location reinforced how imagining one without the other created an artificial divide that weakened the identity of both. When constructing my remembered landscape, I did not pay sufficient attention to this relationship, but it was all too apparent when situated in the physical landscape.

Yet another affective aspect of the weather relates to a sense of jeopardy, vulnerability and exposure I felt on location. I could not help but observe my changing perspective, reactions and feelings about the landscape concerning how the unpredictable weather conditions impacted the terrain and my presence within it. My sense of landscape would quickly migrate from anodyne to threatening as I followed the path of a storm to calculate if I would get caught out by it and drenched. If it were heading straight for me, anxiety levels would increase dramatically. With the weather conditions volatile enough to generate thunder and lightning, my prominence as sometimes the tallest object in a high, open terrain became a significant concern. I noted that in such conditions, how I perceived the landscape altered radically. The necessity to attempt to find shelter in an otherwise exposed location was at times so overwhelming that my affective orientation shifted radically: what formerly felt like a secure environment soon became a hostile one. Embedded memories of this time and place include a daily drenching and respect for the power of nature.

In more generalised terms of difference, some locations I had selected from my remembered landscape did not deliver the affective impact I had assumed they would, considering the evidence gathered at the time of 'mapping'. Nevertheless, most locations met or exceeded my expectations concerning affective weight, some in ways I had not predicted. I found those locations triggered the most robust affective responses and, consequently, were the most satisfying and rewarding locations to experience as I knew their capacity to reformat or reinforce my remembered landscape would be the most productive.

In addition to exploring the site, adding new experiences and laying down new memories in person, I also documented significant landscape encounters through digital photographs. I took a great many of those to fix specific visual data into this symbolic format—symbolic because photographs signify or stand in for something that is not there, as the photograph is not the object itself but acts as a symbolic representation of that object conceptually—to aid and refresh memory recall and memory creation once I had left the site. The photographs were not taken to reference during acts of painting or composing as objects to copy in a representational fashion. As mentioned, I do not paint from life or by copying representational reproductions. I paint and compose only from the memories of places assembled through phases one and two of the 'mapping' process. Photographs were taken to help build and trigger affective responses to the locations that would maintain and contribute to the remembered landscape. To achieve this, the photographs would be automatically interpreted, assimilated into my memories and then embedded as newly symbolised matter. Memories, too, are symbols representing phenomena that are not materially present in the brain. The ongoing process of constructing a remembered landscape involves transforming all somatic data and the feelings engendered into symbolic form. I think of the processes of memory formation as the brain pre-formatting data in a mode suitable for its storage and access. In this context, symbols generate more symbols, like a network of words spawned by the user to conceptualise a sense of meaning for any given word.

My original 'mapping' rituals constructed a conceptual landscape that made me perceive the actual landscapes as familiar. I experienced a sense of orientation and affective expectation, which was duly met. However, the impact of scale and lighting conditions, as well as the instability of my emotional orientation towards the landscape when threatened by extreme weather, generated significant cognitive dissonance between my original 'mapping' and my bodily experience of the locations. My conceptual map was subsequently modified and changed as I examined and re-examined those experiences and memories. The map is still under construction and will no doubt remain so continually. It is in flux. Its affective resonances have also been triggered many times, mainly through the serendipitous mark-making actions of painting, enabling me to feel with some confidence that something of the locations I was immersed in has been embedded in my work. I want to assume that this something is a 'sense of place'. Indeed, a 'sense of place' has been embedded within my perceptual reality. Still, I realise that such specificity or even generic assumptions around any 'sense of place' embodied in my work is subjective and that transmitting this condition to others is unproven. Transmitting an embedded 'sense of place' remains an aspiration, but not a claim I can verify.

## The South Downs National Park and Lymington Marshes

My experiences in those locations differed somewhat from the former because they were framed within the context of an organised residency undertaken with the expectation of producing several outcomes—drawings, paintings, music compositions—that would be publicly shared and documented. The project was called *Look In, Look Out* and was part of *The Observatory* Residencies, organised by an arts organisation called SPUD. My role was identified as Composer-In-Residence to *The Observatory* and operated across two separate week-long periods in the summer of 2015. Although my title focused on composition, I was primarily there to explore how I might transmit embodied observations of the sites through the media of painting and composition in a unified manner.

The approach I took to this residency was similar in many respects to those detailed about the Berkshire Downs but differed in two respects: first, I spent considerably less preparatory time building a remembered landscape, probably because the geographic locus of the residency was predetermined; and second, I generated sketches, drawings and compositional ideas, on paper and in my aural imagination as part of the research process in-situ as the residencies unfolded.

*The Observatory* residency was undertaken as a fully documented, day-by-day diary-style project.[132] Many aspects of the processes and presuppositions of making were considered essential to sharing publicly, if not more so than any finished work or outcome. This requirement contextualised much of what followed, particularly regarding documentation and process. It meant that I needed to express thoughts as I came to terms with them by articulating the insecurities and uncertainties associated with the creative process from my perspective as the artist. In romanticised language, I needed to open a window into my soul. I'm not a romantic type when it comes to my practice as an artist, so I hold phrases like that very lightly, but the point around instantly sharing the machinations of my mind was relevant to how I proceeded.

My documentation solution was to make daily talking-head video diaries where I spoke unscripted about experiences, ideas and concepts, challenges, failures and possible approaches and solutions. I set myself up as a talking work in progress. Issues around objectivity remained unresolved and everything I said, as honestly as I would say it, could only be viewed as a subjective self-assessment. This doesn't preclude the content of what I said from being valid or relevant, but it does mean it could not be externally verified or measured empirically. Nevertheless, the videos, along with landscape photographs and, on occasion, mobile phone audio recordings of sonic environments (I remember the polytemporal rhythmic tapping of metal rigging against aluminium yacht masts on a windy day at Keyhaven harbour as well as a field recording of skylarks, bees and distant church bells at Titchmarsh) became evocative sonic symbolic representations of particular times and places.

The onsite making of work demonstrated a particularly significant difference between this residency and the Berkshire Downs experience, as here, I was attempting to immediately embody my reactions to the landscape in various pieces of work I produced, particularly drawings, while simultaneously attempting to assimilate what for me were the landscapes' affect-triggering components determined through observation (see Figure 14). Although the work produced onsite was very much approached from the perspective of research and the making of preliminary sketches to be worked up into finished pieces in the months following the residency—I thought of those actions as sensing-to-performing documentation identical to how I now appreciate the operation of PK coupling although at the time, beyond my perception of the bodily and embodied experience of working in this way, had no knowledge of a possible theoretical explanation. I was surprised by how much this research activity, particularly the immanent performative pieces (sketches), quickly took on the significance of finished work despite no intentionality for outcomes to be anything other than preludes to richer, more considered creative activities. My attitude to the completeness of those works altered as perspectives around what constituted a finished work changed. I realised that the declared endpoint of any artwork is fluid, self-determined and not externally qualified. Indeed, such an endpoint will not exist when the work can be modified further and where the notion of

---

[132] Access to many documented materials can be found at *The Observatory* Spud Observatory website here: <https://www.lookinlookout.org/marc-yeats> [accessed December 19, 2022].

completion is only one arbitrary line among many that may be drawn under the work ad infinitum. I believe all artworks can be further modified and are never complete in an absolute sense. Nevertheless, I frequently settle upon one of those possible arbitrary lines drawn under work to consider it finished in a practical sense.

Figure 14. Onsite drawing from *The Observatory* residency, South Downs National Park (2015).

To generate located, immanently realised works, I knew it was necessary to actively engage all my senses in an attempt to quickly map a landscape, recognise what about it triggered my affective responses, recognise, too, its symbolic components in association with those responses—in PK coupling terms, very much engaging with my spatio-temporal self-orientation, in relation to other parts of my body and the environment about me and responding to the possibilities for action in that present time—and to further assimilate all embodied impressions into a conceptual landscape through symbolic associations and expression as mark-making. Additionally, through a consciously driven action-based feedback loop, I responded to the sensorimotor embodiment of that moment along with interpretive, symbolic constructions to initiate actions through drawing that, because of their speed of execution and lack of cognition or consideration, felt spontaneous. Those actions were dynamic, responsive, assimilative and recursive. As well as the PK coupling aspects of those actions, I would respond to the mark-making and the symbolic significance it implied as each line was manifested. Seeing the drawing as an addition to my external environment, I again interpreted it and responded through PK coupling and additional hermeneutics. This cyclic process of feeling/performing/interpretation continued until I deemed the activity sufficiently exercised to be complete. The frenzy of scribbling that ensued was, I believe, an example of strong embodiment in action. Here, the notion of coupling feeling with performing and where phenomenality is constituted by the different capacities that feeling involves is embodied into an artefact.

My understanding of what was happening phenomenologically in relation to PK coupling is now more developed than at the time of this residency. Given my awareness of what I was doing then, the added expectation I had imposed upon myself to explain what I was doing and why became an extra performative pressure. I found that being embedded in the moment as an act of total hermeneutic situatedness and a necessary consequence of speed drawing precluded any meaningful notion of being able to assess and describe the actions I was undertaking objectively and impartially. Nevertheless, I attempted to explain my actions as best I could using the language and understanding available to me. It became clear that detaching myself from myself while embodied and immersed in a particular experience was impossible. Consequently, I spoke as an artist in primarily subjective terms. While not ideal for my purposes, such communication was of some use but only in so far as it articulated what I thought was happening from an emotional, interpersonal perspective. Although such a subjectively driven writing style is attractive to a range of readers, a metaphysical or romanticised ideal of how an artist operates allows little room for meaningful analysis or an understanding of the artistic process, certainly on a physiological or neurological basis or in terms beyond the personal. Indeed, it is unnecessary for an artist or an audience to think about or engage with artwork in terms other than the personal to experience meaningfulness. Nevertheless, wishing to describe my practice in objective terms where possible and considering that the act of speed drawing and the self-observation and assessment that immediately followed, all of which would be undertaken in little more than a minute of intense activity, it is little wonder that the brief I had set myself became unachievable and overwhelming.

Figure 15. *Observatory 1h, Near Winchester, Hampshire*. Acrylic on paper, 420 x 594 mm. Marc Yeats (2015).

Although I have isolated speed drawing to examine it in more detail, such levels of simultaneous (or what is perhaps perceived as simultaneous) activity, a sort of read/write programming, or the feeling/performing operation of PK coupling, is part of the ongoing neurological processing that our CNS and brains undertake every moment of every day, mostly out of our awareness. My interest in what is going on neurologically from the perspective of an artist ultimately concerns how any knowledge supports my awareness and understanding of what is embodied and manifests in the artist-making processes of painting, drawing or composition—as physical, measurable, analysable things made up of surfaces, densities, components, structures, vibrations, colours, frequencies, materials, relationships, textures and time.

Together, the in-situ work creation, the pieces of art themselves, walking to explore, walking to compose, talking-head videos, photos and sound recordings provided more data for 'mapping' purposes, each contributing to the construction of my remembered landscapes. As with the Berkshire Downs, the research, data and embodiment of that time, along with my remembered landscapes, became a rich source of stimulation, reference and motivation for the work that followed. I produced around twenty sketches, eight paintings (see Figure 15), two string quartets that I would identify as directly related to the residences and an extensive range of other music compositions and paintings indirectly influenced by the experience over six years. In addition, the conscious methodology of creating remembered landscapes that began at *The Observatory* has continued to develop within subsequent on-location research opportunities, as evidenced by my Berkshire Downs experience. As for embodying what I perceived as a 'sense of place' in any of the works produced during or following this residency, I cannot say I was successful beyond personal terms of reference. However, many of the works produced did succeed in triggering affective associations related to either a generic or, on occasion, a definite 'sense of place' in me as the creator and viewer/listener.

## The Suffolk Coastline

My final example of a residency, or in this case, a relationship with a particular landscape, has unfolded and deepened across nine years between 2012 and 2021. It shares many aspects in common with *The Observatory* residencies and my trip to the Berkshire Downs. For example, as time progressed, I built remembered landscapes in the manner previously described; I created located immanent work onsite; I made video diaries, recorded comments, thoughts and wrote blogs; I took hundreds of photographs; and, concerning those activities, produced two string quartets, orchestral music, ensemble pieces and a host of other compositions as well as a great many paintings I would attribute to material origins generated in this location that have embodied within them the triggers that initiate my affective reactions to this particular 'sense of place'. As a site, the triangular area plotted between Wenhaston, Orford and Kessingland has stimulated the enormous outpouring of work I would associate with any landscape area so far encountered.

Owing to the number of years I have been visiting this location, it is unsurprising that so much work has been created in association with it. Time allows for such productivity, but time alone does not account for the inclination or necessity to make work about any location. For such fecundity to thrive, my affective relationship with the sites must be vibrant and robust. This only comes about when I have generated sufficient interest in its landscape configurations—the features, topography, geology, flora and fauna, weather, the relationship between land, sea, waterways, architecture, archaeological and agricultural imprint—to trigger intensities of affect that transform interest into fascination and obsession. Over time, I have invested my remembered landscapes with a sense of seasonal change, every weather and lighting condition imaginable and a familiarity that only comes through time spent on location. As a result, my remembered landscapes have become multivalent. But another element to this landscape, particularly its coast, drives my fascination even further.

The low-lying sandy cliffs of Suffolk are at threat of erosion by the constant action of the sea, rising sea levels and storms. This coastline has been receding for centuries and is littered with now-submerged towns and farmland. Whole communities have had to relocate or move further inland to escape the encroaching sea. The cycle continues despite attempts to halt or delay this process through scattered, largely ineffective sea defences. My experiences of the ever-changing coastline show that vast chunks of land fall into the sea each season, with those dramatic changes destabilising 'mapping' processes and remembering coastal landscapes.

Relationships between coastal hinterlands, particularly beach formations, the sea and the land, are ordinarily in constant change due to actions of the wind and tide, erosion and deposition. However, experiencing the inevitable disappearance of coastal woodlands, coastal paths and agricultural land from year to year is something else. Those changes make the land and cliffs feel temporary and constantly at risk. Perceiving a landscape as a fragile condition was new to me. Of course, I appreciate that erosion and entropy always happen everywhere, but the speed of change is so significant here.

The repercussions of this landscape instability directly relate to the perceived anxiety I associate with my experiences of the coast. Through that, the radical alterations within landscape configurations introduced new triggers that influenced my affective relationship with place in ways not experienced elsewhere. This anxiety can be summed up as a question: will what is familiar to me, what I have remembered, still be there when I visit? I feel a continual sense of impermanence, loss, fragility and rapid change. Those affects relate to dynamic processes.

Change is dynamic. It operates across time. We perceive changes in multiple simultaneous cycles in our everyday lives. For example, the daily difference between night and day, shadow and light, foliage growth and flowers blossoming, seasons changing, weather patterns and the cycles of the tide, to identify just a few. Change processes that operate over more extended periods, even millennia or deep time, such as the formation or erosion of mountains and oceans; the movement of tectonic plates closer together or further apart (excluding extreme attention-grabbing change events such as earthquakes and volcanoes); or the gradual rise in sea levels or average global temperatures; often pass unnoticed as a day-to-day observation even though change is constantly happening. Along the Suffolk coastline, it is not the fact that change occurs that is of note; it is the catastrophic rate of change that is exceptional.

Notably, I have concentrated on this point because the dynamic process of change is now embedded in my remembered landscapes of this area and the change that dominates my 'sense of place'. My 'mapping' process is undertaken against a backdrop of landscape instability resulting in my acceptance that my remembered landscape may no longer be related in some way to a current physical state and that a particular physical reality may have disappeared. This makes forming a remembered relationship with the coast like trying to hold hands with a ghost: what was once corporal and solid has now become sand and air. Where once there were cliffs or trees, there is now space and sea.

Experiences of the Suffolk coast frequently present me with new physical realities on the ground when expectations projected from my remembered landscape prepare me for something familiar that is just no longer there. Everything about the place has changed apart from the actions of change itself. Encountering this newly configured but familiar landscape results in a significant jolt to my perceptions. It is at first disorientating, then disappointing, then profoundly sad. Finally, it equates to loss (see Figure 16). This jolt is, I believe, my body's reaction to the cognitive dissonance produced when my conceptual, remembered landscape collides with the reality of the physical landscape before me as well as the considerable effort needed for perceptual realignment to adjust from one sense of reality to another in an instant. Over time and now prepared, I assimilate and anticipate change as part of the identity of this coastline and part of what I experience about it. Erosion and impermanence are significant markers of my constructed Suffolk coast 'sense of place'.

Figure 16. *Covehithe Beach, Suffolk.* Acrylic on paper, 297 x 420 mm. Marc Yeats (2016).

The additional challenge of creating work associated with this area is how best to embed my sense of dynamic change and vulnerability into artefacts I produce as a symbolic representation of instability, impermanence and loss. Of course, vulnerability, anxiety and a sense of loss are not felt by or emanating from the landscape itself; the landscape is not (as far as I'm aware) a conscious entity. Instead, those very human feelings are projected from me onto my concept of what the landscape is. Nevertheless, such affective weighting colours my association with the area and, as stated, informs the emotional constructions that signify a 'sense of place' for me. Despite the challenges—the impossibility even—of bypassing the hermeneutics of others to successfully transmit specific emotional conditions as exact values through my compositions and paintings, I remain eager to trigger and replicate such feelings for others to sense in my work. I appreciate that such ambition is unlikely to succeed this way.

The expression of conditions changing over time is ideally formatted within a temporal medium such as music, where material and process can unfold, be constructed, deconstructed and even eroded throughout a timeline and where structural configurations, like those in the landscape, may be altered with all material changes observable through study and analysis of the sonic or notational manifestations of the piece as physical phenomena. Such observations are pragmatic and will not reference the emotional impact such musical structures may have in relation to a 'sense of place'. They can, however, effectively demonstrate processes associated with those places, such as erosion. A series of paintings, too, can illustrate change associated with erosion or even use physical erosion processes, such as scraping or removing layers of material, to reveal others below. Again, those properties and processes, pragmatic and material in nature, will not necessarily ensure any connectivity to a 'sense of place' specific to the Suffolk coast in and of themselves.

I cannot speak of where a 'sense of place' resides other than in the mind of the creator or the receiver of a work. Sometimes, those may be one in the same person. I understand that the physical configurations of landscape and their varied features form a recognisable characteristic that, if referred to symbolically in any number of manifestations such as words, photographs, paintings, musical compositions or the experience of walking, for example, may trigger associations between place and that individual. Triggers are very personal and may be related objectively to physical materiality or emotional senses through the experience of place. Triggers may also couple what appear to be unrelated stimuli with disparate experiences across a range of senses and emotions.

Though not part of the Ximena et al. paper, it may in the future be possible to explore the feeling/performing correlates associated with a 'sense of place', if such exists, in the context of ESMT and PK coupling. Though highly speculative, I find such a prospect tantalising. Away from this speculation, the hypothesis supporting the coupling of feeling and performing within the stated principles and theoretical models of ESMT and PK coupling remains compelling.

Situated within this theory, the artist acts as a bridge between place and audience through what is embodied in the artist's physicality and embodied in their work. I move to perceive and perceive to move can be rewritten as: I create to perceive and perceive to create.

# CHAPTER THREE

# FOR THE LOVE OF CHALK AND OTHER MATTERS

## The White Stuff

Chalk landscapes have a substantial impact on my creative life. My attraction is evident through the work I produce that is connected to them and the time I enjoy spending in those landscapes. I am curious to know why my obsession with chalk began and how it manifests in my paintings and compositions. To answer those questions, I must travel back to my childhood to remember where it all started. If I were a less curious artist, I'd accept my feelings without question and make work. But my attraction to chalk landscapes, stretching over the past five decades, is so powerful that not to discuss what possibly drives me would be to ignore a substantial area of my makeup, thought and operation. Consequently, I wish to examine as much as possible to discover what I can and cannot determine. Thankfully and firmly grounded in fully determinable science, there are two questions I can ask and answer within a factual framework: what is chalk and what are the characteristics of chalk landscapes?

Chalk is a soft, white, porous rock laid down in shallow seas during the Cretaceous geological period, about one hundred million to sixty-six million years ago. It comprises finely grained and often microscopic fossil debris deposited at the time to form a mud-like seabed that, across millennia and a range of geological processes, becomes the familiar white rock seen widely in the landscape across areas of southern England, in particular, Salisbury Plain, Cranbourne Chase, the Dorset Downs, Berkshire Downs, Chiltern Hills, the North and South Downs, the White Cliffs of Dover and widely found throughout Buckinghamshire, Hertfordshire, Bedfordshire, West and East Sussex and Kent and further north into the Lincolnshire Wolds and parts of southeast Yorkshire. The chalk forms much of the upland backbone of Southern England.

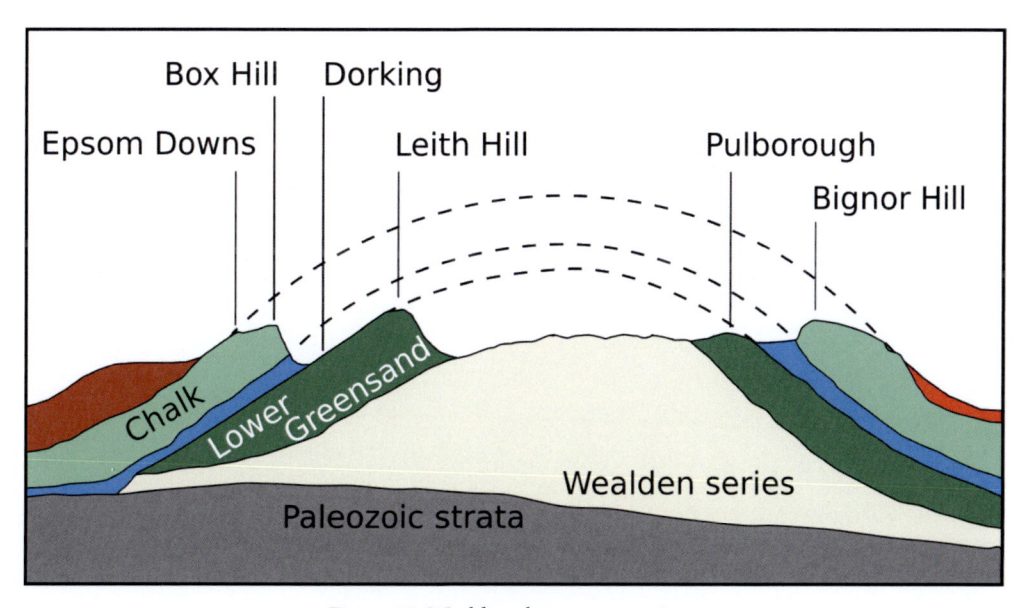

Figure 17. Weald geology cross section.

From its deposition to the modern day, the chalk in Southern England has changed its appearance dramatically. In the first instance, through geological and tectonic activities, particularly those concerning the collision of the African and Eurasian tectonic plates around sixty-five million years ago that led to the formation of mountain ranges from the Alps to the Himalayas—tectonic movements still active today—that have caused the chalk mass to become fractured, folded, faulted and uplifted; and in the second instance, as a direct consequence of the sculpting and compressing actions and forces of glacial movements during the last ice age—between one-hundred and fifteen thousand and eleven-thousand seven-hundred years ago—where chalk formations were located under or near to the southern edge of glacial ice sheets. Effects of erosion and change brought about by the dissolution of the chalk and the action of glacial meltwaters formed the typical chalk scenery we see today, where strata have been raised to the land's surface (see Figure 17 which shows the present-day topography of the chalk, indicating its folded and now eroded original deposition in this Wealden cross-section).

Those ancient processes form the smooth, rolling, characteristic contours of the chalk downs, valleys and plateaus, with their shapes slowly changing owing to ongoing erosion and geological actions. Its dip and scarp slopes are typical of chalk scenery, as graphically represented in Figure 17. Those features are brought about because of the tilt and uplift in chalk depositions caused by the tectonic actions mentioned previously, followed by glacial erosion actions that have resulted in steep slopes—escarpments—occurring on one side of the deposit and a long, gentle slope leading away from this towards other parts of the deposit. Examples of escarpments can typically be seen along the North and South Downs ridges and chalk plateaus, such as Salisbury Plain and the Berkshire Downs fringed by scarp slopes or may have steep escarpments along one leading edge and dip slopes leading away into chalk valleys towards the deposit perimeters. Where the chalk meets the sea, sheer cliffs form, for example, the White Cliffs of Dover, Beachy Head and Flamborough Head or other geological features such as natural arches, like Durdle Door or collapsed arches, such as the Needles off the western tip of the Isle of White or Old Harry Rocks near Swanage in Dorset, can be observed. The topography and characteristics of chalk scenery, its flora and fauna and how the land has been managed for millennia make its landscape characteristics recognisable.

Those features and characteristics are deeply embedded within my entire being. But why am I drawn to this soft, porous, white carbonate rock? Why do I feel connected to chalk landscapes above all other landscapes? To help find an answer, I accessed memories to see if I could locate when I first encountered chalk scenery and what its impact was on me. I cannot be specific, but my first physical contact with chalk was around twelve. I had no memories of chalk before this age, even though the likelihood of passing through and noticing chalk landscapes was high owing to the location of my family home between Greater London and Kent, where chalk scenery is prevalent. Despite this probable contact, my remembered story did not begin until I experienced a strong compulsion to seek out the chalk.

Though young, I was allowed to travel by train, alone or with friends, out of London to walk in the Kent countryside. I remember seeing the chalk along those train routes exposed through quarrying, as white scars on the hillsides or alongside the rail tracks, scrapped away to make railway cuttings. As the train passed through the cuttings, I would see the white stuff close up from the carriage window. I was fascinated. My heart would quicken. Those outcrops of rock promised something I hadn't previously realised I needed. I had no idea why I was excited or what was promised—knowing was not significant. Being close to chalk was. I felt obsessed.

It is likely that on the train route from south London to Folkestone, where I would go fossil hunting along the beach, I noticed extensive chalk cuttings near the station of Knockholt in Kent. Once I had noted this outcrop of chalk, I took the initiative to travel there and explore the chalk I had seen up close and personal. The chalk cutting was not easily accessed from the station. I remember climbing over a few fences; I was on railway property and my presence there was illegal, so I did not want to be seen. I made my way to the outcrop. Upon arrival, I examined the bits of fallen chalk for some time, looking for fossils (I didn't find any). From that initial foray into the chalk, my abiding memory was positioning myself within part of the cutting as if it were constructed like a chair, sitting on the ground, resting against the chalk and looking up at the sky. It was like an act of meditation. I remember vividly. I was feeling, sensing the ground through my body. I also remember the overwhelming sense of relief, happiness, belonging and what I'd now describe as resonance at being this close and in physical contact with the chalk. It was like returning home after a long estrangement. I felt connected and plugged in.

This account is my first experience of total immersion in a landscape, my first experience of the complete embodiment of an environment. Even at the time, I realised that what I had experienced was significant, although I was unable to articulate such thoughts using words. This story is apocryphal; many elements could easily stray into personal mythology and the metaphysical. I appreciate this and shall avoid such connotations as they will not help explain what happened beyond personal experience, wishing first to explore any possible explanations in science.

## PK Coupling, Behaviour and Embodiment

In 'Mapping', I introduce the theory of PK coupling as the relationship between the proprioceptive and kinaesthetic systems and how they learn about body position and movement options during ongoing actions as part of an active, organised system in continuous and dynamic interaction with the environment. Termed strong embodiment, PK coupling theory proposes that some dynamical self-oriented and relational features of the phenomenology resulting from the coupling of perception and action constitute an active and ongoing correlate between feeling and performing. Though still a hypothesis, I can situate my first acknowledged experience of the chalk as a perceptual recognition of embodiment's physiological and neurological action within PK coupling. I cannot claim that PK coupling exclusively explains those phenomena or is necessarily its only component or causality. There are likely to be various other factors I am unaware of. However, based on current science, PK coupling offers the best fit available for me to rationalise those initial and subsequent experiences in the chalk.

I also discuss embodiment as central to my experience of landscape and my actions as an artist, taking the connection between feeling and performing literally. Describing the artefacts I create and acts of walking as performances brings my work as an artist into a direct relationship with the landscape through PK coupling, making sense of my sensations and actions. Similarly, what is embodied in my artwork is a direct consequence of the correlation between feeling and action.

Although I can use words to describe the scientific aspects of this phenomenon as a process, describing its phenomenological aspects in detail remains challenging. As explained in 'Mapping', direct correlates between feeling and performance cannot be fully described. This leaves me asking what sensations are associated with which actions as much PK coupling occurs outside of awareness and often, perceptually as an automated process that, though responsive and dynamic, presents me with an ongoing sensorimotor performance as a fait accompli.

When walking, painting or undertaking any other embodied activity, I have intentionality concerning where I'm going or where I want my limbs to be in relation to whatever functionality I am undertaking. It is clear in physical terms whether I have been successful. For example, with walking, if I am unsuccessful in placing my feet on the ground in a way that also facilitates the necessary fine adjustments of balance throughout my entire body, I would fall over or trip. By looking ahead or down at my feet, coupling vision and movement, my senses will predict the best physical placement while still in motion. If success is unlikely, my senses and body will automatically make all necessary adjustments via the dynamic of PK coupling to achieve or adapt my intentionalities at that moment. A great deal of this activity will function outside of my conscious awareness. I could be absorbed in thinking of something completely other than walking and my sensory-motor system will keep me on track. This is a clear example of PK coupling's adaptive, responsive and dynamic feedback loop. Despite this manifestation of sensing and action as part of my everyday life and functionality, what lies behind the organisation of those actions remains largely beyond my perception. I may focus on the relationship between what I am sensing and my consequent bodily actions at times of risk, for example, when walking on an icy surface, driving a car through a particularly tight and awkward space, or undertaking some delicate or precise movement when painting or composing. Still, my body takes care of what it does most of the time through autopilot. With so much happening automatically and outside of awareness, I do not understand why particular actions result from specific feelings or senses away from the more obvious examples I have given.

Although what I experienced as a child and still experience as an adult in the chalk can be situated within theories of PK coupling, what remains unclear is why I was attracted to the chalk in the first place. As mentioned, the strength of feeling that drew me to go to Knockholt suggests that the urge to have contact with the chalk was already present. I assume that antecedents precipitated my actions, but those remain mysterious, like the exact correlation of feeling to performance in PK coupling. Nevertheless, this lack of understanding does not preclude me from making work. I feel my way forward through my senses, through my body. Alongside cognition, reason and the pragmatic intentionalities concerned with making, I rely on my automated bodily operations in everything I do, including my artistic practice. Processes of strong embodiment enable my body to think about what I am sensing as an automatically coupled activity. I also interpret the outcomes—the performances—of PK coupling as an ongoing hermeneutic process, an action that itself induces further levels of feeling that will correlate with yet more actions to structure a perpetual dance between sensing, performing, interpretation, sensing, performing and interpretation and so on.

As mentioned, intentionality plays a part here, too. For example, the PK coupling that constantly occurs as I move, when I walk, is structured into the overall flow of that walk, governed by the intentionality to travel here or there along a particular route. I continually make choices determined by multiple factors that, away from the global structure of the walk, govern which side of a path I walk on, what obstacles I avoid and what detours I make to ponder this or that. The variants are many. And then, there are the multiple subdivisions of those actions—adaptive and responsive actions—designed to keep me upright on uneven terrain. From the original intentionality to walk to how I walk and how that walk manifests as performance, those actions are influenced by PK coupling and its correlations between what is sensed and felt and movement as performance. Any activities undertaken through intentionality involving the body similarly unfold through PK coupling, be they painting, composing, dancing, observing or listening. Stimuli that generate feelings can be correlated to performance.

Although I have the language to describe aspects of this process through a basic understanding of PK coupling, what cannot be expressed verbally, perhaps the perceptual experience of PK coupling itself, is expressed through sensing and performing as an embodiment in my artwork. The artwork embodies this dance through the particular significance and meaningfulness described as the condition that makes it an artwork. Although rather glib sounding, through writing *Music, Painting, Landscape and Me*, I appreciate that this need to express what I sense through performance, in its broadest context, is the driver for why I am a composer and painter rather than a writer as the primary expression of my self-ecological relationships.

Like the Ximena et al. paper that situates proprioception in action within the contexts of ecological and social interaction, the thought-provoking abstract of a 2019 paper called *The Life of Behaviour* by Alex Gomez-Marin and Asif Ghazanfar also emphasises the importance of contextualising neuroscience within the broader fields of behaviour, environment, materiality, agency and history, illustrating the connectivity of sensing and performing (action) from a different perspective to PK coupling. Though not explicitly related to the Ximena et al. paper and using animal rather than human subjects, this research discusses how the scientific tendency to dissociate the life of behaviour and its rationale when examining stimulus-response phenomena reduces the value and scope of its findings. To emphasise this, the paper's abstract explains:

*Neuroscience needs behaviour. However, it is daunting to render the behaviour of organisms intelligible without suppressing most, if not all, references to life. When animals are treated as passive stimulus-response, disembodied and identical machines, the life of behaviour perishes. Here, we distil three biological principles (materiality, agency and historicity), spell out their consequences for the study of animal behaviour and illustrate them with various examples from the literature. We propose to put behaviour back into context, with the brain in a species-typical body and with the animal's body situated in the world, stamp Newtonian time with nested ontogenetic [the development or course of development especially of an individual organism] and phylogenetic processes [phylogeny is the evolution of a genetically related group of organisms via the study of protein or gene evolution by involving the comparison of homologous sequences] that give rise to individuals with their own histories; and supplement linear cause-and-effect chains and information processing with circular loops of purpose and meaning. We believe that conceiving behaviour in those ways is imperative for neuroscience.*[133]

The references here, mainly to the brain being in a species-typical body and with that body being situated in the world as part of a meaningful 'lived experience', resonates with my perception of the operation of PK coupling within my own physicality, further reinforcing my position on embodiment, sensing and performing as correlates within the rationale of my artistic practice. Considering this connection between neuroscience and behaviour, analysis and descriptions of motivations, behaviour, responses and outcomes from the perceptual, personal and 'lived experience' perspective provide additional contexts that enrich what can be objectively described through the science of afferent/efferent impulses alone. To achieve this, I shall present various behavioural and experiential phenomena that occur when I am in chalk landscapes, remember chalk landscape-related experiences or engage with music, painting, photography and literature concerned with those landscapes, being careful to distinguish between what is known science and speculation based upon that science. First, I will describe my responses to landscape through the involuntary production of what I term sensed sound.

---

[133] Gomez-Marin, Alex et al. The abstract to this paper is cited in full. The definition of phylogeny is separately taken from Waikagul, Jitra and Thaekham, Urusa, pp. 77-90.

# Sensed Sound, PK Coupling and Proprioception

I hesitate to call this sensed sound music, as it is not 'heard' in an organised, musical way, nor are the sounds structured as anything other than drone vibrations, fleeting fragmentations, or dense, cloud-like microtonal chords. The sounds are chimerical. They defy detailed descriptions beyond broad categories but evoke strong emotional signification and meaningfulness. They are produced in and perceived as somatic stimuli through my body, more akin to vibration, oscillation and resonance that is felt as a spontaneous or immanent response to my experience of the landscape. It is an involuntary and aperiodic response that correlates sensation to movement perceived as sound.

My presence in the chalk elicits additional physical sensations along with the sounds. Those feelings may be intense, at times being powerful enough to induce a sense of breathlessness, visceral tremors like the sensation of 'butterflies' caused when in a car travelling over a hump-back bridge or on a free-fall fairground ride or rollercoaster at speed, where the perception of momentary weightlessness is experienced in the pit of the stomach or under the diaphragm, or at their most extreme, a brief episode of over-excited mild heart palpitations. From the perspective of experienced emotions, I would describe those sensations as ecstatic and elating. Though intense, the experiences happen in waves lasting only several seconds to a few minutes. Attempting to locate many of those sensations in any bodily area is challenging. Occasionally, I will experience them in my chest or stomach and at other times, in my limbs or body. Sometimes, the sounds are accompanied by olfactory stimulation and a somewhat metallic odour and tingling sensation in my upper nose, not unlike sensations I have experienced when feeling excitable or anxious, suggesting a possible link to adrenalin production. Those nasal experiences can amplify the intensity of bodily place-initiated emotions and feelings, not least because I have grown to anticipate such affects in those environments. It isn't easy to separate external stimuli from internally generated anticipation that itself stimulates the phenomena.

I do not know what causes those bodily experiences, but I speculate a possible explanation may unfold something like this. In common with many life forms, the human body produces an electromagnetic field. Perhaps the landscape generates similar properties along the electromagnetic spectrum from its physical configurations—its mineralogy and positive/negative electric charges, invisible until experienced when lightning moves between the sky and the earth or jumps from the ground to the sky, for example. Could there be naturally produced material or physical forces the human body has evolved to be sensitive to? Is it possible to have a somatic sensitivity to electromagnetic forces that register at some level in the brain, through the nervous system or at a cellular level?

In a 2023 research paper titled *Essential Elements of Radical Pair Magnetosensitivity in Drosophila* by Adam A. Bradlaugh et al., the researchers discovered that the human body, like our animal counterparts, has molecular components that respond to magnetism in ways connected to those used by birds or other migrating animals that use the earth's magnetic fields to navigate. Although not considered operational at a conscious level in humans, we share a universal chemical found in all living cells that, if sufficiently present and combined with other molecules, may respond to magnetic sensitivity. The latest discoveries imply that this magnetoreception is more widespread in the animal kingdom than previously thought.[134]

Although in no way supporting my own speculations about embodied physical responses to

---

[134] Bradlaugh, Adam A et al., pp. 111-116.

electromagnetic properties found in the landscape, this research highlights how an ever-increasing understanding of the capacity of our bodies to respond to the environment in ways beyond currently understood somatic activities remains possible and even inevitable. Such research may help rationalise several difficult-to-explain bodily phenomena I experience in the landscape or when making work.

There is still much to be discovered about how the brain and nervous system work in the body, its capabilities and its sensitivities. The rationale I put forward for such experiences is a long way away from any metaphysical concepts. I am not proposing that my notions of human sensitivity to landscape-generated electromagnetic forces are correct or scientifically sound. Like all science, neuroscience is continually developing, understanding and reinventing itself with each new theory to encompass much that one hundred and fifty years ago would have been considered the realm of fantasy.

The possible electromagnetic phenomena I refer to are sufficiently affecting to be remembered, whatever their origins. What causes those reactions—my emotional responses—to the landscape is significant enough to be embedded within my concept and memory of that place. I would go as far as to propose that those qualities, among others, define a 'sense of place', setting up an affective loop that reinforces place identity on multiple affective levels when remembering and visiting the location. I believe such emotions and feelings arise as immanent consequences of hermeneutics and the ongoing interpretive actions I undertake when building significance and meaningfulness in the landscape—my excitable experiential state when on location contributes to the intensity of that affective condition. An independent sense of emanation from the landscape is achieved when, through memory, those sensations become projections associated with place, experienced either in or away from the location, within or outside of conscious awareness. In my experience, self-generated emanations such as those are convincingly perceived as an external force. Perceptions are easily fooled. What I 'feel' and what I 'know' are frequently in conflict. They are also potentially very different things. When analysing experience phenomenologically, it is essential to question the origins of all experiences.

Returning once more to 'mapping', I have highlighted the significance of horizons—areas where the land meets the sky. I find those borders of particular interest, primarily because of the strength of emotional impact they hold for me. Chalk horizons are particularly potent in this respect. The smooth lines, either with or without stands of trees, particularly Beech trees, trigger strong emotional responses accompanied by body-wide sensed sounds when observed. There is undoubtedly a link between what I see and what I sense in my body, or perhaps how my body responds to what I see. The physiological responses I describe are further stimulated when landscape configurations combine, particularly lighting and weather conditions, for additional dramatic effect. It is challenging to specify which combination of components elicits the strongest feelings. Like correlates within PK coupling, the correlates of what I specifically feel in the landscape and how related actions, responses and bodily sensations are experienced in an A = B relationship is impossible for me to say. I know when they occur phenomenologically and can gauge their strength and duration in those moments. Perceptually, such phenomena are immanent to my landscape situatedness.

## Expanded Proprioception

Physically, when viewing chalk horizons on location, my sense of proprioception is vastly expanded to fit the scale of the landscape. It is as if my somatic fabric is reaching out to feel and assimilate the boundaries of what I'm seeing and sensing. This physiological response can sometimes feel like an out-of-body experience. It is not that, but the rate of sensory expansion is such that my sense of self expands as the sensory connection to my physical placement on the surface of the ground diminishes. It is as if extending outward makes it impossible to maintain a sense of being grounded. I imagine my brain is experiencing a sensory/stimulus overload and is compensating—prioritising—to manage all the data. I can easily understand how this experience could be interpreted as transcendental or spiritual. But I believe the explanation can be found closer to home through the perceptual awareness of PK coupling correlates in operation.

Figure 18. *Overton Downs, Wiltshire*. Oil on cradled board, 297 x 420 mm. Marc Yeats (2022).

Interestingly, the same sense of expanded proprioception experienced in the physical landscape is sometimes experienced in recalling my remembered landscapes, but more particularly, in the symbolic representation of similar horizon configurations found in my paintings (see Figure 18) or the paintings of others. Here, the potency of the symbolic representation of landscape and weather configurations induces those remembered sensations of expanded space and ecstasy, even if only for a moment. Imagined sounds may also accompany those sensations. There is a difference in the context for those experiences where my situatedness in a physical landscape includes vast amounts of somatic data being received entirely because of where I am—bird sounds, rustling leaves, traffic, temperature, breezes, the texture and firmness of the land under my feet, the smell of flowers, damp earth, crops and decomposition, for instance— and where by comparison, this particular external somatic input is absent when looking at a painting in a gallery or my studio, for example, where the associated and remembered somatic data triggered by the referent nature of the observed image may be recalled momentarily, serving to block out any current environmental interference generated within the viewing space itself, enhancing that experienced moment by assigning the symbology of the image to my internalised landscape symbology which in turn locates the experience of looking at the painting with being present in a similar physical location through memory. Voilà! The floodgates are opened. I am there. I imagine this state is meant by the typical turn of phrase 'being lost' in a painting or piece of music. Those states are transitory, but all are connected visually through seeing on location, visualising or seeing symbolic representations of place and moods, for example, in artwork as a cognitive operation. What is clear is that whatever sensing to performing relationships occur through PK coupling when situated in the landscape, I experience very similar, if not the same, sensations when not physically in the landscape. I wonder how this can be when the sensorimotor environment and the circumstance for similar correlates of feeling to performing have changed radically. I assume that different environments generate different correlates and should support different experiences.

The same triggered experiences I associate with being situated in the landscape also occur when listening to music. Unlike seeing, I cannot identify what symbolic musical configurations are associated with landscape features or even place-specific emotions, as there are no referent aspects to connect sounds with landscape materiality; there are, for example, no definitive sounds, chords, melodies, structures, harmonies or any sonic content that can establish a consistent and shared symbolic representation for a chalk horizon with trees in the manner a photograph of such features can. Nevertheless, certain combinations of sounds perceptually elicit powerfully compelling, often elating sensations of landscape situatedness, at times even more convincing than visual imagery.

However, visual imagery is never far from my experiences of listening. Listening automatically generates visual information in what perceptually feels like a direct correlation between sound and sight. The generated visual matter may be abstract, possibly shapes and colours, textures and forms, but will happily coalesce into familiar, experienced, remembered landscape forms. My imagined landscapes may be recalled or remembered mental snapshots of place-specific features relived in every somatic detail. Those visual phenomena are immanent in the listening experience and are another PK coupling operation.

I speculate that the body's experiences of PK coupling may be recorded as part of their embodiment to be later relived when triggered, explaining the ease at which feelings associated with being in the landscape can be supplanted to listening experiences or looking at photographs or paintings or other matter that triggers PK-coupled memories. If this assumption is correct, it would also suggest a link between symbolic representations found in paintings and music, such as triggers for remembered PK-coupled and other physically situated landscape experiences. As my constant interpretations of internal and external worlds and the interactions between them and me generate ever-expanding symbolic networks that can be remembered, experienced, learned, anticipated and adapted in the most dynamic ways, it is conceivable that feeling and performance outcomes generated through PK couplings themselves become associated with symbolic signification, either through some embodied coupling or through the associations of remembering place and feeling/performing outcomes. Although PK coupling operates largely out of awareness, I am not a totally passive bystander. I register the effect, affect and consequences of PK outcomes in my body as experiences, memories and objectively as the effect on the environments I find myself within and the work I make. If I am cognisant of those outcomes, they can be remembered and those memories and the experiences themselves interpreted and symbolised in the same way as all other phenomena are processed.

## Performance: Embodiment and PK Coupling

Leaving descriptions of my chalk-related experiences behind, I wish to discuss another aspect of internally generated sound; the production of sonic imagery using my aural imagination integral to the compositional act. Although I have experience composing for most instruments, ranging from woodwind to brass, percussion, keyboard and strings, my only experience playing instruments is restricted to my amateur dabbling in playing the descant recorder by ear and occasionally tinkering around on the piano. That's it. The level of my own performance experience cannot be compared to the highly virtuosic writing I produce for my professional music colleagues. I have no direct physical experience playing most of the instruments I write for regularly. I make music for all instruments based on technique and knowledge of the instrument. In the main, this knowledge has been acquired in the first instance, through listening to instruments being played via recordings and sometimes live at concerts and second, from looking at how music is notated and some research gathered from various books about instrumental capacities and playing techniques. However, book research has always been minimal. My approach to instrumental writing has been based upon limited observation and extensive listening coupled with any inherent materiality and physicality I have observed and absorbed. In the main, instrumental writing has been achieved through a projection of imagination rather than any acquired techniques born from the physical experience of playing. I have, it could be said, 'winged it' for some considerable time, reusing those techniques that worked as intended, adopting those techniques that produced unanticipated results I liked and discarding those approaches that failed to achieve any useful outcome. It is a technique forged through trial and error. However, in the following paragraphs, I want to focus on my embodied and imagined physical experiences when writing for instruments and whether this embodiment can be situated within PK coupling theory.

Conceptualising music through remembered sound in the aural imagination is part of most composers' composition practice to some degree at least. Unlike the sensed sounds I produce through apparently involuntary responses to landscape, this manifestation of compositional aural imagery is controlled mainly through acts of will and intentionality. As I compose in my mind, I can muster a range of instrumental sounds and organise those into musical structures, aided either by the visual signification of musical notation or without. My memory carries a vast repository of sounds from a lifetime of listening. Those sounds are accessed and assembled into conceptual structures as part of the compositional process. This aural imagery ranges from clear to vague. Some auralisation of structure involves projection. Where my auditory abilities are insufficient to process a complex structure, educated guesswork is required. When educated guesswork is needed, my mind produces a low-resolution aural output to support the construction's temporal momentum, enabling me to attain a conceptual sense of the composition without fixating on its finer details. I can return to those through different processes at a later date.

However, the aural imagining of my compositions does not involve the conceptualisation of sounds alone. From when I started composing, but more particularly in the last fifteen years, I have developed a proprioceptive sense of what it is like to physically play any given instrument as an integral part of the composition and aural imagery construction process. When writing, my body experiences a range of sensations that include breath pressure, resistance, strain, string pressure and tooth, physical positioning, gestural configurations, material relationships and responses to instruments and a range of other more finely honed sensations that generate a sort of 'mock-up' experience of the physicality of performing my music on various instruments as a conceptual fantasy. I even base how I expand specific performance techniques, extend the performance capacity of both player and instrument and seek to enhance or generate novel sound production based upon those imaginings of embodied materiality and physicality. The projections are based on risk—they are guesswork—as they do not correspond to my physical experience of anything directly related to playing instruments. They feel like embodiment. But the embodiment of what? Still, my readiness to utilise such impressions and the frequency with which I do so suggest a high confidence level in referencing those sensations.

Logic tells me there should be no correlation between my imagined sensing and the physical reality of playing instruments. To further confuse the issue and despite the technical challenges the performance of my music poses any musician, I have occasionally received feedback about how natural my very difficult-to-perform music feels under the fingers or centred in the body of experienced performers during rendition. For example, the virtuoso experimental clarinet player and composer Gleb Kanasevich based his 2020 dissertation titled *After the Genesis: Formation of Identity Through Self-Borrowing and Alternative Musical Forms and an Original Composition Found Objects for Seven Percussionists and a Sound Engineer* around the physicality of playing my work for clarinet, particularly the timecode-supported polytemporal concertante work, *shapeshifter* (2015).[135]

Kanasevich writes in his paper:

*I deconstruct [Yeats'] compositions into compound physical gestures that are comprised not just of notes, rhythms and dynamics, but also of the additional motions that a performer may need to do in order to produce the necessary sounds. The paper aims to illustrate how Yeats' more physical and visual approaches to composition provide avenues for his performers to express queer identities in contemporary classical music more freely and how his formal approaches effectively extend instrumental technique beyond the established veneer of heteronormative virtuosity.*[136]

I do not think of my work as a composer in terms of identity or identity politics. Still, I fully appreciate Kanasevich's consideration of how physicality and my practice as a painter impact my compositional work and its performance.

I have also had wide-ranging correspondence with Markus Wenninger, a highly experienced Feldenkrais practitioner and expert contemporary music interpreter and performer, who has played a selection of my pieces composed for clarinet and flute and, as acts of transduction, has performed my compositions designated for other instruments, also on the flute, reporting that he finds the physicality of those performances along with the music's notational signification, clear, compelling and idiomatic. Markus has also asked how it is possible that I know various, as he puts it, 'tricks of the trade' known only to advanced performers of the flute when I have no direct experience of playing the instrument myself.

I cannot draw any conclusions from this feedback regarding my expanded proprioceptive sense when composing, as it is from a small and specialised sample of players. I fully appreciate that such opinions are relative to each player's technical and emotional situatedness regarding their playing and my music. Indeed, with or without any claims I may make around proprioceptive sensing, my music is often considered difficult or impossible for many trained players to perform. From their perspectives, any notions I may have around the usefulness of expanded proprioception as an aid to naturalistic performance and gesture would appear bizarre and

---

[135] Kanasevich, Gleb.
[136] Goodacre, Simon, [accessed 25 January 2023].

contrary to their experience. Nevertheless, I take such affirmative anecdotal reports from Kanasevich and Wenninger as indicative of some success in how my music is conceptualised, judged and subsequently symbolised in notation to facilitate physical responses during performance.

Many composers attempt to create idiomatic music for the instruments they write for, at least to the extent that the material is playable pragmatically. I am no different to any other composer in that regard. However, the influence that my embedded playing-related sensations contribute to my compositions is substantial, extending from solo to orchestral works, where each is felt as a bodily experience immanent to its aural conceptualisation. My body is literally used as a sounding board guiding and responding to my compositions. Regardless of their usefulness in shaping my work, I am eager to understand those feelings and how they have arisen.

## PK Coupling: Possibilities and Assumptions

As there is what seems an obvious link between feeling and performing, between the imagined sensation of playing an instrument and actions necessary to achieve that physicality through embodiment, PK coupling would appear to fit, demonstrating correlates between imagined sound production and the physicality—the bodily performance—necessary to produce it. However, there is a problem with this assumption. Unlike the PK couplings associated with physical activities such as walking and painting which I have directly experienced physically, operating through a system of continuous feedback and testing (remember how the body knows that it is upright and heading in the right direction because it is obvious at the conscious level that the body is upright and proceeding as planned) and where, through dynamic, adaptive and responsive systems, many variables can contribute to multiple successful physical operations and outcomes (a walk may involve a range of possible step patterns, stride lengths and directional orientations, for example, and a painting may reach a point considered complete via a vast range of variable, adapted and recursive actions), here, within the conceptual act of composing, there is no instant feedback loop to confirm my actions as successful.

With no direct physical experience of instrumental playing across an array of instruments, each with its specific requirements and no immediate feedback loop to indicate whether my imagined physical sensations of playing instruments are indeed correlated to appropriate physical acts of performance, my assumptions should produce an array of arbitrary and chaotic results for the musician, including a host of performative behaviours and technical demands that are impossible or at least inept or exceptionally difficult to produce pragmatically. Opportunities for miscalculation should be considerable.

To reinforce my concerns, PK coupling research clarifies that individual personal experiences enable perception-action loops to develop through ongoing learning, interaction and responsiveness to the world. Specifically, skilled proprioceptive and kinaesthetic coupling plays an important role in the felt perceptual experience of spatiotemporal self-orientation in present action and interaction.[137] With no experience playing the horn, oboe or cello, for example, and, owing to the conceptual nature of composition, no perception-action loops acting in the spatiotemporal domain, immediate feedback concerning the efficacy of my compositional decisions based upon an imagined physical embodiment are absent. When considered, it would seem unlikely that any sense of embodiment I experience in relation to instrumental playing could or should yield useful results in players' hands. Considering their genesis, it is surprising

---

[137] Ximena et al., p. 19.

to receive the affirmations I have concerning my instrumental writing.

It would be misleading to suggest that everything I wrote was technically expedient. It is not. I make mistakes and misjudgements. My embodied sensations do not always lead me to the most efficacious conclusions and actions. There are degrees of trial and error in what I do, generally, because of the extreme virtuosity of my writing and a continued compulsion to push both instruments and performers towards their expressive and technical limits, many of which are undefined. Mistakes and miscalculations are made and I learn from those when music is performed. Performances—the time of reckoning—I consider a delayed felt perceptual experience of spatiotemporal self-orientation in present action and interaction, where the delay between conception and rendition may be months or years after writing has taken place. The result is learning dislocated from action.

If PK coupling is, as I suspect, at play here, it operates without the usual feedback learning loops mentioned. In their absence, I speculate that my very attentive, empathetic neurological system is taking the limited physical experience I have of playing instruments, sympathetically extrapolating and expanding those and using memory, imagination and projection, all connected to the host of sensory experiences associated with listening to and observing performance data amassed across my lifetime, to generate a series of physically sensed bodily phenomena that correlate the imagined production of sound through instrumental performance as feeling with embodied performance. Even though this correlation, if such is in operation, is speculative concerning specific outcomes on instruments, their origins are firmly embedded in my actual experiences of physical performance, no matter how limited those experiences may be.

Considering those factors, my decisions concerning how and what to notate, driven by my proprioceptive, embodied imaginings, are considerably more hit than miss. I can say with certainty that those phenomena sit within *"circular loops of purpose and meaning"* that *"enrich our histories and personal life of behaviour"*, but, owing to the difficulties in spatiotemporal feedback loops and the learning it supports, it is impossible to say whether or to what degree PK coupling is involved.[138]

Throughout this chapter, I have discussed a range of embodied phenomena, all of which directly impact the making of my work but, more centrally, how I perceive the world around me. As is often the case with afferent/efferent relationships that occur cyclically, it is difficult to distinguish whether sensations come before action or action precipitates sensation from the perceptual perspective. Is it my emotional response to being in the chalk landscape that correlates first to actions as physiological consequences of that stimulation or a physiological response to being in the landscape that I feel and interpret emotionally, leading to further physiological responses?

It is difficult to answer this question directly as I suspect that although various neurological systems operate independently, there is an interplay between their consequences from a perceptual and behavioural perspective and how those perspectives enrich the 'lived experience'. For example, as mentioned, I do not associate what I perceive as sensed sound with my hearing apparatus, instead, what I associate with hearing is an awareness of sounds produced in my body, even though the perception of sound is generally associated with a discreet CNS afferent system that is supported through its specialised organs of hearing. Saying I sense sound

---

[138] Gomez-Marin et al.

in areas of my body other than the ears isn't helpful, either, as it further entwines sensation, perception and functionality. Still, such perceptions are commonplace where sounds are imagined, as in listening to or remembering pieces of music or recalling or rehearsing conversations, all of which involve imagined and remembered sounds produced in the mind that, in those instances of production, have had nothing to do with tympanic vibration.

It occurs to me that this bodily sensation of internal sound production is an action correlated to sensing—the feeling—of composing or feelings sensed in relation to being in chalk landscapes and, in this capacity, signifies exactly what a feeling/performing correlate is, a relationship between afferent and efferent signals, but instead of correlating feeling to movement, my body produces a response I perceive as feeling to sound. If so, it implies that my body is composing, by and through itself, without any external modelling or artistic intentionality. This is an exciting and controversial thought.

Sight, too, plays a major role in how I sense and perceive my environment. It is also essential within aspects of proprioception and how I know where my body is in relation to external environments and the objects that comprise them. Sight plays a significant role in my emotional responses to external environments. With sight as a crucial source of somatic stimulation and its contribution to aspects of PK coupling in this capacity, I cannot help but wonder if there is a correlation between what is seen, for example, in chalk or any other landscapes, the feeling—the sense—that what is seen stimulates within me as afferent impulses and, through PK coupling, a correlation between those and the sensed sound as the performing element of that correlate.

I appreciate that this and associated hypotheses are highly speculative and go far beyond what is verified in Ximena et al. Nevertheless, I speculate that what is seen may be performed as sound through a PK coupling correlate that associates the two through embodiment and performance. If proven correct in the future, such a hypothesis would certainly explain why it is so easy for me to think of sight (painting) and sound (composing) as naturally related physical and emotional embedded responses to being in chalk landscapes that I can subsequently embody in my artwork as another performative outcome.

Finally, I would like to know if the sensed or imagined sounds I hear in the landscape are a consequence of PK coupling that correlate and locates somatic impressions with a specific 'sense of place'. Could this 'sense of place' be generated from my engagement with, sensing of and response to a landscape through performing that unique environment as embodied sound? Do those embodied sounds correspond to a sonic 'sense of place'? Do they influence the sound of my formal compositions through how I signify those works and how that signification shapes the interpretation of players and listeners? Is the presence or influence of imagined sounds what triggers recognition of a 'sense of place' in my or other people's music when encountered through listening? My answer to those questions and working hypothesis is yes.

# CHAPTER FOUR

# STYLE, SPONTANEITY, SERENDIPITY and MISTAKES

## Style

In 'Mapping', I discussed how aspects of my process as a painter and composer became ritual-like in their acts of interpretation, reinterpretation and hermeneutic situatedness, along with how I read and responded to my interior and exterior landscapes and the work I produced in connection with them, as an immanent condition of that situatedness. I went on to discuss how, as an artist observing and responding to my actions, my behaviour could be viewed as a self-referential closed circuit that reinforced the identity of its symbolic significance because of me 'painting a picture of myself painting a picture of myself painting a picture' and so on. The analogy works equally well for composition.

It occurred to me that during the ongoing processes of those rituals and when constructing, embedding and practising visualisation to strengthen the identities of my remembered landscapes, for example, a secondary operation was also taking place that concerned the formation and maintenance of style. This activity was not necessarily a conscious style-building act. Still, the consequence of privileging and filtering content to populate my remembered landscapes, along with the subsequent nurturing and reinforcing of impressions and emotional affects associated with those actions and outcomes, guided how I constructed a stylistically consistent perceptual and conceptual view of my work. In turn, this perspective was reflected and embedded in my work, either in or out of awareness, through the influence it exerts on my physical actions, in part through PK coupling, for example, but also through comprehension of my aesthetics, recursive and self-referential choices when making art. Such self-influencing concerns extended to comparing works of the same media during or after they were made.

I am surrounded by previous work—in my painting studio, for example—that constantly reminds me of where I have come from creatively and what I have made. Other work produced across the years is always close and even if it wasn't physically present in the studio, past creations, paintings and music remained embedded in my memory as sights and sounds. Any work I thought about making seemed to flow or develop from previous work and was therefore connected to it. Whether intentional or not, this awareness had a somewhat homogenising influence on my practice. It moved my actions and their outcomes towards what looked or sounded like a cohesive, stylistically related body of work. That my work was never conceived or created in isolation may appear to be an obvious observation. Still, in the situatedness of making, such external reference is easy to overlook in the moment's frenzy to the extent that conscious reference to other work is obscured. My work had my stylistic fingerprints all over it, ensuring, in my mind, that others recognised my paintings, drawings and music as my work. I considered the capacity for recognition and attribution of this kind an aspect of quality control, knowing full well that definitions of quality were entirely personal and had nothing to do with one's ability to homogenise. In all cases, my priority was to ensure that: a) I could sufficiently unify certain qualities of a work and the relationships of those qualities within and between one another to encompass the identity I consider a 'Yeats' oeuvre while b) leaving sufficient heterogeneity evident from the processes of making for new developments, directions and differentiation between works to be present. Actions of this type caused me to walk a tightrope between attribution and not making everything look or sound the same. Ultimately, those outcomes exhibit tendencies towards the heterogeneous while being bound together by an underlying stylistic homogeneity of mark-making, embedded kinetic activity and sonic gesture, to name a few characteristics.

Homogenising activities were neither intensive nor routine. In most works—those that came quickly—there was an immanently arising stylistic consistency that originated through the idiosyncratic practice of making the work. No further action was necessary. However, not all paintings or pieces of music came so easily. Some required greater degrees of contrivance and reworking to enable me to establish their identities. Reworking could achieve very satisfactory results that were often quite distant from any starting points implied in the configuration of matter contained within the work. With those creations, I would constantly reference what I considered the most successful of my previous work to find clues on how to proceed and break the impasse. This approach was often successful but not always. I had to give up trying to rescue work on rare occasions, as I could not satisfactorily manipulate the materials. I would admit defeat. This seldom occurred with music composition but did happen once or twice a year with certain paintings. My painting studio has a corner where I store the corpses.

Comparing past with present work through physical observation or memory is an automatic, sometimes unselfconscious and ongoing referencing back to look forward, making my past body of work continually present in some manifestation or another. Because of this, its influence is constant, acting as a stylistic homing beacon, keeping me in line with my conscious stylistic values and, to various extents, predetermining the scope, if not the detail, of outcomes whether or not I am aware of those decisions. This influence is also sufficiently strong to predetermine many of my physical actions while making work, whether I am aware of this gravity or not. In this way, a movement style is shaped by how I learn to inhabit my body in response to environments and what I do in those environments. I self-condition movements within my bodily design's physical agency and scope to create a habitual and practised kinetic repertoire. Along with this self-conditioning of movement through the conscious and wilful shaping of efferent nervous activity situated within intentionality, there will also be out-of-awareness PK coupling actions with their relationship between sensing and movement, between sensing and performance that would operate without an internal model or intentionality through correlates between afferent and efferent impulses. Assuming those correlates were sometimes stable, outcomes as movement or bodily performance, for example, would hold some continuity that, along with intentional kinetic activities and behaviours, would amount to an embodied, physical style that could be conceived of as performance—a dance, perhaps—associated with various acts of making across media that are both within and without conscious awareness and control.

Dictionary definitions describe style as: *"(noun) a particular manner or technique by which something is done, created or performed [...] a distinctive manner of expression (as in writing or speech) [...] a distinctive manner or custom of behaving or conducting oneself [...] a particular mode of living [...] a distinctive quality, form, or type of something".*[139] Notions of style extend to every aspect of life: from the clothes we wear to the food we eat; from our presentation to our thinking; from the things we make to the things we use; and from how we think to the actions we take. Often, we are unaware of those behaviours and patterns as we are too busy living them daily. My interest in style in the context of this book gravitates around the things I make, how I make and how I think about them. I have understood that in addition to all genetic

---

[139] 'Style', in Merriam-Webster.com Dictionary, *Merriam-Webster*, <https://www.merriam-webster.com/dictionary/style> [Accessed 9 February. 2023].

predispositions and bodily capacities, style is the manifestation and consequence of an iterative approach to acquired or self-generated, self-reinforced assimilated behaviours and thinking operating either in or out of awareness that shape my work. Style is a construction, a filter, an orientation, a concept or all of those. It can also be a confection or an affectation redolent of the artistic dilettante.

The exercise of certain choices made consistently and frequently has become part of my practice and embedded into my actions and thinking. My sense of style is not administered through the ongoing completion of a conceptual questionnaire before, during or after making work, nor am I consciously asking myself a stream of style-related quality control questions to ensure I keep on the identified stylistic straight and narrow. Living and working within a fully assimilated, evolving concept of style, at its most integrated and organic, is an unselfconscious and conscious awareness of processes, actions and outcomes that operate within my genetic and physical makeup, with aesthetic and technical core values and abilities, learned, acquired and assimilated over a lifetime. I do not view this assimilation as ever a finished or settled state. Indeed, my drive to constantly push techniques and outcomes into ever-new territories implies incorporating heterogeneous elements that I choose to embrace or reject as part of my ongoing practice. It is this process of assimilation that grows my stylistic scope through experimentation, adaption and incorporation.

Although the antecedents concerning how and why my style developed as it has are now lost to time, I do not doubt that every stimulus, reaction and consequence across my life experience has contributed to style development to a greater or lesser extent. Those experiences and their comprehension have shaped how I do things now. I liken this process to a caddis flying larva building its protective casing, collecting and fitting together all manner of intricately shaped heterogeneous materials around it throughout its life until the finished shell appears as a cohesive structure. The huge difference separating the caddis fly larva's armour from the human mind is that what we collect around us is a range of mental and bodily experiences, cognition and outcome projection associated with perceived cause and effect, afferent/efferent responses and the consequences and reinforcing actions associated with meeting our physiological needs as well as increasingly more sophisticated concepts such as desires, preferences and taste and where all of those conditions are relational, self-referential and function together as a hugely complex conceptual network that on some level we evaluate, update and reformat every moment of our lives. It is little wonder that much of what constitutes our situatedness within a style concept happens outside our conscious framework. What we comprehend is often just the most obvious tip of a vast, deeply submerged iceberg. This iceberg is also continually adapting and evolving.

Aside from individual genetic predispositions, I assume that a personal style develops from what we encounter throughout life that stimulates and shapes us. For me, this stimulation embraces a broad range of notions generated from a complex relational assemblage of concepts and values, including personal satisfaction, attraction, emotional affect, achievement, technical prowess, consistency, elegance, impact, sound combinations, relational qualities, entanglements, embodiment, transmission, colours, 'sense of place', technique, admiration, structure, projection, harmony, mark-making, individuality, ambience, identity, intensity, statement, disharmony, positioning, shock-value, disorientation, heterogeneity, obfuscation, resonance and many others. The more deeply I explore the components and motivations that position my stylistic situatedness—what stimulates me—the more extensive and nuanced the list becomes. I assume that a range of attributes conditional to style would be common among all those situated within specific cultural, social, ethnic, religious, economic, educational, age and gender-related groups, for example. Still, finely nuanced triggers, motivations and goals would vary considerably from person to person owing to individual life experiences and orientation to those conditions.

As life is experienced and I become increasingly aware of what stimulates me, I attempt to recreate those experiences by bringing myself more often in contact with them. Next, to exercise more control over my environment, I attempt to mimic circumstances and actions that can generate similar conditions that stimulate me as acts of will. As time passes, I move increasingly away from imitation towards generation. I learn what actions bring about the outcome I desire. I play and invent. I experiment. I keep what stimulates me—what pleases me—and discard what doesn't. I draw close to those outcomes that resonate. Through learning, I imitate myself, establishing and experimenting with cyclic actions to reinforce positive feedback loops and make more of the things, outcomes or objects I want to identify with. If I am fortunate, I will like and be stimulated by many of the new things I make. Through more experience and making, through more acts of will, I happen upon more things, self-generated and externally experienced, that stimulate and please me. My 'collection' widens. Heterogenous phenomena become incorporated into my orbit of experience and production. They become associated with me and I with them. The cycle repeats over and over. Identity and style are born.

However, among out-of-awareness phenomena that contribute to my practice, questions remain about the nature and impact of spontaneous activities and how they contribute to style-building. With significant elements of my practice built upon self-programming and a vast, life-long collection of behavioural and neurological antecedents, I am curious to establish how spontaneous my perceived practice-based spontaneity is and what part serendipity plays in constructing style and technique. Ostensibly, I am asking if spontaneity in artistic practice exists outside of what artists, including me, report of their own experience anecdotally. I also want to know if spontaneous activity does exist in my practice, what manner of phenomena it is, how it is defined and how I distinguish its unique qualities from other perceptually similar out-of-awareness phenomena.

## Spontaneity

I have valued my sense of spontaneity, seeing it as a means of keeping work fresh and avoiding overworking and contriving materials. I appreciate work that appears or sounds like it has been produced effortlessly, whether this is the case or not. I have thought effortlessness synonymous with spontaneity, in art at least, with no firm basis on which to base this assumption.

For example, in the early 2000s, in an attempt to support effortlessness in my practice and encourage a more spontaneous approach to making work, I instigated a phase of blindfolding myself during the initial stages of painting. I did this so that I could only rely on my physical sense of mark-making, my capacity to imagine what those marks might look like, individually and in relation to one another and construct a mental map of their assumed physical relationships using memory informed by proprioception—removing seeing from making forced me to rely on memory informed by the feedback of senses other than sight, particularly those involved with the spatial positioning of physical actions, crucial to but often considered of secondary importance or ignored completely when painting with sight. I initiated this approach to free myself from the guiding and inevitably confining stimulus/response cycle that seeing while working generated, particularly in response to the influence of aesthetic and stylistic considerations, to guarantee spontaneity and effortlessness in my mark-making during those initial painting stages. I no longer consider it necessary to deprive myself of sensory input to induce acts that could be spontaneous. That practice did not survive beyond a year. Nevertheless, it felt like the obvious course of action at the time.

I was too intimidated by the prospects of disaster and apparent loss of control over proceedings to continue this strategy to finish work, so I reverted to seeing what I was making soon after the first few layers of activity were applied to a surface. Inevitably, my subsequent sight-driven interventions resulted in degrees of modification or even obliteration of those original marks. Overpainting in this way, like making a palimpsest, is common practice in both my painting and composition, where such actions are undertaken with the understanding that every mark, gesture and trace acts as an antecedent, a stimulus or provocation for what follows, whether the original impetus or signal is visible in the finished work. I can now align that understanding and behaviour with the thinking behind Derrida's notions of what is present being determined by what is absent.

My blindfolded painting was a dalliance with what I thought of as spontaneous actions except that, as I concluded at the time, the range of chance outcomes was considerably less open to widely divergent possibilities than I initially thought. Despite what seemed rather extreme methods to free my actions from pre-determination, it soon became clear that the marks I made when painting, blindfolded or not, always looked familiar. There were signature gestures that ran through everything. Not only that, but the positional relationships of those gestures also conformed to a repertoire of familiar though iterative patterns, shapes and structures.

Looking more closely at my mark-making, I began to suspect that far from being spontaneous, all—or at least a great many—of my actions were being governed by two (there may be more) self-conditioned responses: the first, I would describe as something like muscle memory, where a particular range of physical actions had been programmed through my nervous system to act as an automatically accessed repository of movements initiated through a range of cognitive and behavioural mechanisms and impulses associated with the desire to make, most of which operated out of awareness and could therefore feel spontaneous and beyond premeditation. PK coupling correlates would also have been involved here as all actions are directly related to sensing and performing; the second layer of pre-determined self-conditioning came from aesthetic and style-based preferences so ingrained that my physical movement control responses and the reading of input and response associated with those impulses generated a recursive and almost instantaneous cycle of events equally pre-programmed to the extent that all the choices I made to determine my actions seemed sufficiently out of awareness and therefore spontaneous. I cannot rule out that spontaneous thought may have initiated a particular action or group of actions. However, when assessing outcomes of those hopefully spontaneous activities, it was clear they were situated within my stylistic orbit, leading me to conclude a strong possibility that the original stimuli were, between initialisation and outcome, fashioned to suit a range of familiar and possibly predetermined iterations.

I believe that due to my practice of making through physical movement where mark-making, assimilating the physical, relational and emotional aspects of those marks, responding to them, initiating more movement and making again, over and over in a recursive, assimilative cycle across a great many years, had generated endlessly repeated physical actions that were now embedded into my body as neuromuscular memory; programmed loop responses that were confined by the extent and fashion to which such movements occur within the constraints of my physicality. It is not unreasonable to state that my body wholly shapes those movements— by the pivotal and rotational bone and muscular structures of my arms set on either side of my torso as a bipedal animal along with the finer positional capacities of my hands while, for example, holding a paintbrush, that worked in unison with hand-eye coordination and that those familiar movements were then initiated through automatically triggered muscle memory impulses embedded over years of repetitive operations or initiated through direct acts of will.

Owing to their physical configurations, neurological and physically embedded limitations, those actions develop as self-limiting responses confined to a particular vocabulary of fixed gestures that are further embodied in the art itself through the physical acts of making as a record of authorship that, like a fingerprint, function as an unselfconscious signature. Additionally, the outcomes of my work are limited to the physical properties of the materials I use—their materiality—that, combined with my bodily and cognitive boundaries, constitute a field of possibilities defined by their multiple agencies. Of course, part of the artist's role may be seen to move beyond those confinements to make work where such conditions are rendered invisible, perceived as advantageous or where the very materiality and agency of the work's components become the focus of the work itself. Even so, traces of those fingerprints are everywhere to be observed or heard in an artist's work.

There will inevitably be a great many circumstantial and conditioning factors that lie beyond my detection, awareness and current understanding, predetermining my actions. Far from being spontaneous, this kinetic and cognitive choreography is just a form of out-of-awareness, previously self-programmed influence where the repertoire of many activities is defined among most artists by their shared physical capacities but, more particularly, determined in detail by subtle individualised stylistic considerations Nevertheless, questions still need to be answered around how much of my work is genuinely spontaneous and how I differentiate spontaneous thoughts and actions from those that are influenced or predetermined yet remain out of awareness. Unfortunately, my objectivity in those matters is self-limiting because I cannot recognise either spontaneous or out-of-awareness actions through self-analysis, as in both cases, I cannot ascertain their presence, origins or rationale.

I had established to my satisfaction that many of my actions were predetermined in some way and at some level of consciousness. But what of spontaneity? I was no closer to answering any of those questions. Beyond my work, it was clear that former artistic movements had been preoccupied with encouraging spontaneous, internally generated impulse-driven behaviour and responsiveness when making art, often employing methods designed, in theory at least, to circumnavigate the conscious mind. In the early 1960s, the Romanian-born American artist, sculptor, author, educator and engineer Jacques Schnier wrote on this matter:

*Since the discovery of psychoanalysis, much has been written on the role of free association or free expression in art. Investigations along psychoanalytic lines now reveal that this mental activity is one of the essential processes by which the artist and scientist creates. By enabling the creative mind to roam the mental highways and byways unhampered by conscious restrictions, free association provides it with a flow of ideas and impressions, relationships and patterns and a world of imagery unattainable by merely intellectually directed efforts alone.*

*This principle, frequently referred to as automatic in the literature of art criticism, has come to be so thoroughly accepted and integrated in the general philosophy of much of our contemporary art that it seems to have dwarfed into insignificance the other aspects of creativity. We hear much of free art, automatic art, the stream of consciousness, unloosening the emotions, pouring out the soul and expressing inner feelings. So much so, that the impression is created that organisation, design, sustained composition, mature control of medium, the element of communication, or any of the other synonymous expressions by which the term 'form' is referred to, is of considerably less importance for the artist, the spectator, or the work of art itself.*[140]

The psychoanalyst in question was Sigmund Freud. It was his technique of free association, where his clients were encouraged to let their thoughts wander freely and without inhibition to create a range of connections between random phenomena manifesting as a stream of consciousness that revealed profound inner truths and subconscious states not accessible via other means. Along with automatism, a concept borrowed from physiology to describe the automatic, subconscious actions of breathing, digestion or sleepwalking, those ideas became hugely influential among Surrealists who, in the early 1920s, explored the techniques to access the subconscious as a source of creative material. Initially popular among Surrealist poets such as André Breton, Paul Éluard, Robert Desnos, Louis Aragon and Philippe Soupault, such approaches encouraged *"writing in a hypnotic or trancelike state, recording their train of mental associations without censorship or attempts at formal exposition".*[141]

Ultimately, Surrealist poetry made little impact. However, automatism found more success and lasting significance as an approach used in Surrealist painting. It developed from automatic drawing that, like automatic writing, used Freudian psychoanalytic theory to encourage the production of symbols, gestures and marks considered to be a true reflection of the individual's psychic state and, therefore, significant.

In addition to free association and automatism, Surrealist painters such as André Masson, Arshile Gorky and Max Ernst, developed supplementary techniques to incorporate chance procedures into their practice, no doubt to further expand the expressive range of work produced through the avoidance of conscious control. The images created were either left 'as is' or actively enhanced and worked up into more consciously elaborated pieces, or perhaps more contrived, depending on one's perspective. Such actions might suggest dissatisfaction with those approaches automatic and chance outcomes, with the artists seeing them merely as starting points to work rather than an end in and of themselves. Whether the outcomes of those processes were a true reflection of the subconscious 'speaking' without conscious intervention remains to be proven. Success in those matters would have been a personal perspective for the artists and their audiences.

Later generations of painters were also drawn to the creative potential of automatism, in particular, a group of American artists in the 1950s called Action Painters, including Jackson Pollock, Willem de Kooning, Franz Kline, Jack Tworkov and Bradley Walker Tomlin.[142] *"Pollock [...] was widely noticed for his 'drip technique' of pouring or splashing liquid household paint onto a horizontal surface, enabling him to view and paint his canvases from all angles".* Pollock also *"covered the entire canvas and used the force of his whole body to paint, often in a frenetic dancing style. This practice was also called 'all-over' painting".*[143]

Pollock and his contributions to 'Action Painting' offer a representation of the painter as an expressive actor operating in an activity where the paint was 'thrown about' spontaneously in a highly charged, even abandoned physical manner. Those paintings, away from Freudian psychoanalytical free association, automatism, Surrealism and particularly Jungian symbology

---

[140] Schnier, Jacques, pp. 61-74.
[141] Britannica, The Editors of Encyclopaedia, 'automatism'. *Encyclopaedia Britannica*, 3 Mar. 2014, https://www.britannica.com/art/automatism-art. [accessed 2 April 2022].
[142] Ibid.
[143] 'Jackson Pollock', *Art and Artists* in *Tate*, Tate.org <https://www.tate.org.uk/art/artists/jackson-pollock-1785> [accessed 25 September 2022].

and concerns around the expression of the subconscious mind, hold a position in my imagination and possibly in the popular imagination as examples of spontaneous making.

However, despite the frenzied acts of painting, notions of spontaneity are irretrievably confused with conscious and out-of-awareness predetermined and potentially rehearsed automatic actions. Although I am not in a position to research this assumption and such investigation is not the focus of this book, I would base any such research around questions concerning forethought, particularly where that extends to when and where the activity would be undertaken; what denotes the start and finish of the act; the previous physical experiences that determine types of movement; the previous intellectual, emotional and perceptual experiences the artist has undergone to shape their conceptual orientations; decisions around what techniques, approaches, materials and colours were to be used; what the scale of the painting or arena of activity would be; if similar approaches to making had been enacted or rehearsed before; how life-long preconditioning of the artist's body and mind would influence the physicality of those processes; how all necessary means to make the work were configured in space and what kind of preparation that entailed; to what extent any expectations around the finished work were formulated in advance; and finally, the artist's predetermined intent to create work in such a manner in the first place, a decision redolent of aesthetic and stylistic premeditation, as Roberto Zenit confirms:

*Like most painters, Jackson Pollock went through a long process of experimentation to perfect his technique. [...] What we were trying to do with this research is figure out what conclusions Pollock reached in order to execute his paintings the way he wanted.*[144]

Considering all of those factors and the vast array of unknown past influences that may predetermine actions and intent in some distant way and taking into account a range of chance operations that may not be attributable to innate human spontaneity but to factors of physics, chemistry, velocity, viscosity, trajectories and a range of mainly other calculable forces concerning the manner and rate of paint application and the objects or devices used to apply it set in motion by the artist, I would question precisely how spontaneous this spontaneity was. In the same way, I would ask how free, free association is when meticulously examined. Perhaps that's a disingenuous attitude to take. Maybe my perspective pays too little regard to the word 'spontaneous' in everyday contexts and how the word is unconditionally used without specific scientific qualifications. I am not claiming there is no spontaneity involved in those acts, just that unpacking what actions are and are not spontaneous seems to be of little concern in the overall impression—romanticisation, even—of an artist as a spontaneous actor, where taking the unquestioning view that if an artist jumps around or uses large amounts of kinetic energy in their work, they must be acting spontaneously.

I appreciate that taking the type of behaviour displayed in 'Action Painting' at face value demonstrates the potential for a great deal of freely expressive and what appears to be a spontaneous activity, certainly more so than would seem apparent with artists who work in a similar, more buttoned-up vein to my own, but and making no assertions about Pollock's claims for his work, I still have a suspicion that any artist headlining their work or others commenting and declaring that creation to be spontaneous, use the word either incorrectly or at best, somewhat loosely, focusing only on their *sense* of the work or its associated practice rather than

---

[144] *Scientists Reveal the Physics of Jackson Pollock's Painting Technique* in *News from Brown*, Brown University <https://www.brown.edu/news/2019-10-30/pollock> [accessed 15 February 2023].

the *actuality* of the processes themselves when considered within a more comprehensive behavioural, cognitive and neurological framework. On the other hand, perhaps a sense of the nature of the activity is all the word requires to determine its meaning. For some, this is no doubt sufficient. I find such self-determined definitions unsatisfactory. Reference to the dictionary does not provide greater clarity. This Merriam-Webster definition is typical:

1. *proceeding from natural feeling or native tendency without external constraint.*
2. *arising from a momentary impulse.*
3. *controlled and directed internally: self-acting spontaneous movement characteristic of living things.*
4. *produced without being planted or without human labour: indigenous.*
5. *developing or occurring without apparent external influence, force, cause or treatment.*
6. *not apparently contrived or manipulated: natural.*[145]

Examining the definitions above in turn: Point 1, frames spontaneity within the context of *"natural feeling"* without defining what natural feeling is or is not. The definition uses words that separately need considerable unpacking and that together offer only vagueness in distinguishing spontaneous actions from any other behaviour that originates from *"unconstrained natural feelings"* driven by all manner of needs or desires. Point 2, *"arising from a momentary impulse"* is equally vague as there is no attempt to identify if antecedents are conscious or subconscious impulses or what generates those impulses in the first place and bearing in mind that so much human operation arises from momentary impulses—our senses are bombarded by impulses constantly and our brains generate impulses constantly—this definition tells us nothing useful. Point 3, again, refers to the internal direction of behaviour common to all living things (does *"all living things"* include plant life, single-celled organisms, bacteria and the like?) but makes no attempt to identify pre-determined or responsive, reflexive movements from spontaneous movements, all of which are directed internally and self-acting at some level of operation. Point 4 suggests that spontaneity exists without external influence being "planted," meaning that it occurs without any preconceived suggestion or influence from outside sources. It doesn't explore whether self-awareness influences spontaneity or if complete detachment from internal factors like subconscious motivation is necessary for spontaneous actions. Point 5 echoes much of the previous definition but introduces the concept of *"without apparent external influence"* implying that spontaneity may exist if the antecedents are hidden and unverified (not apparent), but from whom this apparent influence is hidden—the subject or the observer—is not made clear. Finally, point 6 once again uses the wildcard *"apparently"* to condition whether something is contrived or manipulated, implying we may never know the true status of a spontaneous action—is it or isn't it? This leaves the phenomena open for us to evaluate, therefore we choose its status. Equally, the word 'natural' is useless in this context as its meanings and implications are too extensive to be relevant to spontaneity unless associated with its thermodynamic context in the natural sciences, discussed shortly.

With no clarity offered through the above definitions and a sense that spontaneity as a concept in general speech is being conceived as any behaviour that cannot be accounted for consciously, I am no further forward. The everyday and artistic use of the word spontaneous is sufficiently flexible to be adapted to suit any self-defining personal circumstances and meanings. Alternatively, the scientific definition of spontaneous and spontaneous processes is precise but challenging, if impossible, to adapt to an artistic practice context. Chemistry LibreTexts provide

---

[145] 'Spontaneous', in Merriam-Webster.com Dictionary, *Merriam-Webster*, <https://www.merriam-webster.com/dictionary/spontaneous> [accessed 10 February 2023].

an accessible scientific description of spontaneous processes that says:

*Processes have a natural tendency to occur in one direction under a given set of conditions. Water will naturally flow downhill, but uphill flow requires outside intervention, such as the use of a pump. Iron exposed to the earth's atmosphere will corrode, but rust is not converted to iron without intentional chemical treatment. A spontaneous process is one that occurs naturally under certain conditions. A nonspontaneous process, on the other hand, will not take place unless it is "driven" by the continual input of energy from an external source. A process that is spontaneous in one direction under a particular set of conditions is nonspontaneous in the reverse direction. At room temperature and typical atmospheric pressure, for example, ice will spontaneously melt, but water will not spontaneously freeze. The spontaneity of a process is not correlated to the speed of the process. A spontaneous change may be so rapid that it is essentially instantaneous or so slow that it cannot be observed over any practical period of time.*[146]

Establishing a verifiable scientific definition of spontaneity based on the principles of thermodynamics is a relatively clear-cut matter. Measurable indicators, criteria and processes occur in specific and predictable ways. Observations can be made and repeatable empirical results can be produced and analysed. But what of how spontaneous activity manifests in the mind? And what of attempting to disentangle one's actions as spontaneous or non-spontaneous through subjective self-observation without empirical results or reference to thermodynamics?

The mind, unlike the brain, is not a physical entity. The mind is the product of our thoughts, our aliveness and consciousness. It generates thought energy through electrical charge impulses that proliferate the brain's physical structures and move across the nervous system via various biochemical exchanges through neural transmitters and synapses. Thought = energy. The brain uses around 20% of bodily resources to maintain and function. Though separate conditions, the mind and brain are interdependent. Without the mind, our brains and physical bodies would be useless, inactive tissue. Without the brain, consciousness would not be possible, but consciousness cannot be reduced to the brain's actions alone. The mind exists and operates through the brain within a vast and possibly limitless network of relationships within its neural structures. Although not a physical object, the actions of the mind continually alter the physical makeup of the brain. For example, the energy the mind generates through sensing, feeling, decision-making, calculating, remembering, reasoning, experiencing and responding—through all thought-making processes bundled together as 'living and experience'—is recorded through protein-based physical connectivity laid down in the brain to reorganise and rewire it effectively. Though more active in childhood, this rewiring or reprogramming, called neuroplasticity, continues throughout our lives from moment to moment. It characterises and differentiates us from each other.

Neuroplasticity ensures that our minds are not pre-existing 'natural conditions', in the same way as gravity in the scientific example of spontaneity above. Many actions, thoughts and behaviours away from the autonomic and root functionalities of the brain do not move from A to B, with the predictability of water moving down slopes or ice melting at room temperature. The mind is not a disinterested force with no goals, proclivities, polarities, bias or agenda, hidden or otherwise. The mind is a system that evolves, learns and adapts through varied environmental

---

[146] *Spontaneous Processes*, article available from *Chemistry LibreTexts* website 18 June 2021 <https://chem.libretexts.org/Bookshelves/General_Chemistry/Map%3A_Chemistry_The_Central_Scien ce_ (Brown_et_al.)/19%3A_Chemical_Thermodynamics/19.1%3A_Spontaneous_Processes> [accessed 8 April 2022].

encounters. Its biological functions adapt through behaviour and biological processes shape its behaviour. It is not a constant and predictable physical or chemical law.

My confusion grows deeper. I cannot interpret the scientific definition of spontaneous actions within the context of my practice or 'lived experience', nor am I satisfied with the criterion for identifying spontaneity within human responses and behaviour based solely upon the subject's level of self-awareness about thought-driven internal/external energy sources. If this 'aware of = nonspontaneous action' and 'unaware of = spontaneous action' equation was all that was necessary to differentiate spontaneous from non-spontaneous responses or 'naturally occurring' from 'externally driven', it would result in most of my operations being spontaneously originated owing to much of my functionality occurring outside of awareness. I do not believe this to be the case.

Neuroscience research has proved considerably more enlightening. In a 2018 paper by Aaron Kuchi et al., titled *Spontaneous cognitive processes and the behavioural validation of time-varying brain connectivity*, greater light has been cast upon spontaneous activity within the brain. Although I am not equipped to give an in-depth explanation of the results of this paper from the perspective of a neuroscientist, I feel it is beneficial to summarise those findings relevant to a clearer understanding of spontaneity within cognitive processes "*where cognition includes basic mental processes such as sensation, attention and perception and complex mental operations such as memory, learning, language use, problem-solving, decision making, reasoning and intelligence*" and the implications those findings hold for my work as an artist.[147] The paper states that:

*In cognitive neuroscience, focus is commonly placed on associating brain function with changes in environmental stimuli or actively generated cognitive processes. In everyday life, however, many forms of cognitive processes occur spontaneously, without an individual's active effort and in the absence of explicit manipulation of behavioural state. For example, thoughts that are unrelated to the current sensory environment, such as involuntary memories, are estimated to comprise ~30–50% of waking life [...] and thus likely represent a significant source of variation in ongoing brain activity [...].*[148]

The authors explain that the terms "*spontaneous cognition*"—freely emerging thought, experience and/or sensation that is not initiated by active control or by an immediate external stimulus—and "*spontaneous thought*"—a type of spontaneous cognitive process that involves conscious awareness (e.g., mind-wandering, rumination)—have frequently been used in neuroscientific literature to identify "*conscious, inner experiences, with some acknowledgement, that there are discrete subtypes of such experiences (e.g., mind-wandering vs intrusive/ruminative thoughts [...]*". This paper defines "*spontaneous cognitive processes that include, but are not limited to conscious experiences and also include processes that are spontaneously initiated and that subsequently occur unconsciously*". The authors propose "*multiple forms of spontaneous mental processes [a freely emerging neural process that is reflected in a behaviour or experience (a spontaneous cognitive process is a subtype)] that can be described in terms of discrete categories, of which a subset are 'cognitive' in nature*". They go on to describe spontaneous mental processes as including "*affective state, arousal/wakefulness, hunger/thirst, sexual drive, vigilance, attention, memory (reactivation/replay), level of full consciousness, current conscious contents and processes*

---

[147] Ranade, Anagha, et al., pp. 445-467.
[148] Kucyi, Aaron, et al., pp. 397-417.

*that mediate the onset, maintenance and transitions of spontaneous thoughts".*[149]

In describing spontaneous mental processes as interrelated, the authors present examples of arousal and vigilance or more independent states, such as an affective state's attention and valence (degrees of pleasure or displeasure) and what they describe as *"multidimensional"* conditions. For example, they tell us that:

*Affect can be described on low versus high intensity or positive versus negative continuums. Moreover, differences in the content and nature of spontaneous thoughts (e.g., thoughts about the past vs. future, positive or negative) can be independent of one another and have diverging relationships. Whereas some spontaneous mental processes are clearly in the 'cognitive' category (e.g., attention, memory), such a classification for others is less clear (e.g., wakefulness, affective state).*[150]

The paper focuses on spontaneous processes that are unambiguously considered to be cognitive in nature and examined in the context of time-varying functional connectivity, that is, time-varying—where a change in functional connectivity across independent or semi-overlapping time windows within an individual occurs and functional connectivity—meaning statistical dependence (e.g. correlation) between the activity levels within two brain regions. Those include attention, memory reactivation and perceptual processes.[151] The evidence presented by this paper suggests:

*Certain subtypes of spontaneous cognitive processes—those that are likely to occur frequently during any given session of wakeful rest—are detectable in specific patterns of time-varying functional connectivity. Studies of attentional fluctuations, memory reactivation and the relationship between baseline brain activity and variation in perception have each shown that spontaneous and transient changes in BOLD FC [blood oxygenation level dependent functional connectivity, measured using magnetic resonance imaging (MRI) that show an increase in blood flow and blood oxygen levels in active brain cells] are relevant to behaviour and experience.*[152]

This research is a compelling and fascinating insight into how spontaneous thought arises and is measured in the brain. Neuroscientists acknowledge that study in this area is still at an early stage and that further research is necessary across a broader base of cognitive functionality to increase confidence in current findings, but what is discussed here is the closest to helpful information supporting the occurrence of spontaneity in the human mind I have found. Despite shortcomings, the revelation that thoughts unrelated to any current sensory environment are estimated to comprise ~30–50% of waking life is significant even though there is, as far as I can tell, no conclusive evidence to suggest all those thoughts are attributable to spontaneous generation. Regardless, the fact that the brain does generate spontaneous activity seems beyond doubt. I can conclude that some percentage of my artistic practice and output will similarly comprise and embody this spontaneous generation. However, exactly how, how much and where this happens is unknown.

That my brain—all brains—generate spontaneous thought does not detract from the contribution antecedents play in shaping a great deal of thought and behaviour at the conscious

---

[149] Kucyi, Aaron, et al.
[150] Ibid.
[151] Ibid.
[152] Ibid.

and subconscious levels, whether that thought has been generated spontaneously, consciously or subconsciously. Antecedents, their influence, effect and affect contribute to predetermining my actions no matter how removed from awareness such antecedents may be. As discussed, I believe it is inaccurate to label actions as spontaneous just because I am not aware of their origin, as if with every moment of fading memory, the definition of specific actions, behaviour and phenomena migrate from being initially classified as distinctly predetermined to becoming spontaneous when their origin is lost. Because of this, I cannot confidently say that my actions are performed or occurring because of an impulse or inclination and without premeditation or external stimulus. Impulse or inclination, yes, I can even make assumptions that those impulses are not initiated by external stimulus, but without influence or premeditation—at any level—it is far harder to claim with certainty for the reasons I have explained.

Despite the usefulness of this research, phenomena identified through neuroscience as spontaneous may appear as a broader category of impulses than is the case owing to a current lack of extensive observable antecedents or causative factors. We see only as far as research permits. As research into spontaneous generation increases, the causation for such phenomena may either expand or contract as our knowledge increases to reflect which brain impulses can be attributed to spontaneous actions. We learn through continual unfolding.

Amid neuroscience and its findings, I cannot distinguish spontaneous from nonspontaneous action as a 'lived experience' when those phenomena originate out of awareness—predetermined out of awareness and non-predetermined (spontaneous) out of awareness. It seems inevitable that I will never be able to distinguish what is genuinely spontaneous in my work as an artist and that all thoughts on the matter will remain speculative. Moving forward and on this basis, I do not feel a high level of confidence attributing *all* actions and outcomes that emerge outside my awareness (and those that possibly account for the ~30–50% of thoughts unrelated to any current sensory environment populating my waking hours) to spontaneity. Therefore, I need to reconsider the hitherto assumed dominant role of spontaneity in my practice and ask what similar experiential phenomena coexist and how I can distinguish between the two. I believe the answer lies in immanent instantiation.

In painting, for example, I have thought of spontaneity in the context of being immediately responsive, either subconsciously, through muscle memory, self-programming, automaton-like actions, or an act of will, possibly initiated via a spontaneous thought that may not have been triggered out of anywhere but by some manner of internal stimulation or influence that has been generated randomly. However, I remain unconvinced the word random, in all its enormity, is applicable or appropriate in this context as such a concept requires there to be no antecedent, no matter how deep-rooted or obscure, that would have acted as a stimulus to the initial 'spontaneous' impulse. As a condition, I am now of the opinion that much of this responsiveness isn't necessarily the result of spontaneous activity but immanent instantiation—that is, the making, bringing forth or identifying of an act or thought that has arisen from a combination, relationship or fusion of conditions and phenomena in a particular moment or multiple moments immanent to a universe of stimuli and responses within or outside awareness.

Still, from neuroscientific evidence, spontaneity will likely occur in making and rendering my work. I appreciate how spontaneous impulses can be precisely and irrefutably identified as such remains distant. I comfort myself in the understanding that knowing or not knowing how spontaneity works as part of my activities will not change one aspect of how I produce that work.

With the contribution and extent spontaneity plays in my practice shared with a concept of immanent instantiation, I have re-evaluated my relationship to a previously held association between spontaneity and serendipity where I understood that serendipity flowed from, or rather, was made more likely if my practice embodied spontaneous outcomes. Now, I assume there to be connectivity between serendipity, immanent instantiation and spontaneity. Understanding immanent instantiation is crucial to my thinking going forwards, not least because it is sometimes possible for me to describe the antecedents, assumed or otherwise, of specific behaviour that falls within cognition alongside those impulses that fall outside my awareness.

## Serendipity and Mistakes

Key to the artist's success as a serendipitist is their ability to recognise potential-rich phenomena suitable for assimilation into their practice, style or concept. This skill for finding phenomena and recognising their value is reflected within definitions of serendipity. For example, *"the faculty or phenomenon of finding valuable or agreeable things not sought for"* or *"an aptitude for making desirable discoveries by accident"*.[153] The words *"aptitude"* and *"discovery"* are of particular significance for the artist because it is this flair to find, identify and subsequently assimilate what may be valuable that can significantly contribute to various aspects of artistic development. This aptitude—a particular skill that can be nurtured—also places serendipity beyond the vagaries of mere luck. However, I do not attribute all serendipity to the happy, accidental find and believe it is possible to engineer an environment that can generate more significant opportunities for serendipity.

Creating such an environment has been a conscious part of my practice for several decades. I call it 'an environment of possibilities', or EoP for short. It is an arena within which I experiment, combine, relate, juxtapose, amalgamate, alter, repel, replace, blend, amplify or nullify and build phenomena and structures as an artist. This environment could be the surface of a painting like a board or canvas, a piece of paper, manuscript paper, audio or sequencing software, notation software, a collage, montage or bricolage, or any digital or virtual environment and extends to external locations, walking and the interiority of my thought and conceptualisations. From a practical perspective, an EoP creates an area or space for me to place, throw, collide, mix, obliterate, play and explore all manner of phenomena in relation to one another to see what emerges from the process. There are no rules. I can be as experimental as I wish. Mayhem and mess are good. The point is to generate the unexpected.

Importantly, this creative space allows for multidirectional relationships between immanently instantiated, spontaneously or previously generated heterogeneous and homogenous phenomena present or brought into an EoP to interact in ways that move beyond what I might have imagined as possibilities and certainly beyond my normal and pre-programmed range of actions I would generally take. I want to be surprised by the outcomes of my activities. Such an immanent environment can be compared to those discussed in free association as many of its actions and outcomes are shared even if the rationale for action—accessing the unconscious mind, particularly for psychoanalytic purposes—is not the priority. Rather than Freudian free association or automatism, I prefer to visualise those relationships being activated within a Deleuzian rhizomatic-type EoP network entanglement where any phenomena can relate directly to or freely associate with any other phenomena anywhere in the rhizome. This connectivity is achieved through associations of difference.

---

[153] 'Serendipity', in Merriam-Webster.com Dictionary, *Merriam-Webster*, <https://www.merriam-webster.com/dictionary/serendipity> [Accessed 11 Feb. 2023].

In music composition, this translates to bringing together a range of notation materials—originally generated or self-borrowed and transformed musical materials—immanent actions, sonic matter, processes, memory, recordings, practice techniques, listening, aural imagining, books, calculations, paper, pencils, drawings, computer software, thoughts, ideas and experience, for example; and in painting, mark-making, gestures, paints, brushes, photographs, surfaces, lighting, digitally altered images, memories, remembered landscapes, painting materials, their materiality and my physicality, all brought together within acts of frenzied speed and urgency—perhaps even spontaneous thoughts and action that arise out of the process—in such a way as to privilege ongoing action over analysis but where, inevitably, those actions will be filtered through my incumbent preconceptions and stylistic positions, influencing all manner of perceptions and afferent/efferent recursive and adaptive loops, whose interactions in this melting pot will hopefully throw out content I can later happen upon serendipitously. I am looking for resonance, connotation, affect, structures, cells of material, ideas and intimations of new expressive or technical possibilities. I'm looking for anything functional, desirable, pleasing, radical or confrontational related to my remembered landscapes, life experiences, observations, aesthetic sensibilities, techniques, concepts and future creative aspirations, perhaps even aspirations I do not consciously know I have. I'm also looking to be surprised. I keep what I like from this process and discard what I do not. This is not a process within which one should feel precious about outcomes. Everything within it is expendable. The best results are achieved through the least care and most thoughtless actions.

Actions within an EoP are both planned and unplanned. I can plan which materials, such as audio content, to throw into the mix or what colours and gestures to use as initiators to the process, but my responses to the stimuli, including those associated with PK coupling correlates, are not so easily predicted as they are emergent properties, either unknown or immanent to the actions and stimuli themselves. Despite feverish execution, I assess and modify all phenomena encountered and produced as a speed-of-thought ongoing, recursive process until I deem the activity complete. Although comprehended internally or externally generated antecedents will shape my intentionality to govern responses, such as my physical and some emotional reactions to the marks or sounds before me, there will be other deeply embedded subjective responses and behaviours where the rapid cycle of stimulus and response generates immanently instantiated content only to obscure their origins. Because of this, it will prove impossible to distinguish out-of-awareness antecedents from what is and is not spontaneous activity. Although an EoP is the location of this entangled activity, it is not the EoP that determines which outcomes are valuable. To determine that value, the skills of the serendipitist are required.

Using my aptitude for serendipity, I search to identify valuable, useful, agreeable, resonant, affecting and desirable things generated in an EoP. This search is not undertaken at the end of a process of making. Serendipity operates throughout the process as soon as activity commences in an EoP. Opportunities to serendipitously identify useful and compelling products of my actions may present themselves at any time and several times throughout. Identifying something of value through serendipity indicates that a particular trace or sound, phenomenon, object or value configuration needs to be preserved for fear of being lost or altered by further activity. Finds may be localised within the work area and easily preserved by continuing EoP functions around them. Sometimes, serendipity may identify a significant, even total, work area that needs to be maintained. At this point, all EoP operations cease so as not to lose any valuable outcomes. In all events, serendipitous finds change the working dynamic of an EoP as they accumulate and impact my responses around the direction of subsequent actions, influencing how my responsive, assimilative and recursive processes continue. In relation and response to my afferent/efferent, cognitive and subconscious actions, an EoP grows its shape, dynamic and content over its operational time. It develops an identity and characterisation. A precarious balancing act remains between working quickly and being sufficiently vigilant for my faculties to use serendipity to yield and capture optimal results. One action too many can destroy something of significance. Focus and abandonment must coexist simultaneously in this workspace.

There is nothing purposefully psychoanalytical or 'psyche inducing' about how I generate opportunities for serendipity to flourish within an EoP. However, aspects of free association probably do play a part. The entire scenario is wilfully manufactured to meet specific aims. It feeds upon the same stylistic, physical, cognitive and conceptual predeterminations, preconditioning and self-referencing confinements already discussed. It may also include a little luck concerning how effectively I can produce valuable outcomes. What supports the likelihood of serendipity is the mixing of so many components that I would not have foreseen the outcomes or necessarily arrived at that exact point through other means.

Although, as stated, there are no right or wrong actions within an EoP and thereby, no possibilities for activities to be categorised as mistakes, actions considered mistakes occur at any time of the making process outside of an EoP. A mistake is only one outcome of many possible results of my actions. Sometimes, if positive, the consequences of a mistake can shake up a whole work, showing a different way forward or a new technique or approach to acknowledge and assimilate. Such an outcome may solve a problem I didn't know I had or cause a rebalancing of relational factors throughout a work. In this way, the potential of a mistake as a positive force to further enhance a work may be seen as a serendipitous act. With some luck and effort, the hitherto unforeseen antecedents that generated a mistake can be analysed and recreated to reproduce the same outcome, moving the initial status of the action from that of a mistake resulting from happenstance to wilful intentionality that enhances technique, for example. As such, I have learned much through my mistakes and value their occurrence, realising that what defines a mistake is a matter of perspective determining if an outcome is an error, disaster or opportunity. Not all mistakes are helpful. They can sometimes open a less productive path or cause catastrophic failure. Such failures have resulted in me abandoning work as irretrievable owing to a catalogue of errors I cannot usefully modify.

Along with all other skills required of an artist to choose what actions to keep and which to disregard, the artist's ability as a serendipitist assists in knowing what is and is not of value. Serendipity and mistakes have often enabled me to improve my technique, practice and stylistic concepts. It is through serendipity and mistakes that, on occasion, I have seen my understanding of how I work and, more particularly, new ways of working occur through a sudden leap forward rather than process-driven, tentative, stepwise advancement. What I have learned through serendipity and mistakes has surprised and resonated with me. I anticipate serendipity and the assimilation of mistakes into my technique will remain at the heart of my practice.

# CHAPTER FIVE

# AN ENVIRONMENT OF POSSIBILITIES

## Introduction

I have written about how I operate within an EoP in general terms of making activities but have not described where those activities occur. All aspects of making, from concept to artefact, happen within my four studios. Those studios comprise, first, my composition studio, a dedicated room in my house with a computer housing Sibelius notation software and Logic Pro sound manipulation, production and sequencing software, an amplifier and speakers for playback from that software and pencil and paper for scribbling ideas and working outs, all situated on my composition desk; second, my painting studio, a space in a converted agricultural barn in Dorset complete with easel, paints, brushes and daylight spotlights where I have the freedom to move about, paint and make a mess; third, the great outdoors, where I walk, map, think and explore; and fourth, knitting external and internal environments together, my mind and body, the centre where and through which, thinking, sensory data, action, realisation and outcomes are processed and enacted. Together, those are my working environments and the four studios that comprise my EoP.

Although my composition and painting studios are physical spaces facilitating work-making in each medium, the making processes of composition and painting are not restricted to those places. As I paint, I think of musical compositions; as I compose, I think of painting. I do this in the built studios but also, as previously explained, when I am out walking, 'mapping' and exploring landscapes and, in general, as part of my ongoing thought processes wherever I happen to be or whatever I am doing. This back-and-forth thinking is a natural outcome of my hermeneutic makeup and open interpretive nature that is designed to transduce my actions in one area of experience into another, for example, in PK coupling, from sensation to movement and in the case of my practice, from one media into the other, either conceptually as thought experiments, projections and imaginings or through the actions of making, materially realised as compositions or paintings.

As is often the case, products of imagination, concept and speculation need to be tested in material production to see if they work, or at least work in ways I find satisfactory, either by fulfilling expectations or being surprised and delighted by unforeseen outcomes. Thinking continually generates ideas and approaches that originate in one practice area that are later adapted and applied to others through trial-and-error testing. This self-referential process is how I learn and grow as an artist. It is how I remain inspired. Interpretation is my response to all immanent and subjective experiences. I think through interpretation and create through interpretation as an ongoing cyclic process, continually interpreting and reinterpreting my interpretations. This is the hermeneutic circle, building meaningfulness, understanding and knowledge. In this respect, an EoP is as much a time, a duration, an ongoingness or a moment as it is a physical location. Making is a physically located and temporal activity. It can be both immanent and, once the experience has passed into cognition and memory—into past time— subjective because I also learn through reflecting on what I have experienced and made and, through those reflections, devise other approaches to build new understanding and meaningfulness.

In this chapter, I shall lay out the plethora of my making techniques and, where cognisant of them, identify similar methods between composing and painting that, although adapted to suit the categorical differences of each medium, show a consistency of approach. I have experience working with art mediums such as drawing, watercolour and acrylic painting. However, I mainly focus on oil painting in my practice and it is oil painting I shall focus on here. Although I cannot pragmatically describe the value of my actions regarding their meaningfulness for others or, much of the time, for myself, or for the same reasons, not demonstrate that actions in one medium have a meaningfulness equivalency to actions in another, the material result of those actions, namely the work produced, will show that connectivity can manifest in stylistic traits, gestures, structures and the processes of making.

A central question in *Music, Painting, Landscape and Me*, is how painting and composition are connected in my practice. My elevator pitch is that afferent data is received via my sensory system and processed by my CNS. Various efferent pathways are determined, some automatically out of awareness and others within the conscious domain, resulting in the cognitive and physical actions necessary to produce artwork. But what exactly do I mean by this?

As discussed in earlier chapters, afferent nerves gather information from my environment and transmit those to my brain and spinal cord, where they are processed and analysed. This lets me perceive sensations such as touch, temperature and pain. Efferent nerves then carry signals from the brain and spinal cord to my muscles and glands, allowing me to respond to the sensory information I've received. For example, if I touch a hot stove, afferent nerves signal to my brain that I'm feeling pain and efferent nerves then signal to my muscles to quickly pull my hand away. Afferent and efferent nerves work together to create a feedback loop that helps me interact with my environment and respond appropriately. In the case of making art, afferent activity involves my sensory experiences as the artist, such as what I see, hear, feel and imagine. Those sensory experiences are translated into efferent activity through motor commands that direct the muscles in my hands, fingers and other body parts to create artwork. For example, when I am stimulated by something I have seen, heard or felt in the environment, it would be through the afferent nervous system that I sense those phenomena and subsequently, my efferent nervous system is used to create the brushstrokes or music notation that interprets those stimuli through whichever medium I chose. Similarly, in terms of interpretation, afferent activity involves the sensory experiences of the viewer, such as what they see, hear and feel when viewing artwork. This sensory information is then translated into efferent activity through motor commands that direct their responses to the artwork. For instance, a viewer might see a painting or hear a piece of music and feel moved by what it embodies. Receivers would use their afferent nervous system to sense the artwork and their efferent nervous system to generate an emotional response reflecting their interpretation of that artwork. Afferent and efferent nervous systems are integral to creating and interpreting art, enabling anyone to translate sensory experiences into meaningfulness expressed through creative acts and emotional responses. Creating artwork involves acts of making and viewing. It is worth reminding myself that before anyone else sees or hears my artwork, I am my only audience. It is through the constant process of reviewing, interpretation and response using afferent and efferent capabilities that an artefact is made.

Of course, the accurate picture of what is happening within the CNS is far more complex and involves all manner of internal loops, feedback responses and adaptive, dynamic learning. I understand that my brain receives a continuous input and flow of somatic data through my senses as inbound afferent activity. This data is immanent to experience. I am aware of some of this somatic input but not all of it. Much of it is filtered at source by my brain to not overload my consciousness. As described in 'Mapping' and For the Love of Chalk and Other Matters, CNS functions like PK coupling, for example, organise how my body automatically responds through movement and other efferent correlates to the external environment. This automated, genetically and environmentally conditioned formatted response correlates somatic sensing and feeling to performance. The differences in those performances, a vastly complex and varied range of physical reactions, constitute part of my making processes operating out of awareness where all that is manifest of their action is what is embodied in the work I make through the physical movements—the performance, or taking the analogy further, the dance—they provoke. Also crucial to creating work are those efferent actions that I am aware of or initiate through intentionality and cognition in response to my ever-changing external or internal environments.

Following the immanence of various CNS functionalities, subsequent efferent outcomes that I am aware of are subject to further conscious interpretation and analysis, often through subjectivity with realisations that lead to more efferent outcomes incorporated into the various conscious physical actions necessary for making artwork. Efferent actions, whether consciously or subconsciously produced or correlated, will inevitably affect and change my external and/or internal environments that, in turn, will generate more PK coupled and conscious efferent responses. Like the hermeneutic circle, this process is recursive, adaptive and dynamic and, through the process of interpretation and building meaningfulness, results in learning. This is interpretation through mind and body. It is how I operate and experience as an artist and human being on a physiological, emotional and performative basis. Through this constant adaption and learning, I have produced artefacts across my life that, as a body of work, continue influencing how I make subsequent work.

Operating within this rich environment of somatic input, I am bombarded with sensations of sight, sound, smell, touch, texture, temperature, taste and many others at every moment. From the perspective of making work, whether the initial received somatic data is sonic or visual is unimportant. What is important is how I respond to that stimulus. As mentioned, I respond to some of this data at the conscious level, but much is processed out of awareness. What is essential in making work is how my mind and body respond to that afferent input and how those impulses are embodied into my work when transduced to materiality through efferent pathways and actions. What do I mean by transduced to materiality? I refer to the process of taking one kind of afferent input and, through creating an artefact, changing those impulses from nervous activity to what is materially embodied into an artwork as its constituent material parts, such as a painting's surface comprised of textures and colours or in the mark making of music notation and the sounds those marks elicit through performer interpretation. Those are material outcomes that have been transduced from impulse to artefact. Embodied with this materiality is meaningfulness as 'signified' through the artefact's properties. However, the nature of transduction, of transmitting and transforming a 'message' from one state to another, in this case, from nervous activity to a painting or musical composition, becomes impossible to pragmatically identify as a direct correspondence of value and meaningfulness owing to the interpretive actions of maker and viewer. Nevertheless, transduction is a way of considering the transformative outcomes possible when afferent input becomes efferent output—bodily movements, such as physical gestures realised in paint, notational signification, sound, movement, ideas or concepts.

To summarise, somatic impulses constantly pass into my body, they are processed, in and out of awareness and that processing leads to physical action that manifests, among other ways, in making art. Whether an outcome becomes a piece of music or a painting is determined by the physical medium through which those impulses are expressed, transduced, interpreted and embodied, not in the specific category of afferent impulses themselves. This is why I can move freely between music and painting. This is how, when I am walking in the landscape, responses to somatic input may occur as internally generated sounds or imagined visualisations with little conscious effort on my part. It is why I can instantly make a drawing to interpret what I see symbolically through line and gesture but switch to imagining what I see as sound by responding to those images. I can even interpret the landscape as a drawing and then interpret that drawing as sound or, alternatively, draw what sounds I hear. Whatever the afferent input, my mind and body can interpret and transduce them in multiple ways and through any medium I have the experience and facility to employ. Though categorically different, what is embodied in a painting or a piece of music stems from the same source. That source is me. Through their makeup, cognition, afferent and efferent relationships and their correlates, my mind and body can process my sensory data, create symbols and symbolic networks in sound and paint that meaningfully express my response to those phenomena.

Afferent and efferent systems demonstrate how integrated and correlated sensing is to performance. It is important to note how seamlessly this system operates before writing about specific techniques of making for painting and composing that, by the nature of that description, tends to isolate one from the other. I appreciate that materially, temporally and technically, composition and painting are categorically different things. However, from my perspective as the artist interpreting the world around me as a performance, they are alternate manifestations of the same experience and phenomena. I aim to illustrate this connectivity by highlighting the correspondence between my behaviours, rituals and techniques—the dance and performance of making—across both art forms. I begin with an analysis of how I compose music, followed by descriptions of how I paint, illustrated using figures where helpful, to examine existing similarities and differences between the two. Along the way, I shall discuss how my EoP benefits from using digital technologies, photography and the indivisibility of artwork as a self-generating property. Before that, I would like to be clear about where I locate the start and endpoint of making work, as the terms starting and finishing a painting or piece of music are used frequently.

It is easy to think of making a piece of art, be it a painting or a composition, as beginning when I start generating composition materials on my computer or putting paint on canvas or board, I feel the artwork is complete when I have reached the material's potential expression in that work. I also think of any research activities associated with making art as part of the process. Nevertheless, the conceptual lines I draw to consider a work started or finished are not fixed. For example, at what point does the true nature of starting an artwork begin? Is it in the material activity of making, in the research, in the experiences that triggered inclinations to make work, in antecedents deeply embedded and shaped across a lifetime of interpretation and response or in the artworks that proceeded it? Sometimes, doodling or sketching can transition from being incidental, possibly arbitrary mark-making or note jotting to coalesce as an artwork or at least, something that prefigures an artwork. What then of starting points? Where exactly does that point of 'this is not an artwork' and 'this is an artwork' lie?

From my perspective as an artist, I believe artwork is artwork when, through interpretation, I determine it belongs to the category I define as 'artwork' or where through intentionality, I have made something that I differentiate from the 'noise and signals' that surround it to be categorised as an artwork. However, whether others consider it art depends on their interpretation and criteria for what constitutes an artwork. It is as if phenomena and conditions I can interpret as art objects always surround me. Those conditions may be on a continuum between art objects and non-art objects flowing in a state of perpetual 'becoming'. Still, it is not until certain hermeneutic conditions are achieved that I recognise my activities as artwork separate from the overriding afferent signals I constantly receive as environmental noise. I am not clear what those conditions are pragmatically, but I am clear that I can interpret and recognise them.

Deleuze proposes that the creation of artwork begins at the moment of its inception by the artist. However, he emphasises that the creative process is not linear or predetermined but instead involves a process of experimentation and transformation. He argues that the start of artwork is not a fixed or determinate moment but an ongoing process of 'becoming'. An artwork is never truly finished because it is always open to new possibilities and interpretations. This view resonates with my experiences that making art is a continuous activity. I would also add that along this continuum of experience, there are times when, let's call it inspiration, or concepts or experiences reach an intellectual, expressive or emotional critical mass which precipitates the making of work as a materialisation of those thoughts and experiences. This is where the artwork manifests as an artefact outside of the artist and the point at which the process of making an artefact is generally considered to have begun. In the context of making art, I'm reminded of the term 'event horizon' borrowed from astrophysics, where an event horizon marks the boundary beyond which nothing, not even light, can escape the gravitational pull of a black hole, can be metaphorically applied to describe a pivotal moment or turning point in the creative process signifying an important stage or breakthrough in an artist's work or creative journey. It represents the point at which an artist moves beyond previous boundaries, explores new ideas, or achieves a transformative breakthrough in their work. It can be a moment of inspiration, self-discovery or the culmination of intensive exploration and experimentation. This moving beyond is a unique and powerful way to express myself as a product of my imagination. I take raw materials and turn them into meaningful symbols representing my experience. I do not create something out of nothing. I transform matter—somatic input, experience, genetics, biases and environmental and social conditioning—into form.

Like Deleuze, I consider that an artwork is never truly finished in a finite and pragmatic sense. There are always revisions, a bit of touching up in a painting here and there and the 'improvement' of a phrase, notational signification or structure that can occur indefinitely after a work is deemed to be finished. A work's traits, ideas, techniques and influences may be continued and further explored in the following work, generating a continuation rather than termination of activities. As time passes, my interpretation and opinion of my work invariably alter. This changed perception may provoke me to rework a painting or composition somehow. It may even result in the withdrawal or destruction of an artefact or, at the very least, a repurposing. This is the meaning I take from Deleuze's 'becoming'. Owing to this realisation, I see the notion of work as being finished as somewhat arbitrary, like drawing a line on a surface continually moving away to show where that movement has stopped but where the movement continues out of sight. When I use the terms start and finish about making work, I do so mindfully of the above but, for the sake of convenience, refer to when the physical act of making or the immediate research that concerns it begins or, concerning the completion of work, when I decide to move onto the next project.

## Music Composition

Across the last thirty years of my compositional life, I have used various techniques to generate musical materials. Through trial and error and my evolving understanding of how I need my musical material to operate, I have developed a range of techniques that transform notational materials. Those transformation processes are foundational to my timecode-supported polytemporal compositional method, a way of composing music that now occupies most of my output away from works for solo instruments. I have referenced timecode-supported polytemporal composition throughout this book concerning polytemporal composition, flexible performance approaches, temporal flexibility, 'jelly' and flux. To fully explain my compositional processes as part of an EoP, I must present how I compose timecode-supported polytemporal music from the perspective of its 'bricks and mortar' and how those processes are embedded in various software and transformational actions.

Timecode-supported polytemporal music has no score and no conductors, is performed from parts alone, supports decoupled, simultaneous, independent temporal trajectories for any number of players and enables the composition of sonically complex, hyper-dense, through-composed and fully notated polytemporal music in such a way that structural integrity is maintained in performance using confined yet flexible performance approaches, organised using only part-embedded timecode mediated in conjunction with loosely synchronised mobile phone stopwatches. Players perform from fully notated parts within which the embedded timecode indicates minutes and seconds above each barline to achieve this temporal autonomy.

All parts are created in Sibelius software, with the timecode automatically added. Once calculated, the timecode proliferates the part. To begin the performance, all stopwatches are loosely synchronised at the piece's start. From then on, performers reference and loosely synchronise their relative notational timeline positions in the music to their timeline positions displayed on the stopwatch as clock time, adjusting their performance speeds as necessary to ensure their playing position along the composition's timeline is as close to the clock-time position indicated by the stopwatch as possible. The mobile phone stopwatches can be thought of as independent but loosely synchronised metronomes for each player where, as well as tempo markings, the timecode provides players with a temporal framework that prevents performance from being too fast or too slow, thereby ensuring each player, regardless of their independent tempi, is in roughly the right place at approximately the right time. This flexible yet confined placing of musical events in time allows the compositional structure to be maintained in performance through flexible interpretation.

With each player following their own temporal trajectory and no unifying pulse or beat, there is no need for a conductor. By reading the timecode in their parts in conjunction with their stopwatches, each player is responsible for their pulse. They are their own conductor. And as there is no universal pulse synchronisation, no synchronised score is produced for timecode-supported pieces. The flexible relationships between all instrumental parts cannot be usefully represented in a fixed and synchronised score format. What is 'signified' in notation does not usefully relate to what is heard in each unique performance iteration. It is the condition of those compositions that they can only be experienced as immanent sound and cannot be previewed conceptually as a notated musical score. Consequently, no score is produced and music is performed through parts alone.

As individual parts are decoupled from one another and not synchronised into a score, assigning independent tempo values to any or all instrumental parts is straightforward. The same rhythmic notation will support a multitude of notation-tempi values. The material will just be rendered faster or slower. Timecode in all parts provides the loose synchronisation and temporal framework that holds the compositional structure together, not the rhythmic notational relationship between parts, as would be the case in a polytemporal score.

Timecode-supported polytemporal compositions are assembled using materials generated through recursive and often obsessive self-borrowing actions to support this multi-layered temporal density. Borrowed materials may be individual instrumental strands, sections of individual strands or complete works or, as is often the case, a combination of original materials combined with other or the same self-borrowed materials that have been subject to one or several forms of transformation. Transformative processes include tempo transformation, rhythmic transformation, time stretching, pitch transformation, transposition and voice reconditioning. Transformative functions may be recursive, where original materials are first transformed in one new compositional assemblage only to be further changed when those transformed materials are incorporated into another unique compositional assemblage. Because transformed and untransformed self-borrowed materials bring 'inherited' notational, rhythmic and sometimes pitch characteristics, all pieces using self-borrowed materials produce highly unified sonic outcomes. Once compositional materials are generated, they are ready to be prepared for organisation into a compositional structure called The Model.

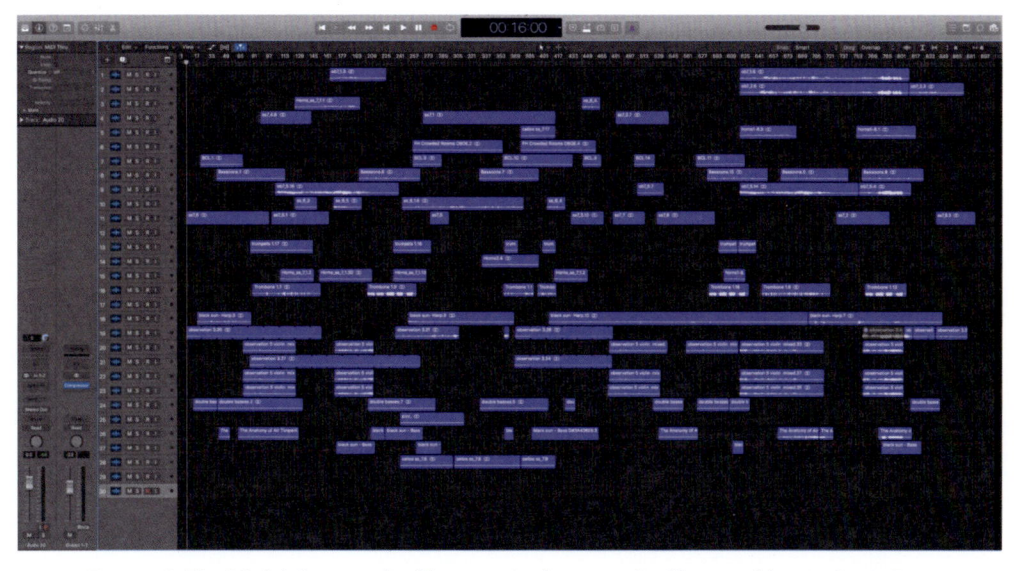

Figure 19. The Model shows audio files organised as an audio file assemblage in Logic Pro.

The Model comprises audio and notation components (see Figure 19). The audio components are generated through the playback and recording functionalities of Sibelius, where each part is recorded and exported as an audio file. Those audio files are then imported into Logic Pro, a sequencing software, where the audio files are assembled into compositional structures. Those structures are known as audio file assemblages. An audio file assemblage contains multiple audio files organised vertically for density and horizontally for duration. A polytemporal audio output is produced when those recordings have materials rendered at different speeds simultaneously combined through playback. This output is also exported as a digital recording called the audio model. The audio model is a rendition of the piece that is identical in every way each time it is played back or recorded. It is the fixed manifestation of the composition.

The notation component of The Model, the notation network, is not visible as it would be in a score. It is only visible as a network of audio files in software where those audio files act as placeholders specific to the notation materials they are rendered from (see Figure 20), which illustrates the relationship between notation and the electronic rendition of it formatted as an audio file placeheld within The Model. Notation is visible, however, when the instrumental parts are extracted from this network to make the materials for players to perform from. The parts themselves will exhibit no notational relationship to each other, as would be the case if organised into a synchronised score. Consequently, structural relationships are only revealed as sound from playback of the audio model or, ideally, in live performance.

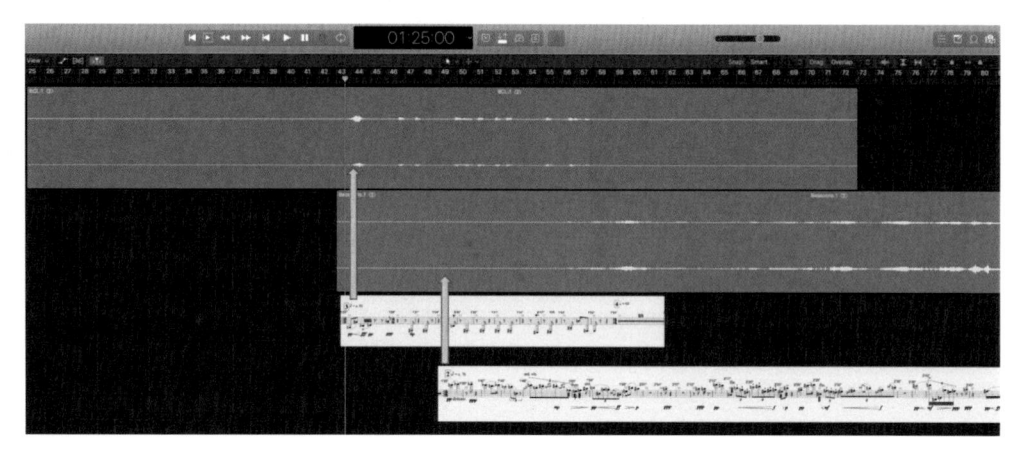

Figure 20. Audio files in Logic Pro act as notation placeholders.

The duration of any notation materials calculated by timecode and the length of their concomitant audio file measured along Logic's timeline is the same. They are identical. As such, the timecode position of any point in any audio file and its progenitor notation are precisely linked and can be exactly located along the piece's timeline. The fixity of the relationship between the notation network and the audio model measured as clock time and 'signified' as timecode constitutes The Model. It is the framework timecode provides that binds The Model together. The timecode framework also binds players to The Model by mediating that timecode in performance. Those performance outcomes are the human, flexible manifestation of the piece.

Aside from conceptualising and imagining musical compositions, the notational signification of any composition is executed within the software on my computer. This is my primary compositional EoP. As discussed, I use Sibelius notation software and Logic Pro to typeset and manipulate my materials and build my final composition models. My approach blends algorithmic and intuitive transformative methods developed through years of experience in composition and performance. The core of this approach is a recursive process that repurposes and transforms materials over time and across multiple pieces, imbuing them with a rich legacy embedded in my compositions' components. Almost all transformative actions are undertaken within Sibelius and use a range of available plugins to generate the transformative outcomes I find helpful.

As the term self-borrowing implies, I write little new material. Occasionally, I will generate new notational content by writing a solo piece. Still, even then, I am unlikely to begin with a tabula rasa as at least some aspect of the material I start with is likely to have been self-borrowed from elsewhere. I do not like seeing blank pages before me, whether of paper or virtual pages generated in notation software. They hold too many possibilities, the scope of which can prove daunting to penetrate. I prefer taking materials I already have and repurposing them. From my perspective and interpretation as the composer, self-borrowed materials transformed in the ways I shall describe tend to blend seamlessly, regardless of their placement within a piece. This is due to the relational connectivity and inherited semiotic richness that supports their correspondence, allowing them to be confidently fixed within a composition in multiple ways. Like distantly related family members, all my materials are interconnected across time and compositions, even more so when each has been transformed multiple times. As a result, materials will, notwithstanding the variabilities of interpretation through performance, always sound cohesive, stylistically consistent and appropriately placed when rendered during a performance, especially where degrees of temporal flexibility are called for in timecode-supported polytemporal music performance. Even though the parts used in creating new compositions may have originated from various sources, the unique qualities of those parts are transformed when combined to create a new and distinct work whose contextual material relationships are entirely different to the context, instrumentation, tempo and duration of the original self-borrowed materials. This new creation is greater than the sum of its parts. It becomes the sounding music, where the emergent properties of the whole are more significant than the individual components themselves. As I have been using material self-borrowing and transformation techniques to generate content for some considerable time now, I shall focus on two aspects of this approach that can be found in all compositions of the past few decades. Those are tempo and pitch-to-rhythm organisation.

## Tempo Transformations

I frequently play and experiment with tempo changes. One of the advantages of computer software is the ease with which one can experiment with distortions and repurposing of musical material, making slow music playback faster and vice versa, for example, to experiment with tempo extremes that go way beyond human capacity. Although I don't use the outcomes of those experiments, they are part of what I do in an EoP. I want to discover extremes of possibility and be surprised by how the perceptual nature of a given musical line will dramatically alter as its tempo is revised faster or slower. Although a basic technique, such transformations yield a range of possibilities when applied to monophonic material lines that are later recombined with other materials to generate new vertical harmonic relationships. Those newly time-stretched or time-contracted materials can be combined in multiple ways to create new assemblages with their own identities. When adjusting the tempo of self-borrowed materials, it's essential to consider the instrument's capabilities, the player's abilities and practical concerns like breathing and articulation. Ultimately, the tempo must be feasible for the instrument and the player to perform effectively. This is particularly so when materials from one instrument or instrumental family are transformed and repurposed for another.

In generating and transforming notation materials for inclusion into timecode-supported polytemporal compositions, I consider rhythm an independent component that structurally characterises materials. This is particularly so when organising pitches and other notations related to expression rhythmically. Consequently, there is little to no change in rhythmic notation when using self-borrowed or self-similar transformed materials. Despite other notational changes, the bar lengths, beat patterns and pulse structures remain essentially unchanged. However, the rhythmic identities of primarily monophonic instrumental parts can be modified through significant alterations, such as deleting or adding bars of material from related or unrelated instrumental lines. This process is like film editing, where time is shaped within specific materials and throughout a composition's overall structure.

## Pitch Transformations

Unlike rhythmic entities, which are generally autonomous and untransformed, pitches are subject to free organisation and transformation without predetermined systems for creating harmonic continuity. This capricious approach transforms pitches from their initial rhythmic placements to any new pitch configurations of interest in subsequent transformations. Whether all pitches or only certain ones are changed depends on maintaining a particular pitch array across transformations to preserve the identity of a designated feature, line or gesture. This transformative process is not complex or sophisticated; pitches are altered through randomised algorithmic processes, inversions, pitch-shuffles and a range of intuitive actions with interesting transformations kept and others discarded. In addition, any generated pitch constellations may be freely changed to suit their rhythmic positioning and dramatic context post-transformation more sympathetically, considering the nature of the recipient instrument, its agility and other relevant factors.

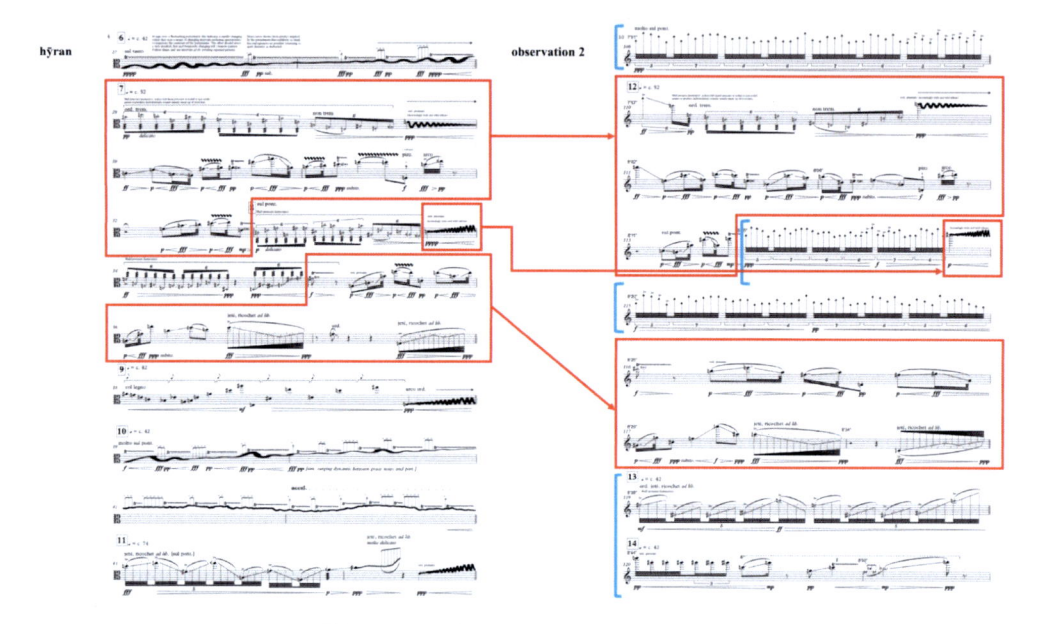

Figure 21. Self-borrowing: from *hyīran* (2013) to *observation 2* (2015).

For example, Figure 21 shows a complex mixture of pitch-transformed self-borrowed materials operating across *hyīran*, a piece for solo viola from 2013 to the violin 1 part of the 2015 string quartet *observation 2*, contained in the red boxes and newly composed materials, identified by blue right-facing brackets. For instance, bars 110-113 in *observation 2* are pitch-transformed materials borrowed from bars 29-32 of *hyīran*. Those bars are followed by new material that overwrites the original material from *hyīran*, only to bring back *hyīran*-borrowed original material from bars 35-37 at bars 116-118 of *observation 2*, once again, pitch-transformed before moving on to new materials. The actual materials of *hyīran* have been erased or overlain by the new materials, only for them to emerge again, creating a notational surface much like a palimpsest.

Combined in new ways, the interplay between fixed rhythmic elements and varying pitch materials has similarities to medieval isorhythmic practices. During that time, the terms 'color' and 'talea' denoted the melodic and rhythmic units. As Margaret Bent describes in her *Grove*

*Music Online* article, *"'Isorhythm' is [a] modern term applied with varying degrees of strictness to the periodic repetition or recurrence of rhythmic configurations, often with changing melodic content, in tenors and other parts of fourteenth and early fifteenth century compositions, especially motets"*.[154] In this methodology, color and talea distinguish between combinations of pitch and rhythmic materials where the pitch materials undergo frequent change. Though not Isorhythmic in the medieval sense, transformations of pitch 'hung' on fixed rhythmic configurations yield consistently fruitful results and an endless source of material that I can generate through compositional play. It is this act of play that is central to the operation of an EoP.

## Constructing Compositions

In true EoP style, utilising the functionalities of Sibelius and Logic, I throw together a range of musical materials to see what happens. Much of this throwing together is driven by happenstance. What materials I select, where I place them, how they are layered vertically to create polyphony and harmony, for example, and sometimes I will choose materials for combination and experimentation based upon ideas generated as concepts and notions developed while walking or ruminating on such matters. Frequently, a composition originates from a blend of randomness and deliberate choice, or in the absence of intent, my best estimate of how I can attain a favourable result. I cannot know or judge specific outcomes at this stage as the combination of musical elements is not known to me in their complex relational configurations, only as a mental sonic sketch which needs to be realised to be proven. Musical structures and characteristics emerge from this building process through chance and play. It is through serendipity that something special may emerge and be noticed. The outcomes of my compositions are not known in advance. Only the broadest confines, such as instrumentation and duration, are considered in composition planning. Everything else is up for grabs. So how do I discover which materials work best together from my perspective, considering there are multiple combination options?

To create a composition in Logic, for example, it is necessary to render the transformed self-borrowed materials 'signified' as notation in Sibelius as sound using the software's inbuilt playback facilities. Those generated sounds are in no way the piece of music or a substitute for performers' genuine mediation of notation materials. This rendering provides a sonic representation of those notation materials as 'interpreted' through the software's algorithms. Realising notation as sound enables me to play with audio files when they are imported in Logic, where I can use them as sonic building blocks. When combined into a structure—the audio model—because it can be 'performed' as sound through the software. This build is also an assemblage of audio files comprising the components—the transformed, self-borrowed materials—constituting the composition. This assemblage serves as a workspace and prototype construction until it is finalised. It is my compositional EoP.

Finalising a composition involves two fundamental operations: first, the audio recordings are imported into Logic and combined in various ways to determine the best materials for the audio file assemblage. Much experimentation, addition and deletion of audio files are necessary to find a compelling compositional structure. Fortunately, Logic makes it possible to play back any number of audio files simultaneously, regardless of their placement or the tempo of the materials placeheld, with each audio file synchronised to the digital clock displaying the timecode positions of all audio files. This playback allows for a comprehensive audio impression

---

[154] Bent, Margaret, p. 1. [accessed 9 June 2021].

of polytemporal music.

Second, the reviews of audio renditions may lead to further modifications of the notations. This sometimes requires recomposing or modifying materials in Sibelius, where once rendered may be reimported into the audio model in Logic for further review until the desired outcome is achieved. This creates a cycle of importing, playback, evaluation, modification and so on between Sibelius and Logic. The building process is in a continual state of adaptation due to incorporating new materials and ideas. This affects eventual outcomes until the compositional process is deemed complete. As a result, there is no sequential building of compositional structure from start to finish. The process is responsive, reactionary, intuitive, risky, unpredictable and sometimes messy.

Creating an audio file assemblage based solely on playback in Logic proves to be challenging as there are no scores or visual indications of notational relationships to reference. It requires extensive experimentation in arranging and rearranging materials and reviewing the audio to determine which structural inventions hold the most potential at any given moment and in multiple configurations. The initial conceptual process of combining materials using aural imagination and guesswork is transferred to the computer to uncover interesting relationships through playback. This process allows for compositional play in a diverse EoP, revealing combinations of tempo, pitch, harmony and rhythm previously unimagined and now rendered materially as sound that can be sculpted.

Between 2010 and 2012, working particularly on a project called *On a Theme of Hermès*, before I developed timecode-supported polytemporal composition, I experimented with modular composition methods that involved composing fragments of instrumental music that were later recorded and combined in various ways, again in Logic to create new compositions. Unlike timecode-supported polytemporal compositions, those pieces were not designed for subsequent live performances, so no attempt was made to generate performing materials from the constructed Logic models. Instead, composition work focused entirely on combining multiple instrumental recordings as sonic building blocks that would then be mixed and mastered as finished tracks. As the individual musical fragments were all performed at different tempi, the simultaneous playback of their various combinations as audio models in Logic produced polytemporal music. With no attempt to correspond those tempi with timecode, the sonic results were asynchronous polytemporal recordings. Through working with audio recordings of this type, I became aware of the potential for using the method to construct and organise audio content on any compositional scale. I then presumed that if I rendered electronically typeset notation through software to create audio materials that were strictly linked to timecode in that notation, I could organise those materials in all manner of ways using Logic Pro's timeline to build audio models for polytemporal compositions. A few experiments later and timecode-supported polytemporal music was born. Significantly, in using Logic as an EoP, taking risks, experimenting and mainly through play, I was able to generate unforeseen compositional results from the combination of fixed (already recorded) materials. Imagine the fun I could have generating compositions where the notation was transformable and its interpretation, mediated by humans in performance, develops a range of additional expressive and structural possibilities. Although technology played an essential part in realising my ideas, the development of the concepts in the first place and the imagination and drive to explore gave me the momentum to experiment. Combining mind and technology extends foreseen possibilities into new unforeseen territories that grow my compositional project through continued experimentation and risk-taking.

In timecode-supported and asynchronous polytemporal compositions, all the materials I initially created and subsequently transformed had been developed without sight of a result and little appreciation of their combinatorial potential apart from the belief that potential existed. For all intent and purposes, materials were generated blind in the trust that they would prove useful and compelling. To this day, I continue to create new materials and material combinations and transformations through self-borrowing and never cease to be amazed at the variety and expressive potential those transformations elicit on materials that, in some cases, are over twenty years old. My work and processes continue to yield results that surprise me. This surprise shows that my notion of a healthy EoP remains alive and kicking.

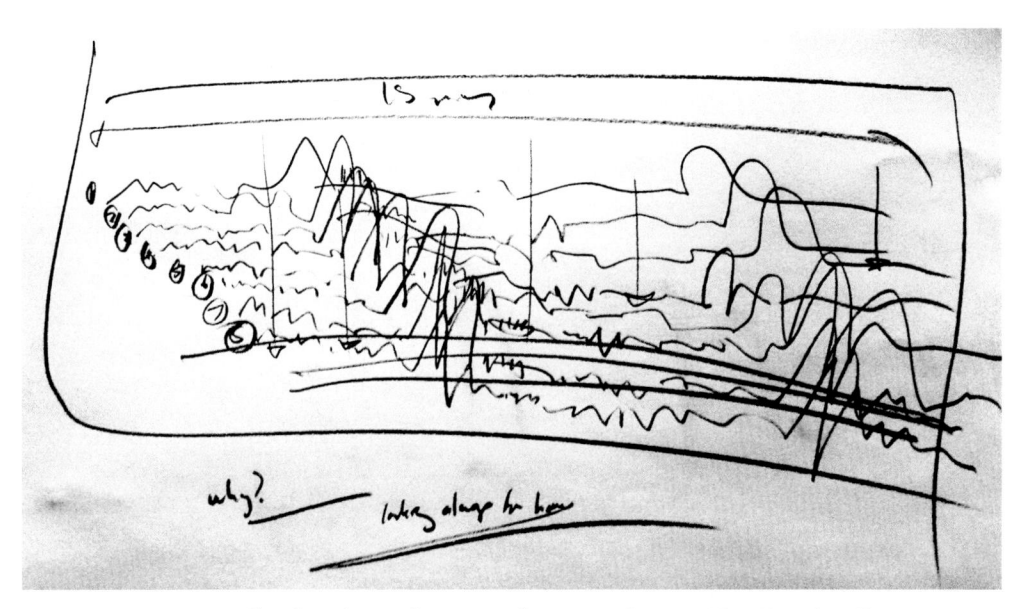

Figure 22. Sketch outlining the proposed structure for *oros*. Marc Yeats (2013).

The final contribution to describing my composition methods is transitioning from making musical compositions to painting and drawing. It concerns drawing as a graphical text used to prefigure the signification of a composition using European classical music notational conventions that I call drawing to scoring. I have spoken about this technique of interpreting thoughts and concepts with great speed when in the landscape to symbolise what I see and sense in line on paper in 'Mapping', particularly about my Composer in Residence to *The Observatory* experiences, where drawing is considered a performance that is the embodiment of correlates between sensing and movement. Using this technique, I can rapidly transfer thought and sensation to line, embodying my thought through efferent actions. Using drawing to scoring as an example of compositional research, I will illustrate how I turned concept to notation in the 2013 piece for eight voices, *oros*.[155]

Before beginning notational composition on *oros*, I played around with several ideas of how the work may be structured. To achieve this, I produced sketches that offered a way to externalise and compare structural options. As graphical significations, those sketches, of which Figure 22 is an example, could, if my compositional intentions had been different, be performed directly

---

[155] Further information and a recording of *oros* can be found at 'Marc Yeats: Composer' website: *oros* <https://www.marc-yeats.com/oros-2013/> [accessed 14 May 2023].

from the drawing where the drawing would be considered the score and performer interpretation would be open regarding pitch, rhythm and tempo, to name a few parameters. However, I was keen to use European classical music notation to signify my ideas in a way that directed performers and interpretation in a more confined manner. What survives from the drawing into its music notation expression is the canonic construction implied in each of the lines circled 1-8 that represent voices 1-8 in their movement from the left to the right of the page, signifying the durational aspect of the piece along with the iterative and flexible nature of the imitative structure. Lines marked 1-8 clearly show a similarity in shape, gesture and kinetic energy, but as they were drawn by hand very quickly, they are not identical. This iterative, flexible canonic form was reflected in how I slightly varied materials from one voice to the other and where the temporal relationship of the voices, though imitative, would only ever approximate each other in performance. This approximation, coupled with the 'felt' tempo changes of each line that were staggered in performance, resulted in an asynchronous polytemporal outcome.

## For 8 voices: SSS AA T BB

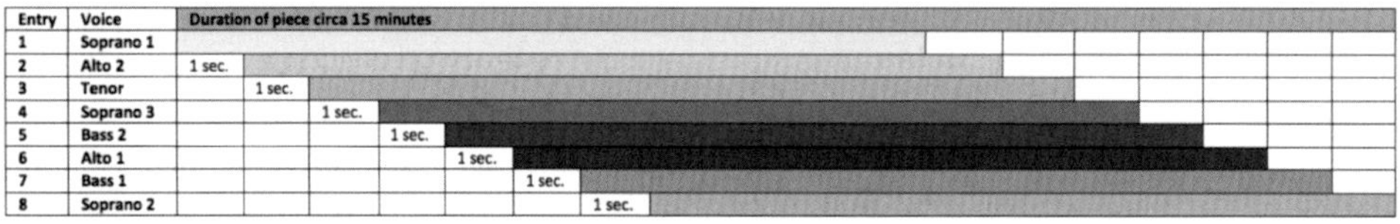

| Entry | Voice | Duration of piece circa 15 minutes | | | | | | |
|---|---|---|---|---|---|---|---|---|
| 1 | Soprano 1 | | | | | | | |
| 2 | Alto 2 | 1 sec. | | | | | | |
| 3 | Tenor | | 1 sec. | | | | | |
| 4 | Soprano 3 | | | 1 sec. | | | | |
| 5 | Bass 2 | | | | 1 sec. | | | |
| 6 | Alto 1 | | | | | 1 sec. | | |
| 7 | Bass 1 | | | | | | 1 sec. | |
| 8 | Soprano 2 | | | | | | | 1 sec. |

Each voice enters approximately one second after the other in the order stated. This distance is maintained as closely as possible throughout the piece [canonic distance]. Subsequently, the same order is observed for singers to finish their material with soprano 1 being the first to finished followed by alto 2 and so on until soprano 2 completes this cycle as the last voice to be heard. Ideally, there should be [approximately] a one second difference between each voice finishing sequentially i.e., soprano 1 finishes first followed by alto 2 finishing their material 1 second after soprano 1, followed by the tenor 1 second after alto 2 etc., until all voices have finished. In reality the time difference between voices finishing will be more flexible but should still occur in the sequence stated.

Figure 23. Performer instructions for canonic structure in *oros* (2013).

Figure 23 shows that asynchronous polytemporal canonic outcomes were explained in performance instructions within the notation of each singer's part. There is no connection between the exact signification of the notation that makes up the singer's parts nor the actual structural contours and ebb and flow of the piece between the drawing and the formal composition. Any implied relationships remained subjective and the processes of generating materials through self-borrowing and transformation mentioned earlier drove the process of what notation comprised the piece. However, the overall canonic structure and aspects of the relationships between the parts are seen here, with more detail concerning the execution of the temporal aspects of the piece given in text form under the graphical canonic representation. This structural relationship between drawing and scoring illustrates how quickly and easily I could capture certain conceptual elements of the piece, embody those ideas on paper and later use them to support subsequent notational detail.

I do not sketch out all my compositions in this manner. Most remain conceptual until I generate materials in software, bringing materiality to those ideas as notation and sound. Still, I frequently use pencil and paper to solve localised problems or articulate ideas differently to help me find solutions. Making concepts of sound physical through drawing, transducing their sensation to performances on paper where that performance is the movement necessary to interpret sound as motion, connects me to and generates alternative meaningfulness so I can comprehend what I am doing more clearly. The act of composition involves utilising any tools I have at my disposal where those tools range across my imagination, my body and software, combined and related through acts of play and experimentation to aid the construction of the piece and any meaningfulness it and the processes that generate it, hold for me.

## Making Paintings

Starting a new project can be daunting, whether a blank sheet of manuscript (digital or paper) or a canvas. However, the blankness of the surface is not what scares me but rather the infinite possibilities it presents. With so many ways to approach a painting, I often feel overwhelmed and paralysed by the flood of ideas that come to mind. I ask which approach will yield the most exciting results and my brain attempts to imagine multiple outcomes simultaneously. This sense of possibility can be inhibiting and prevent me from starting new work.

To overcome this, I begin by making marks on the canvas quickly and with as little care as possible. This first act of mark-making provides a context against which I can anchor an interpretation. Signification is meaning. From there, all manner of marks are triggered in response and counter-response, building upon each other until the canvas is transformed from empty to full. I employ many indeterminate approaches to mark-making during this stage.

As I wait for something to emerge that I can focus on, colours, textures and brushstrokes are perceived as symbols of various kinds. Those symbols contain degrees of meaningfulness that, at some point, will come together as a relationship or network of symbols with some referent connection that I can hold onto and then work with. I call this a meaningfulness network. Isolated marks will contain significance and meaningfulness, but that meaningfulness can be enhanced and expanded further by adding other marks. However, like a form of writing, the meaning of a work of art is never fixed or stable but is always subject to ongoing interpretation and analysis. So, like words generated to qualify other words, I add brushstrokes to build meaningfulness.

When I paint, I sometimes consider my work holds sufficient meaningfulness to be finished at the sketch stage. This is when the initial outcomes of my actions within an EoP are unprocessed. If the artwork meets my standards for expression and aesthetics and falls within what I categorise as an artwork, I consider it complete. I accept the actions and the artwork's condition as the final product. I strive to incorporate spontaneous and intentional elements to achieve balance in my paintings. It can be challenging to strike the perfect balance, as the freshest and most unworked marks are often made at the beginning of the painting process. However, I must ensure that my goals for the finished work are met and that it is adequately developed.

Nevertheless, I am sometimes asked by a viewer, "*Is it finished?*", implying that what constitutes a finished painting is as much a point of view as a statement of intent on my part. Despite different notions of what finished might be, each subject I paint requires a unique approach to capture my interpretive ambitions and I alone must decide when to stop. There is no guaranteed formula for success, so I keep working until I feel satisfied. Although the balance point cannot be calculated in advance, I rely on interpretation, intuition and reasoning to guide me. Like my compositional practice, I approach my work through play and embrace unexpected results, spontaneity and serendipity. This approach ensures that each painting I create is unique.

Figure 24. Comparative mark-making.

Over the years, my painting techniques have evolved significantly. In my twenties, I painted with a meticulous approach aimed at creating photo-realistic illusions. Now, I focus on producing abstract expressive landscapes. My painting techniques are largely unchanged since this stylistic shift; however, the context in which I use those techniques have evolved. I continue to use similar brushstrokes, gestures and mannerisms that I developed through my physicality and muscle memory. However, the meaningfulness networks of those marks have become increasingly abstract and open to interpretation. My current work consolidates those mark-making techniques into contextual relationships related to landscape symbols. This includes referent symbols associated with the sky, trees, fields, grasses, light, shadow, aerial and linear perspectives, seasonality and general landscape configurations.[156] Whatever techniques I use, I

---

[156] Aerial or atmospheric perspective is a visual effect that occurs when objects become less defined and appear bluer in colour as they move farther from the viewer. This phenomenon happens because the

aim to create form from interpretation and this form arises from combinations of my mark-making. In Figure 24 I have included examples of paintings from 2003 to 2023 to showcase this. The images depict details from Figure 28, *movement towards no.4* (2003), Figure 29, *Box Hill, Surrey* (2021) and Figure 30, *East Kennet* (2023), arranged from top to bottom.

Despite the colour variations of the brushstrokes and mark-making in Figure 24, each mark displays a smooth, flowing movement in either an upward or downward direction or from left to right and vice versa and may be curved or straight. In the first instance, those gestures are determined by the kinetics and physicality of the movement that initiates them as a response to whatever impulses triggered them and second, by the thickness of the brush and the amount of paint on it. The speed at which the gesture is made and the pressure with which it is applied affects how much paint meets the surface, whether wet on wet or wet on dry. The gestures are used to signify all manner of landscape-associated objects. They are often left raw and unworked, placed one upon the other in various densities and sizes to imply detail and enhance structures or focal points. Sometimes, I may smudge gestures to create further blending or paint more gestures over the smudging to give the illusion of three-dimensionality, as seen in the top image comprising Figure 24.

Figure 25. Detail from *Overton Downs, Wiltshire*. Oil on cradled board, 297 x 420 mm. Marc Yeats (2022).

In some of my paintings, I like to leave the white surface of the canvas or board visible between brushstrokes, as shown at the bottom of Figure 27. I may also drag the palette knife across the surface of those marks while still wet to generate a contrasting textural surface. Once dry, I may glaze over the pre-marked area using a transparent pigment mixed with quick-drying media, permanent rose, sap green and raw sienna, for example, changing the tonal characteristics of the underlying brushwork and moderating the white of the board that now appears to illuminate the painting from within as it reflects light to the eye through the glaze (Figure 25).

In the top example in Figure 24, taken from *movement towards no. 4*, I frequently used a palette knife to carve out sections of the painted surface, whether wet or dry. I then filled the scraped area with the same brush stroke gestures as seen in the other examples in Figure 26, but the paint was only applied to fill the scraped-out area. Sometimes those areas were left naked. In

---

Earth's atmosphere scatters light, with shorter wavelengths (blue and violet) scattered more strongly than longer wavelengths (red and orange). As a result, distant objects may appear less defined and bluish than closer objects. This effect is widely observed in landscape paintings and photography and helps to provide a sense of depth and distance in a composition.

my current work, there are instances where I have scraped away layers of paint to create a shape into which new paint is applied and I also use a range of scraping techniques to imply movement or detail of some kind. Scrapping is also used if I am unhappy with an area of a painting and wish to remove as much of the surface paint as possible. What is left behind, the trace of that action, can produce a new referent surface or imply unforeseen trajectories to explore.

Figure 26. Detail from *Bramfield, Suffolk*. Oil on cradled board, 50 x 50 cm. Marc Yeats (2023).

Aside from scraping, thought is also given to the various optical temperatures I wish to depict concerning symbols representing reflected light or where the light falls, particularly warm sunlight and its contrasting cooler colours to suggest shade areas, as shown in Figure 26. Pigment temperatures range from warm to cool, corresponding to transitions across the entire colour spectrum, including those from reds to blues crucial to creating the illusion of aerial perspective. Such illusions are particularly apparent when painting the blue of a sky that transitions through several cool to warm blues to suggest representational differentiation between a distant horizon and the closer sky above.

I am not a slave to any of those techniques. I can mix up and contradict colour relationships and combine all the techniques mentioned to create other illusions that take their significance from their structural and contextual positioning in a painting rather than the physics of aerial perspective, for instance. I can play and experiment in any direction my imagination takes me because painting is not a passive reflection of reality; it is an active process of construction and deconstruction that challenges my preconceptions and assumptions about the world. Any of my paintings will demonstrate this construction and deconstruction as the process of making in an EoP and how my concepts of the landscape are 'signified' in paint using all those techniques within localised areas or across an entire work.

Finally, though not a brushstroke, I draw directly into and onto my paintings using various marker pens compatible with oil paints. Not all paintings have this mark-making, but it is prevalent among some. Using marker pens is exciting because of their fluid and continuous action. This action is excellent for converting my kinetic gestures into marks that bring energy, movement and spontaneity to work, as shown by the pink line in Figure 25 and the pink, purple and black lines in Figure 26. Additionally, marker pens help add aspects of detail or fine lines where they are called for.

As I revisit the mark-making details displayed in Figure 24, I examine them within the context of the paintings they were taken from. Despite their material similarity, I aim to demonstrate how the arrangement of those brushstrokes and movements into various meaningfulness networks can influence my perception and interpretation of them.

Figure 27. Detail from *Lyme Bay*. Oil on cradled board, 30 x 30 cm. Marc Yeats (2021)

For example, the brushstrokes shown at the top of Figure 36, taken from *movement towards no.4* according to my interpretation, lack an obvious association with landscapes or their features, despite being highly kinetic and expressive and predominantly using the colour palette of green, a colour often associated with plants and landscape painting. Some viewers have interpreted a macro-micro-organic subject matter in my paintings of that period, likening them to "*looking through a microscope*", "*pond-life under water*" or "*viewing the world from space*". Although I did not intend to provoke those vivid images, all interpretations are valid. What is certain is that while the *stillness in movement* series of paintings, including *movement towards no. 4*, was inspired by my experiences in the Orkney Islands landscapes, I did not intend to create landscape referent paintings in response.[157]

Now, seeing the remaining mark-making in Figure 24 in the context of their complete paintings shown in Figure 29 and Figure 30 has different associations for me from those in *movement towards no. 4*. My intention with those paintings was to create meaningfulness networks that referenced the landscape. Although I didn't know where the paintings were heading when I started making them, the interpretive process of creating soon led me to consolidate the marks within contextual relationships that symbolised various landscape features in the overall symbolic dynamic of those artefacts. This contrasts the lack of referent or iconic symbolism in *movement towards no.4* to the organisation of symbolic forms within Figure 29 and Figure 30, which differ significantly.

---

[157] More information and images from can be accessed from Marc Yeats's website at <http://www.marc-yeats.com/blog/stillness-in-movement/> [accessed 22.05.2023].

Figure 28. *movement towards no. 4*. Oil on cradled board, 122 x 92 cm. Marc Yeats (2003).

From my interpretive perspective, it is fascinating how similar gestural activity, mark-making and texture can be used to imply or signify different things contextually; in this case, in *East Kennet, Wiltshire*, a foreground full of implied detail that was not meticulously constructed but created quickly using bolder, more entangled marks, the intensification of colours and the contrast between them to generate the optical illusion where the lower half of the painting signifies objects closer to the viewer than those found elsewhere in the painting. *In Box Hill, Surrey*, the most kinetic and gestural activity is in the middle horizontal band of the image, from my perspective, representing horizons, trees and entanglement of hedgerow and foliage, with the suggested foreground only patchily worked and degrees of this gestural activity continued into the area representing the sky. Those different illusions are generated from very similar mark-making, but in each example, their organisation suggests a different contextual relationship within the overall structure of the paintings. In recent years, I have increasingly incorporated stronger referent symbology into my work, further enhancing the significance of my meaningfulness networks.

To summarise my journey so far, I have moved from iconic symbolic simulacra to a degree of abstraction that made no direct reference to landscape, only to return to landscape painting with a newfound appreciation for the gestural charge, freedom and colouristic intensity used in non-landscape painting. This approach allows me to break free from iconic representation and imply landscape phenomena through abstract expressionism, emphasising openness, gesture and colour. I still incorporate a sense of architecture, form and perspective from my photorealistic days, which provides the structures for the expressive components of my art. From my interpretive perspective, this context relates every mark I make to my experience of the landscape.

Figure 29. *Box Hill, Surrey*. Oil on cradled board, 18 x 24 inches. Marc Yeats (2021).

Figure 30. *East Kennet, Wiltshire*. Oil on cradled board, 420 x 594 mm. Marc Yeats (2023).

Like words, brushstrokes can have different meanings in different contexts. This means I can weave multivalent meaningfulness through a relatively confined repertoire of significations where the marks' limitation and familiarity materially embody the hand that made them in the work produced as a style of execution and vision. As such, the meaning of a work of art is not something that can be objectively determined or discovered but is instead embedded within the work itself, waiting to be interpreted and brought to light through the act of engagement where meaning is an ongoing and open-ended process that is never fully resolved or completed but is always subject to revision and reinterpretation. I view how I paint as a form of invention or creation that brings forth new possibilities and meanings rather than simply reflecting or reproducing what already exists. My paintings are not reproductions of what I see or sense. As interpretations of what I experience filtered through my style and mannerisms of making, they are categorically different. Style and mannerisms aside, what, then, are the processes involved in creating paintings and constructing meaningfulness networks away from mark-making?

## Becoming

My brushstrokes are unique to my style and reflect my physical movements and artistic preferences. My technique involves translating sensory input into PK coupled and other immanent responses alongside intentional actions to create the specific marks that form my artwork. But how do I choose and organise those marks to construct a cohesive painting?

When I begin work on a painting, I can't predict which of the three journeys I outline here my creation will take. The immanent unfolding of events dictates the course as I paint rather than a conscious decision taken before I begin work. The three possibilities are: 1) a smooth progression from initial marks to completed work in just a few sessions; 2) a more extended period of mark-making undertaken in the hope that a subject will emerge; 3) returning to a painting considered finished to reshape it into a representation that better reflects my interpretation of the subject. The third process highlights that art is never complete and can be revised or incorporated into new versions as my understanding of its meaning evolves. Those journeys demonstrate my work's experiential, experimental, adaptive and playful nature, where spontaneity and serendipity shape its form through action.

To illustrate this, I want to share the journey of three recent pieces and how they evolved from blank surfaces to completed works. Each painting starts with a sense of possibility, utilising various techniques incorporating brushstrokes, overlaid paint, scraping, rubbing in and out, glazing, overpainting, drying and thinking time already described. The process is always adaptive, responsive, dynamic and recursive. The difference between the three journeys and the paintings they produced is the time it took to finish them.

Suppose a painting doesn't meet my interpretive expectations or takes too long to coalesce in a way that interests me. In that case, I place it in a designated area in my studio that I jokingly call the 'naughty corner'. If it's been particularly 'naughty', I turn it to the wall so I don't have to look at it. After a period of 'punishment', I revisit the painting, hopefully with fresh eyes and look for new possibilities and ways to improve it. It returns to the naughty corner indefinitely if I still can't find a solution. Although it can be frustrating to have paintings in the naughty corner, I view them as opportunities to learn and gain insights whenever I finally resolve their issues. Ultimately, the success or failure of a painting is a result of my actions and decisions. But the joy I feel when I liberate a painting from the naughty corner is palpable and an empty naughty corner is always a cause for celebration.

Figure 31. Making: Journey 1. *East Kennet, Wiltshire.* Marc Yeats (2023).

Figure 31, *East Kennet, Wiltshire*, is an example of Journey 1. This picture took a few weeks to produce and most of that time was spent waiting for the paint from the previous session to dry before I could begin painting again. The initial mark-making in frame 1 was immediately visible as well-developed referents, resulting in a quickly shaping conceptualised landscape. I did not have a pre-determined image or exact memory of a location in mind when I began painting. Instead, initial brushstrokes set the context for subsequent mark-making, which was intentional and directional. Within an hour, frame 1 was complete. Once dry, I moved on to frame 2, where I applied glazes, particularly in the greens of the lower half of the painting, to add depth and enhance the aerial perspective. Frame 3 involved the consolidation of cloud formations and balancing tonal areas in the sky, with trial-and-error adjustments of lighter and darker areas in the middle ground. Finally, I removed the tree-like element and made highlighting and colour intensity adjustments, resulting in the completed work in frame 4.

The speed of execution and method of making for *East Kennet, Wiltshire*, is unusual. Typically, a painting's emergent properties require several processes of trial and error to materialise in a way that I find useful. However, this painting came together with ease. Although some areas of a painting may come quickly, it is rare for all aspects to consolidate their significance simultaneously. I often struggle with certain areas or elements of a painting, experimenting and reworking those that are troublesome in the hope of breaking through any impasse. Problems are not always obvious and it can take some time for me to identify them; as always in an EoP, trial and error are a central tenant of operation.

Figure 32. Making: Journey 2. *Powerstock, Dorset.* Oil on cradled board, 50 x 50 cm. Marc Yeats (2022).

Figure 32, *Powerstock, Dorset*, was a year-long project that began in July 2021 and was completed in June 2022. The journey of creating this artwork showcases the typical painting process in my EoP. Initially, the painting was constructed from an entanglement of brushstrokes with no predetermined imagery or focus, only a decision on which colours to use and a dense layering of mark-making. Marks were laid down impulsively and in response and interpretation to previous marks. As the stages of the work progressed, the final painting emerged, as shown in the snapshots of the process from left to right and top to bottom of the two left-hand columns of Figure 32. The image was developed by blocking out and reducing the original complexity of lines and gestures to consolidate and contextualise what remained. Through the colours I chose and the blocking out process, the painting opened with areas signifying the sky, which, based on my interpretation and experiences of the landscape, further indicated flooding the work with suggestions of light, shadow, time of day and ambience, creating other symbolic associations. I amplified those characteristics by emphasising and reinforcing tonal and colour contrasts, which ultimately developed the meaningfulness of the original mark-making.

As the artist, every brushstroke and decision I made contributed to the outcome of the painting, whether visible or not. My reactions, interpretations and actions all played a crucial role in shaping what the viewer and I saw. It's important to note that even the things that are not immediately visible in the painting are equally significant to those that are.

Figure 32 showcases the processes I frequently use to create my paintings. Although each piece starts similarly, the combination of marks I make creates a unique work of art. I don't follow an assembly-line technique for painting, as each piece presents challenges and opportunities for growth. While I may use some tried and tested steps to address issues or bring an artwork closer to completion, no universal solution applies to every painting. Through experience, I have learned that each painting requires a personalised approach. Sometimes, the best solution to perceived problems is to take radical and destructive action to create a new work of art that incorporates all the previous mark-making in some way yet is utterly transformed.

Journey 3 of my making process consists of two phases illustrated in Figure 33 and Figure 34. The first phase shows the many stages of Journey 2 that *Bramfield Suffolk* went through between June 2021 and May 2022 until I thought it was finished. However, after some time, I realised that it did not fit the style of the family of works I had been producing at that time and didn't signify the kind of landscape interpretations I aimed for. Despite ignoring my feelings of disquiet, they grew and I moved the painting to the naughty corner. The painting remained there for many months, with no resolution in sight. Retrospectively, I realise that the many iterations of this work indicate my restlessness and discontent with what I had produced. The images illustrate an EoP in action but an action that did not make the desired results. As with any activity in an EoP, there is no guarantee of success, just a multiplicity of possibilities that may prove useful.

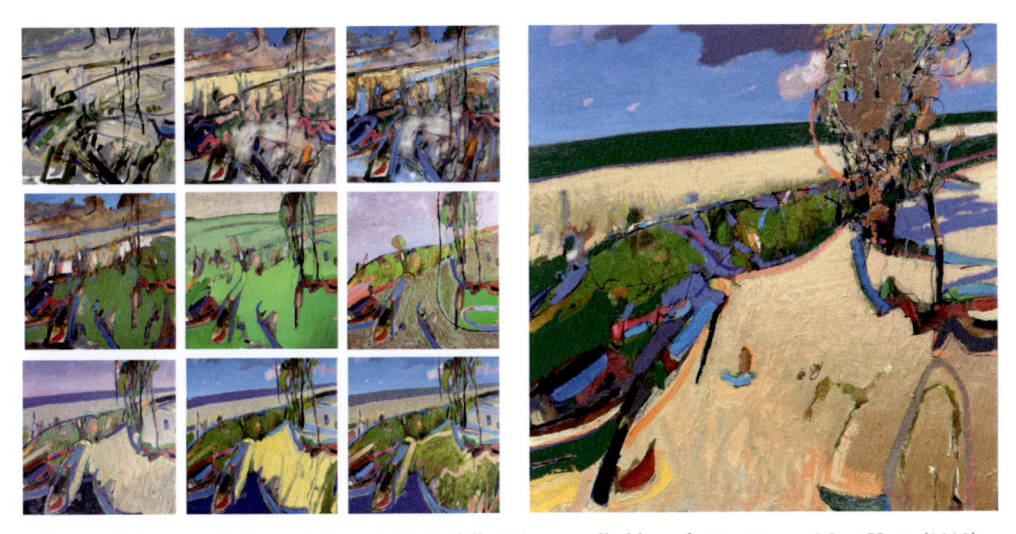

Figure 33. Journey 3, Phase 1. *Bramfield, Suffolk*. Oil on cradled board, 50 x 50 cm. Marc Yeats (2023).

In the second phase of Journey 3, Figure 34, I experienced a breakthrough in my thinking. *Bramfield, Suffolk*, had been freed from the naughty corner and was back on my easel. Despite my initial reworking of the painting, I still wasn't moving in the desired direction and felt stuck. I managed to enhance and restructure the greens to depict light on the grass and experimented with the scale of the tree-like structures. However, the painting still lacked the balance and dynamic energy I sought. I worked on the areas I believed were successful interpretations of my intended vision, but some parts continued to disappoint me. Fortunately, everything changed when I introduced the illusion of elongated shadows from the left to the right of the painting. Acting as indexes, they implied that something out of view was blocking the light. This addition gave a strong impression of light direction and intensity, bringing a radical breakthrough to the painting.

Next, I decided to change the horizon level and add dark green paint to the upper third of the painting, creating the impression of trees and branches. This change transformed the overall balance and dynamics of the piece, altering its context. The addition of dark paint suggested trees in the shade, emphasising the distribution of light and dark throughout the work. By intensifying the contrast between the light and dark areas that represented grass, the painting's light and colour became more vibrant. After adding a few finishing touches, the painting was complete, including colour highlights and intensifying complimentary relationships between blues and greens. The journey from 2021 to 2023 was long, but I learned much about my practice. By taking risks and overpainting what was once a finished picture, I created a new work that pushed my painting technique and interpretation into new territories. Every brush stroke and stage of the painting process contributed to its physical integrity and the embodiment of my thought within it. The painting is a history of making, intentionality, mistakes, false starts and abandoned trajectories. Every aspect, from the texture captured by a brush stroke to the composition structure, was born from interpretation and response. This process highlights the dynamic relationship between the parts and the whole in the process of interpretation, emphasising how preconceptions shape understanding and understanding in turn shapes preconceptions.

Figure 34. Journey 3, Phase 2. *Bramfield, Suffolk*. Oil on cradled board, 50 x 50 cm. Marc Yeats (2023).

Preconceptions certainly govern when I consider a painting to be complete. Reviewing the images presented here that show the different stages of a painting becoming finished demonstrates just how subjective such considerations are. I say this because I believe any iteration of any painting could be considered complete at any point in the artwork's journey when viewed in isolation from its process; in other words, not viewed or anticipated as incomplete. As the maker, I can stop the making process at any point and declare the result as finished. Who's to say if I'm right or wrong?

Those thoughts raise the question of which of the iterations shown here is a truly finished work, if any, or are all versions considered complete? For example, any of the iterations in Figure 33 and Figure 34 could be presented as finished works if the viewer had no previous knowledge of what my finished work looked like and took on trust that the work was finished because I had declared it so as the artist. Equally, if the painting were encountered in a gallery, hung and displayed professionally with no accompanying information, it would be accepted as a finished work owning to the condition and context of its display. The version I have chosen to signify completion is just one of many possibilities. Whether the viewer considers the displayed artwork successful is a different matter entirely.

This applies to music composition, too. I may publish a work as complete and then, sometime later, remove or add bars and publish another version as complete, but which is truly finished and who is to say further revisions may not follow? Even without publication, the works in progress that populate my hard drive are constructed and deconstructed as an ongoing process with only my inclinations as a guide to when that process should or could finish. Suppose a performer omits certain bars or even sections at the premiere of my composition. Will the audience know the difference between my finished work and what they have been presented as finished purely from the material fact of what they hear? An art object does not inherently hold information to proclaim it is finished, nor does it embody a universal condition that identifies it as artwork. Such interpretation arises from cultural, historical, environmental, educational and experiential preconditioning. One person's art is another's noise or scribble.

For example, at first glance, a palette may appear as a simple object, a vessel for holding and mixing colours. Its surface, covered with splotches and layers of paint, bears witness to my creative process, becoming a testament to my presence, actions and gestures. It is a physical trace of my hand and a residual of my process. But what separates this surface from the palette a painter or decorator uses? Why is one possibly an artwork and the other not?

Figure 35. Palette detail. May 2023.

As I progress through my work, the palette becomes a layered palimpsest, showcasing the multitude of colours employed and the variations in their proportions (see Figure 35). It becomes a historical archive, a repository of my experimentation and exploration. The dried remnants of paint reveal my evolving choices, reflecting the emergence and disappearance of specific hues, shades and tones. Moreover, the palette embodies the physicality of engagement with my materials. The smudges, drips and paint splatters on its surface are traces of my gestures, movements and bodily presence. It bears witness to the energy necessary to make a painting, reminding me that painting is a deeply embodied and visceral experience. Furthermore, the palette carries the memory of previous paintings. As I sometimes reuse a canvas or board, I often repurpose my palettes, allowing the remnants of one painting to mix with the colours of the next. In this way, the palette becomes a bridge between different works, a tangible link connecting the past and present. It echoes previous artistic endeavours, infusing the current painting with subtle intertextuality and a sense of continuity.

Simultaneously, the palette also signifies absence. The palette gradually loses its initial vibrant hues as colours are mixed and applied to the canvas or board. It becomes marked by the absence of certain colours and the emergence of new ones, showcasing the constant transformation and transience inherent in painting. In this sense, the palette is a record of what is no longer present, a repository of my choices and decisions and a testament to the ever-changing nature of making.

Importantly, the palette can be seen as a site of potentiality, a space where colours converge and interact before being transformed into artwork. It is a liminal space between the absence of untouched colours and the presence of their application. As I navigate this space, make deliberate choices, mix pigments and manifest my actions and intentions, the palette becomes a site where absence and presence merge, where my symbolic vision takes shape through the interplay of various elements. This understanding encourages me to reconsider the hierarchy between the artwork and my painting tools. In foregrounding the palette as an artwork, I recognise its significance in the creative process and the complex interplay of absence and presence it embodies. The palette ceases to be a tool and instead becomes a visual representation of my process, a tangible record of my choices and a dynamic entity embodying the trace of my acts of making. Whether those considerations amount to my palettes being considered artworks remains a matter of interpretation and intentionality.

## Technology, Photography, Prints and the Feedback Loop of Image Generation

My music composition technique relies on technology for many aspects of its generation. Conversely, painting does not. However, I have been using image manipulation software since the mid-2000s to develop my paintings by experimenting with and manipulating digital imagery. It is useful to discuss the role of photography generally in my artistic practice before delving into the significance of photo manipulation software.

The advent of digital cameras, especially mobile phones with built-in cameras, has revolutionised the way I work. During the 1980s, when I used to paint in a photorealistic style, I took photographs of landscapes, including trees, clouds, hills and plants, to use as sources for my paintings and would paint directly referencing those images. Although I visited, experienced and sketched at nearly all the sites I painted, I copied images from photographs and rendered them as paintings. Because of this, my love for landscape photography grew alongside my painting and I took pride in how closely my paintings resembled photographs of the landscape when captured on film. Although I still take photographs of landscapes for reference purposes, I no longer copy images from photographs to make paintings, preferring to paint from memory, referencing my remembered landscapes as discussed in previous chapters. Nowadays, my landscape photography is a free-standing activity that complements my painting work but doesn't directly contribute to it. I now use photography to make images of my finished work that, captured as digital data, can be transformed using software. It is those image transformations that are central to my practice.

Figure 36. Limited edition print *1a: from stillness in movement*. Marc Yeats (2005).

Figure 37. Limited edition print *6e: from stillness in movement*. Marc Yeats (2005).

In 2005 following the *stillness in movement* exhibition, I realised I could take high-resolution photos of those paintings and crop smaller details, transforming their colour relationships to make new, iterative images. I was intrigued by the concept of hidden paintings waiting to be noticed and appreciated as standalone artworks. In fact, the images in Figures 33 and 34 could easily be presented as complete works on their own. The fact that they are cropped or divided from the original painting does not diminish the value of the original or the new artwork. While physically cutting up a painting into smaller sections to create multiple works is a valid creative act, I prefer manipulating images through cropping as a more versatile approach to generating multiple works from one original. By the end of 2005, I had generated a series of images I was marketing as limited edition prints. In those prints, I was focusing on the types of gestures and brushstrokes discussed above, but where the focus of the new images was only on those gestures without reference to their original context (see Figure 36 and Figure 37, for examples). As the frame of reference had changed from entire paintings to singular or a small collection of gestures or a particular texture, for example, the meaningfulness of the image had similarly altered to reflect its new compositional dynamic.

The question of whether an artwork retains its status as such when divided or cut up is complex and depends on various factors, including the context, the artist's intention and the specifics of the division or fragmentation. Dividing or cutting up an artwork can significantly change its meaning and impact, creating several unique artworks instead of a singular coherent one. For instance, if a painting is split into pieces and treated as separate artworks, each part may have new meanings and interpretations that differ from the original. Nevertheless, some artists intentionally create artworks meant to be fragmented or transformed over time as individual elements are added or removed. In such cases, dividing or fragmenting the artwork is a crucial part of its concept and meaning and may challenge traditional notions of artistic unity and wholeness. Ultimately, whether an artwork remains an artwork when divided or cut up is subjective and open to interpretation because the unity of an artwork is not set in stone but depends on the relationships between its various elements. This includes the effects of dividing or cutting the artwork. Such actions can alter the artwork's relationship to its context, create new interpretations and meanings and disrupt its symbolic form. However, any interpretation or meaning is ultimately subject to change and dividing or fragmenting an artwork can create multiple new artworks, each with its unique identity. It's unclear how far such a division can go before it is considered a mere fragment and no longer an artwork. Ultimately, those decisions are a matter of interpretation. I have 'zoomed into' my paintings and extracted multiple images for manipulation but not to a degree where the fragmentation is extreme.

Figure 38. *Box Hill #4*. Digital print. Marc Yeats (2022).

In recent years, I have created many images from within images to generate prints and non-fungible tokens (NFTs), all of which have involved various degrees of image manipulation, particularly in colour and contrast fields such as in Figure 38 and Figure 39, both extracted from

*Box Hill, Surrey*. I delight in finding what I perceive as complete landscapes hidden among the wider mark-making of a painting.

While my primary goal is to create new artwork, those experiments using technology also influence my painting practice. Using technology to transform images has allowed me to create faster and more diverse experiments than I could with traditional paint, which often inspires new directions for my work without simply copying the manipulated image. Instead, I use what I learn from those experiments to generate new concepts and explore new directions. Imitating myself, or rather, imitating the results of my experiments, opens exciting possibilities outside of my usual field of imagination. For those reasons, I consider photo manipulation an essential tool for play, experimentation, risk-taking and learning and it is at the heart of my artistic practice and EoP.

Figure 39. *Box Hill #2*. Digital print. Marc Yeats (2022).

## Shared Making Processes

Both composition and painting involve exploring creative possibilities through technology, but their approach differs. Regarding music composition, the software allows for creating multiple copies of electronic notation materials (scores) by duplicating their data without compromising the integrity of the original file. This means that transformative processes and editing can be applied to those copies to generate new materials without affecting the original data. Conversely, creating physical copies of a painting that can be manipulated to produce multiple versions is impossible through technology, as modifying the physical form of a painting requires altering its material composition, resulting in a new entity altogether. However, digital images of a painting can be created through photography and edited in various ways to produce multiple digital iterations. In this way, a painting can exist alongside digital copies of its image, whether transformed or not. What the electronic components of the composition and the digitisation of images provide in common are the opportunities to play with their data to create new possibilities, whether through structured research or happenstance. Both extend and develop my technique by offering outcomes I can appropriate to my practice.

Another shared advantage of working digitally comes when reviewing my work. For example, rendering my music through software enables me to listen in real-time and from a different perspective than that generated using my aural imagination to comprehend the sounds. When I compose music in my head and 'perform' it mentally, it varies based on my priorities, focus and mood. However, when I write music down, the fixity of the marks—the trace—I make as notation becomes a more stable entity than my imagination and memory alone, despite the flexibility around the meaningfulness that notation signifies and my understanding that performers will interpret work uniquely. Nevertheless, what is important here is how software can 'read' electronic notation to generate playback that I can review. This rendering allows me to hear my work differently than through my aural imagination. It enables me to adopt the role of an observer rather than a creator, which can be advantageous for evaluating my emotions towards the piece, its structure, and how they develop over time. This perspective also helps in identifying new creative pathways, even amidst the considerable constraints of software playback. While I appreciate that this rendition is not the piece, it does provide me with a useful material iteration. What is critical to mention is that notwithstanding my ever-changing interpretive fabric, rendition from the computer is identical with each playback. It provides a still point in the turning world of my aural imagination.

In a similar way, as listening to the computer rendition of my music creates distance between what I hear and what I produce when interpretation shapes aural imagination, reviewing my paintings through mobile phone photography also provides interpretive distance where I exchange looking directly at the work with looking at a replica of the work scaled down and through a phone screen for a new perspective. I undertake such reviews frequently while painting in the studio, where my observation, interpretation and understanding of those photographs direct subsequent actions. I also photograph work at the end of each day's painting to take home for review. I find that leaving time between the last in-studio look and reviewing any photographic images at home allows the preformatting of expectation and memory to fade and my perception of what the image shows to be fresher. I am in search of alternative perspectives. Conclusions from those reviews shape the following day's painting and often point to future developments. Before the advent of computers and mobile phones, I would look at my paintings in a small mirror for the same purposes as photographing the work. The mirror, reversing the image, showed all structure and design relationships hidden from direct view. Accordingly, I would act on those findings. The mobile phone camera has replaced the mirror, but reviewing my paintings in the studio and reflecting on photographic images at home remains central to my practice.

My fear of starting work from the position of an empty stave or a blank canvas is also shared between composing and painting. My attempts to avoid this as a starting point have led to several strategies. My staves come ready filled with transformed, self-borrowed materials that can be rendered and combined as audio files in software, while in painting, I quickly create surfaces full of mark-making. Those techniques generate perceptually dense and complex visual and sonic surfaces that I overload with content. What follows is a technique shared between composing and painting that I consider constructing or deconstructing density. I load my composition with extreme layers of simultaneous activity and my paintings with entanglements of mark-making. Once I have determined a sufficient point of material saturation, I refine the work's symbolic fabric by carving into the depths of sound or layers of paint. This involves removing, moving, scraping away, deleting, blocking out and refining until I find a point of meaningfulness that is significant enough to indicate that I'm on the right track. In both instances, that point of meaningfulness may be reached when symbol recognition and resonance have been interpreted between what is embodied in sound or paint and my remembered landscapes or any other significant experience. I can uncover multiple layers of details, events and timelines through excavation. Revealing in this way alters my perspective of the work, creating an ebb and flow of dynamics and tensions between the work's symbolic unity. This is narrative construction. It is building a story of change, difference and 'becoming'.

Excavation as a process of revealing what lies beneath has aspects in common with creating palimpsests. A palimpsest refers to a writing material or manuscript that has been modified or reused by scraping or erasing the original text and writing new content on top. This term can also be applied metaphorically to various other contexts, such as painting, where the technique refers to several layers of paint being applied to a surface, with each layer partially or completely visible beneath subsequent layers. This creates a visual depth and complexity as previous layers peek through the uppermost ones, giving the artwork a sense of history and evolution.

Creating a palimpsest in painting involves building up layers of paint, allowing each layer to dry before applying the next one. As each new layer is added, I may use transparent glazes, rub out, or partially scrape away materials to intentionally reveal sections of the underlying layers to expose different colours, textures or compositional elements. This layering and removal process can be repeated several times, creating a rich, textured surface.

In composition, the layering of different materials and speeds of material unfolding at the outset of the composition provides the many layers necessary for subsequent overlaying with other sounds that allow what exists underneath to be audible. It also allows the removal of layers of sounds through deletion or volume (dynamics) and density changes to expose underlying materials. Unlike the physical actions of overpainting and scraping away necessary when painting, the virtual and conceptual removal or addition of musical layers in software involves processes of deletion, volume regulation or the moving around of materials in relation to one another.

The beauty of employing the palimpsest technique is that it enables me to achieve various effects and build different meaningfulness networks by symbolising the passage of time as a materially embodied history of making in much the same way a cliff fall exposes different geological time layers. It provides a fascinating and complex interplay between the visible and the hidden, the audible and inaudible. Revealed layers might hint at previous compositions, sketches or concepts, offering glimpses into my creative process. Moreover, the palimpsest technique can add interest and depth to a painting or sonic composition, as the interaction between the different layers creates a sense of texture and complexity. It allows me to explore the interplay of colours, shapes and forms, giving the artwork a unique and intriguing quality. Overall, using palimpsest in painting and composing provides me with a versatile method to create layered and visually compelling artworks that invite viewers to explore the surface and uncover the hidden narratives within the layers of paint and sound.

## Gathering Thoughts: Functional Relationships

At the start of this chapter, I described an EoP, where it is situated and how I operate within it, emphasising the unity and flow between afferent and efferent systems and how they, through the relationship of sensing to performing and thought to embodiment through action, were essential to interpretation and the making of art. This interpretation and embodiment are how I explain the seamless flow between composing and painting and why I view both media as different embodiments of the same somatic input.

For the purposes of description and analysis, I separated mark-making and material generation from its wider contexts within compositions and paintings, behaviours and rituals from the fluid and recursive process of interpretation and making. I also looked at the overlaps between the building techniques I used commonly for composition and painting. Despite similarities in my making behaviours, I have not established relative or relational values, associated meaningfulness, Intersubjectivity or truth values between the categorically different phenomena comprising a music composition and a painting. Each is a formative singularity that differentiates itself from the experiential noise surrounding it. Those singularities have a unique ontology I determine through hermeneutics to qualify as artwork, but despite both media being art forms, physics determines optics and acoustics as radically different.

Even so, everything I have written about making techniques needs to be viewed in the context of functional relationships, by which I refer to the dynamic interaction between the parts and the whole within a hermeneutical context. As I have stated, understanding is not a passive process but rather an active engagement where the interpreter interacts with the text, artwork or any object of interpretation. In this context, a functional relationship refers to the reciprocal relationship between the parts within this context, an art object and its meaningfulness networks generated from the overall meaning that emerges from their interaction. In this way, understanding is not simply a matter of extracting meaning from a piece of music or a painting; instead, it involves a fusion of horizons between the interpreter and the interpreted.

As the composer or painter, my relationship to the work I produce is that of both interpreter and the interpreted. I bring my preconceptions, biases, and historical context to ongoing interpretation, including the construction of meaningfulness networks. Meanwhile, the art object I am making or viewing offers back its own richness and significance, forming a loop between the two. A dynamic process of understanding occurs through the functional relationship between those elements that are not viewed in isolation but are understood in relation to the whole. The meaningfulness I construct is not fixed or predetermined but emerges through the reciprocal ongoing dialogue and interpretation between the interpreter and the interpreted within its processes of transformation and 'becoming'. It involves the mutual imbrication and corresponding influence of various elements, which continually interact and modify each other. It emphasises the immanence and emergence of new forms and possibilities through the interactions and connections between components.

One of those components, as emphasised, is that chance and unforeseen outcomes play a vital role in my practice, offering valuable insights and avenues for exploration. Those unanticipated results, emerging from the interplay between afferent and efferent functionality and internal and external environments, serve as catalysts for new perspectives and transformative experiences that challenge my established assumptions and invite alternative interpretations. I navigate the intersection of creative intentions, sensory stimuli and expressive output across my four studios as another functional relationship, a relationship that functions so I can produce art objects. This functional relationship has a hermeneutic perspective where actions undertaken in my EoP become transformative agents, prompting reassessment, enabling fresh perspectives and initiating a cycle of interpretation and reinterpretation that deepens my understanding of my work and how I make it. Unforeseen outcomes provide opportunities for deconstructing established boundaries and conventions, encouraging the exploration of new directions and re-evaluating existing paradigms while highlighting the transformative potential of symbols that transcend their original meanings to evoke unique and unexpected responses from me as the maker and interpreter of my work. This 'shaking up' of my thinking and established techniques generate unexpected symbolic forms and meaningfulness networks that take on the character of symbolic resonance, often associated with my remembered landscapes. By navigating the delicate balance between intentional action and unpredictability, happenstance shapes and informs my artistic trajectory, ignites the spark of imagination, challenges conventions and facilitates new avenues of artistic expression. It reminds me that while degrees of planning and technical proficiency are important, embracing the unexpected infuses vitality into the creative act, fostering transformative and meaningful experiences embodied within the artwork I produce.

Finally, my studios, too, share a profound functional relationship, a dynamic interplay that shapes the creative process and influences how my work is made. My four studios are an extension of my mind, thinking space and body, becoming physical manifestations and embodiments of my practice. In those studios—my EoP—I am immersed in the artistic process, exploring ideas and experimenting with various techniques and materials. The studios provide an environment that protects me from external distractions, allowing me to experiment and explore. Having said that, I cannot leave my mind, thoughts and emotions at the studio door to blank out everyday life and its preoccupations. I cannot switch to a brain that is concerned only with art. When I enter the studios, I bring everything I am with me. Everything I think and make is filtered through my being.

My studios also function as a repository of tools, materials, resources and locations to walk that support my practice, comprising various physical landscapes and places, brushes, instruments, paints, computers, cameras, pencils, paper and other implements essential to my work, the familiarity of which fosters a seamless flow of making, enabling me to translate thought into an artefact. There is reciprocity, too. My presence and activities infuse my studios with a sense of purpose and artistic resonance embodied in the physicality of the place, how it is organised and the content and work it houses. This embodiment is witness to my making history that, in turn, influences and subtly shapes my artistic output. This interplay between me and my studios creates an intimate dialogue, a dynamic exchange that enriches the creative process. In essence, this functional relationship encompasses a symbiotic exchange. My studios serve as a space where ideas take shape. In turn, I bring articulation and presence to the studios forging a harmonious entity that facilitates creative expression and serves as the backdrop to my making journeys. This is my environment of possibilities.

Throughout this chapter, I have provided an interpretation of my actions and outcomes and what they symbolise to me. I stress that, from my perspective, there are no hierarchical structures, fixed identities or absolute starts and finishes to work. This functional relationship is not necessarily understood in terms of a harmonious interaction or always purposeful arrangements of elements. Instead, it is inherently paradoxical and always accompanied by a certain degree of non-functionality or 'aporetic' moments. These moments are subject to multiple interpretations and disruptions, generating a site of tension in each artwork. They also open the possibility for construction and deconstruction, where stability and fixed meanings are destabilised. Those alternative interpretations include the meaningfulness interpreted by the reader concerning what I have written of my process and what constitutes an EoP and how the two function together.

# CHAPTER SIX

# THE CONSOLIDATION

## Introduction

Writing this book has taken me on a journey that uncovers the functionality and rationale behind my artistic practice. Throughout its pages, I have focused on establishing evidence to support an understanding of the 'how' and, whenever possible, the 'why' behind my creative process. By exploring diverse fields of inquiry encompassing neuroscience, science, 'Fuzzy Logic', interpretation, objectivity, meaningfulness, memory, resonance, affect, intention, indeterminacy, superposition, philosophy, metaphysics, ontology and more, I have amassed valuable insights into my practice, revealing the underlying mechanisms behind my artistic choices and actions.

At the start of writing, I asked what compels me to make paintings and music compositions per se and why the processes, methods, concepts, rituals, antecedents and behaviours I have developed and acquired shape the way I approach making paintings and musical compositions. I also asked what influence concepts of affect and a 'sense of place' play in the outcomes I produce and how those may be embodied into the work and transmitted to others. Crucially, I asked how music and painting are connected and how both relate to my engagement with the concept of landscape. The answers to many related questions are now developed and scattered throughout the book's chapters. To summarise:

Landscape emerged as a central theme throughout my research. I explored its significance through hermeneutic situatedness, proprioception, embodiment and a 'sense of place'. Chapters like 'Mapping' and For the Love of Chalk and Other Matters became platforms for speculation on the correlations between landscape, somatic experience and embodied sonic and visual experiences and how they helped construct my remembered landscapes. I also explored the influence of a 'sense of place', resonance, PK coupling, flux and indeterminate outcomes within music composition and the creation of visual art. Through this exploration, I aimed to prove my assertion that painting and composition are linked expressions of the same somatic and emotional input and thought, manifesting through different artistic media.

I consider my research into the causal factors of neuroscience, somatic functionality including afferent and efferent relationships, PK coupling, particularly its automated functions, perception, cognition, memory, the material and physical capacities of my bodily operation, the preconditioning of genetics and behaviour shaped through environmental factors have provided valuable answers on 'why' I paint and compose as I do from the 'how' I paint and compose perspective. As introduced in The List, discussed in 'Mapping', The Love of Chalk and Other Matters and concluded in An Environment of Possibilities, causal factors and relational forces supporting interpretation, transduction, PK coupling and sensing to performance, some hypothesised, explain how I move seamlessly between composing music and making paintings as a hermeneutic, interpretive and physical activity. In this science-related context, I have established a plausible answer to how and why I paint and compose as I do.

During my exploration, I became increasingly aware of the 'lived experience' and its profound impact on artistic creation. Sensory perceptions and bodily sensations emerged as integral components of the creative process. Neuroscience became crucial for understanding the mechanisms behind perception, memory, embodiment and emotional responses to my work and the landscape. Together, they provide explanations of 'mapping' and embodiment, constructing a 'sense of place'. As I considered my experience of phenomena from multiple perspectives, the lens of philosophy played its part too. Notions concerning an intrinsic equivalence of meaningfulness between the significations of different media were abandoned and fuzzy values, as introduced by 'Fuzzy Logic' highlighted the interplay between subjective experiences of truth values and broader contextual understandings. Interpretation and objectivity became significant areas of examination as I delved into the role of artist statements, titles, intention and indeterminacy in shaping the perception and understanding of artwork by me and others.

Hermeneutics, interpretation, transduction, meaningfulness construction, intentionality and transmission formed a crucial framework within which I explored various elements of artistic practice. Those elements included memory, resonance, affect and the influence of past experiences and emotional connections on the creation and reception of art. I inquired into the dynamics between composer, performer and audience in music composition, addressing intentionality, interpretation, transduction, transmission, convention, deterritorialisation and the construction of meaningfulness. The notion of polyphony for the eye and the ear emphasised the multi-layered nature of artistic expression and the diverse interpretations that can arise across different sensory modalities. Through my creative practice and autoethnography, I further investigated style, spontaneity, serendipity and the significant role of mistakes in learning and experimentation. Topics such as 'hallucination' allowed me to explore the human capacity to construct selective realities and biologically generated simulations of reality, blurring the boundaries between neurology, cognition, perception and imagination and their influence on artistic production and perceptions of reality. I also considered the act of observation and its relationship to artistic creation through the lens of the observer effect in quantum mechanics.

Drawing those diverse threads together, my conclusions point to the complexity of transmitting artist intentionality to the receiver regarding meaningfulness equivalency. While my intentionality is evident in the art itself, manifested through its structures and materiality, the interpretation and meaningfulness triggered in the receiver or performer are shaped by their social, cultural, genetic, physiological and experiential makeup. Although there may be moments of overlap between the intentionality of the maker and the interpretation of the receiver, mainly where those actions are situated in convention, the receiver's interpretation is not solely a consequence of, or intrinsic to, the maker's intentionality nor under the artist's control. However, the receiver's interpretation does stem from the meaningfulness embodied in the artwork. It is through signification that interpretation finds its ground.

Through this immersive investigation, my writing has shed light on the motivations and processes that drive my artistic creation. It has emphasised the interconnectedness of various disciplines and aspects of human experience, encompassing the cognitive and neural dimensions of the creative process, the philosophical and ontological dimensions of artistic expression, the subjective and emotional forces at play and the dynamic interplay between perception, interpretation and communication in art. This synthesis of knowledge invites readers to embark on their journey of exploration, embracing the rich tapestry of art and its profound resonance with the human experience.

However, the answers and speculations I have formulated when writing *Music, Painting, Landscape and Me* offer an incomplete picture of the multiplicity of my operation. They only partially explain the phenomena and immanence of the 'lived experience' of being an artist.

They say little about the intrasubjectivity such an experience involves, particularly concerning how emotional forces drive my work. To go further, I need to ask why I paint as I do through the symbolic forms of philosophy and ontology, each with its different modes of expression and unique way of embodying and expressing meaning that, in combination with the knowledge from the scientific domain, may together answer my questions more thoroughly.

## Ontology and Being

As previously described, ontology is a branch of philosophy that examines the fundamental nature of being, existence and reality. It explores questions such as: What exists? What is the nature of existence? What are the basic categories or types of things that exist? Ontology seeks to understand the structure and organisation of reality and the relationship between different entities.

On the other hand, being refers to the state and quality of existing or being alive. It encompasses the concept of existence itself. In philosophy, 'being' is often discussed in terms of different categories or levels of existence. Those categories include physical objects, living beings, abstract concepts, properties, relations and fictional entities. Each category of being may have different qualities or characteristics that define its existence. Questions such as *"What compels me to make paintings and music compositions per se and why do the processes, methods, concepts, rituals, antecedents and behaviours I have developed and acquired cause me to make work the way I do?"* concern ontology and being. I will attempt to bring some insights through both perspectives—first, ontology.

The ontology of the artist can be approached from different perspectives and philosophical frameworks. Here are a few aspects I have considered:

- Existence as a human being: Ontologically, I exist in the world. I possess a physical body, have thoughts and emotions and interact socially and culturally. My existence is tied to biological, psychological and social dimensions.
- Creative agency: I am partly characterised by my creative abilities and capacity to construct forms of expression. From an ontological standpoint, my creative agency is a distinctive aspect of my being. It involves my ability to imagine, conceptualise and transform ideas into artistic creations.
- Materiality and Embodiment: My ontology is deeply rooted in my practice's physical and sensory aspects. My engagement with materials, techniques and the physicality of my creative process contributes to my ontological existence as an artist.
- Artistic identity: I have a sense of identity tied to my artistic practice and output. My identity is a part of my being, encompassing my artistic aspirations, values, beliefs and aesthetic sensibilities. It shapes my creative choices, influences my worldview and impacts my self-perception.
- Artistic Practice: My ontology includes engagement in artistic practice. This encompasses various activities such as conceptualising, planning, executing creative works and experimenting with different mediums, techniques and styles.
- Reflexivity and Self-Reflection: My capacity for self-reflection and critical engagement with practice involves an ongoing process of self-examination, questioning and self-awareness. My ontological status is shaped by my ability to reflect on my intentions, assumptions and creative choices.

- Relationship with Artworks: My ontology is also intertwined with the artworks I produce. The artworks posses their ontological status, existing as physical or conceptual entities. My relationship with my artworks involves a sense of authorship and shared authorship in music performance but no responsibility to communicate intentions or evoke specific emotions through my creations.
- Constructivism and Intentionality: Intentionality and my active construction of meaningfulness through the shaping of artistic expressions play a central role in imbuing artworks with significance and contributing to their ontological status.
- Social and cultural context: My ontology intertwines my relationship to broader social and cultural contexts. I exist within a network of artistic traditions, movements and institutions and cultural norms, historical influences and social interactions shape my artistic practice. This social and cultural context influences my ontology by providing a framework for my creative activities and artistic identity.

From an ontological perspective, my identity as a painter and composer emerges as an integral part of my being, deeply intertwined with the nature of who I am and how I relate to the world. My making produces modes of expression that enable me to connect with and make sense of reality. For example, as a painter, I engage with the visual realm, using colours, lines and forms to signify my thoughts, emotions and perspectives. Through painting, I interpret the world through my networks of signs and offer a different lens through which others can experience and interpret reality. It is a means of connecting with the world and revealing new insights.

Similarly, as a composer, I immerse myself in sound and rhythm. Through music composition, I shape abstract ideas into tangible sonic landscapes using components such as time, silence, sound, rhythm, pitch, texture, colour, form and structure that performers subsequently interpret to produce what is heard as the sonic fact. Music and painting express my thoughts and ideas categorically differently than words.

My creative activities are not merely external expressions but intrinsic to my being. From an ontological standpoint, painting and composing are essential facets of my existence, enabling me to gain a deeper understanding of myself and the world around me as the act of making unfolds through a transformative journey of self-discovery, providing a medium through which I can construct truth that may otherwise remain hidden to me. Through those activities, I navigate existence, forging meaningful connections between my external environment, my inner world and the external manifestations of my artistic expression.

While an ontological exploration of why I am a painter and composer is profoundly personal and subjective, it does not diminish the value or significance of the insights that arise. The subjective nature of those answers is a consequence of the intimate connection between my existence and creative activities. Through introspection, self-reflection and examining the meaning and significance of art and making, I can understand the ontological aspects of my identity as an artist.

Closely related to ontology is being. I have acknowledged a sense of being an artist through *Music, Painting, Landscape and Me.* Fully articulated here, this sense of being arises from an exploration of the 'lived experience' and interplay between subjectivity, embodiment and the world, investigating how my perception of intrasubjective relations and embodied engagement shape my understanding of 'being', but also how cognitive processes, consciousness and sense of self are inseparable from my bodily interactions and environmental contexts. At the same time, I acknowledge the contingent and constructed nature of identity, knowledge and reality and how the complexities of power dynamics, language and social constructions shape my understanding of being.

There are multiple philosophical interpretations concerning the nature of being. No one perspective is dominant and some contradict each other. I have drawn my interpretation from how I perceive and rationalise my 'lived experience'. Though not aligned with any single position, the following description does reflect my thought at the time of writing. Consequently, I comprehend my sense of being an artist from multiple perspectives. I shall break those down.

First, through subjective recognition and acknowledgement, I self-identify as an artist. This self-identification is closely tied to an awareness of my creative intentions, including a conscious desire to engage in the creative process and to communicate or express ideas, emotions or experiences through artistic means. This intentionality drives my artistic practice as a composer and painter and significantly shapes my approach to artmaking. Closely aligned is my sense of artistic vision that shapes those creative endeavours. This vision encompasses ideas, concepts, cognitive and physiological dispositions and aesthetic sensibilities. It is built through my distinct perspective on the world and a desire to share those through my artwork. Artistic vision is my interpretation of reality. It evolves and develops over time. It is closely tied to my sense of being.

Second, I would further describe my sense of being as follows:

- A comprehension of multiplicity, where I reject the idea of a unified and essential identity, instead seeing myself as a multiplicity of intensities, ideas and creative potentials that I access to create works that interpret the richness and complexity of experience.
- An interpretive and dialogical process where I engage in an ongoing discussion with my artistic intentions, physical materiality and cognitive/CNS makeup, the artwork itself and the viewer's interpretations, together focused through hermeneutics, interpretation and understanding of the past, other cultures and different artistic traditions that draw upon my background, experiences and cultural context through an iterative process of creation, reflection and reinterpretation, particularly with my practice.
- A transformation and 'becoming', where I see everything in a state of flux and adaptation, where my creative practice involves a constant process of 'becoming', exploring new possibilities and experimenting with different forms of expression that do not fix me in a particular identity or style but situate me in a perpetual state of 'becoming' something different and new.
- 'Différance', specifically, where reality is not composed of stable and fixed entities but of differences and variations that I engage with to create personal forms of expression that may disrupt my established order and open new thinking and experiences.
- My aesthetic and emotional experiences can provoke intense sensations and transform my perceptual capacities.
- Play and playfulness, where my sense of being involved in embracing the freedom and spontaneity of the creative process allows me to explore new avenues, experiment with different forms of expression and break free from rigid conventions; and finally,
- All the above constitute the environment from which my sense of being emerges and how, through my physicality and making work, reciprocity between mind, body and action enhances and further develops my sense of being.

I make work the way I do to construct meaning and unravel the complexities of my existence. I paint and compose to experience truth, to tap into a deeper understanding of truth, not merely as an abstract concept but as a tangible experience that engages in the process of 'becoming', where meaning is not fixed but constantly in flux. Rather than striving for a singular truth, I immerse myself in the infinite possibilities that arise from the interplay of external and internal forces. I paint and compose not to represent a predetermined reality but to tap into my immanent world experiences, channelling them through interpretation and expression. I create not to stabilise the experiential flux but to unleash its transformative potential. To achieve this, the canvas and the musical score become sites of experimentation, where I engage with the materials and sounds, allowing them to unfold and evolve unhindered by fixed notions of form. I make art to challenge the conventional boundaries of perception and invite multiple interpretations. They invite viewers and listeners to actively participate in the creation process, forge connections and derive their meanings through interpretation. In so doing, sharing my work creates multifarious relationships with others and connects me to them. It is not about imposing a singular truth or perspective but rather about generating a network of possibilities and multiplicities. As others encounter my work, they interpret what is embodied through their unique experiences and perceptions to catalyse the emergence of diverse perspectives and alternative ways of being. In addition, I make work to attain a sense of self-affirmation. By engaging in the creative process, I actively participate in life, affirming my existence and physicality as an exploration of interpretive potentialities. Pleasure and satisfaction in making work do not arise from a fixed end goal but from the manifestation of a dynamic process of 'becoming', of embracing multiplicities and connections within the world. I create art because it makes me feel complete and connected to reality. Significantly and most simply of all, it brings me happiness and satisfaction.

## Science or Ontology?

At the start of writing, I believed that objectivity, fact and science, with their intersubjective frameworks, were superior and more valuable mechanisms to answer my questions than the intrasubjectivity of experience and feelings. I was looking for verifiable truth or, at the very least, facts. However, along the way, I became increasingly aware that this drive for fact supported self-imposed dualistic attitudes that anticipated science being able to illuminate and answer more than it could while devaluing ontology and pushing its contribution further out of the frame. Through my readings of Derrida, I also became aware that fact and everything built upon it is ultimately unstable. Together, those understandings have changed how I think about the relationship between science and ontology, science and the arts and what fact and truth are. This, in turn, has shaped the answers I now give to my original questions. I shall explain why.

As a systematic and empirical approach to understanding the natural world, science primarily establishes descriptive and explanatory truths rather than ontological ones. Ontological truth pertains to the fundamental nature of reality and existence. Science seeks to uncover regularities, patterns and causal relationships in the natural world through observation, experimentation and the formulation of theories. It aims to provide accurate and reliable explanations of natural phenomena based on empirical evidence and rigorous methodology. Even so, the knowledge produced by scientific inquiry is provisional and subject to revision as new evidence emerges.

While science successfully uncovers descriptive and explanatory truths within its domain, it has inherent limitations when establishing ontological truth. The scope of scientific inquiry is confined to the empirical realm and is focused on the observable and measurable aspects of the natural world. Ontological truths often deal with questions beyond the reach of empirical investigation, such as the nature of consciousness, the existence of abstract entities or the ultimate origin and purpose of the universe. Those questions often fall into the domain of philosophy, metaphysics and speculative reasoning, which may rely on different methods and approaches than those of scientific inquiry.

For example, Positivism, with its rigid criteria for determining facts and knowledge, fails to acknowledge the richness and significance of human experiences beyond physics. According to Positivism, only facts that can be proven and reduced to the laws of physics are considered valid. However, this narrow perspective neglects the invaluable insights and understanding that can be gained through art and other forms of human expression.

When we read a book, explore the poems of Emily Dickinson, immerse ourselves in a symphony by Peter Maxwell Davies, engage with a sculpture by Michelangelo, or witness a play by Shakespeare, we encounter profound aspects of the human condition that cannot be reduced to simple physical laws. Those experiences give us unique perspectives, emotions and connections that contribute to our knowledge and understanding of the world.

Furthermore, Positivism fails to address the subjectivity of human perception and interpretation. It fails to account for the variations in individual experiences and how they shape our understanding of truth and fact. For instance, Positivism cannot determine if the perception of yellow by one person is identical to the perception of another person. This highlights the limitations of Positivism's criteria for objective truth and factual accuracy.

Contrary to Positivism's claims, our understanding of the world is profoundly influenced by our 'lived experiences'. The knowledge we gain from engaging with the world, interacting with others and reflecting on our encounters holds greater epistemic value in our day-to-day lives than a mere awareness of abstract theories or reductionist scientific explanations. However, this disconnection between science, ontology and the 'lived experience' may not be as clear as it initially seems.

While writing *Music, Painting, Landscape and Me*, I found great value in the thought of Ernst Cassirer (1874-1945), a renowned German philosopher and historian of ideas. His works have played a pivotal role in shaping and confirming my thoughts on the relationship between art and science. Cassirer's significant contributions to philosophy, cultural anthropology and philosophy of science have profoundly influenced my understanding and provided a foundation for exploring the intricate connection between those disciplines in my project. He is best known for his work on the philosophy of symbolic forms, a theory that explores how human beings create and understand symbolic systems such as language, myth, art and science. Cassirer's approach emphasised the role of symbols in shaping human experience and culture and he argued that those symbolic forms are fundamental to human understanding of the world. He believed that through symbolic forms, human beings construct and interpret their reality and that those forms play a crucial role in cognitive and social development.

According to Cassirer, science and art represent distinct modes of human expression and cognition, each uniquely contributing to our understanding of the world. He argues that scientific knowledge, grounded in empirical observation and rational analysis, seeks to uncover causal relationships and establish general principles. Science aims to provide objective natural phenomena descriptions and explanations based on systematic methods and empirical evidence. It is concerned with uncovering the underlying mechanisms and laws that govern the physical world. In contrast, Cassirer sees art as a symbolic form that operates in a different sphere, transcending the empirical and engaging with the subjective and expressive dimensions of human experience, where artistic understanding arises from the expressive power of symbols, images and aesthetic forms. Art captures and conveys aspects of human emotion, imagination and subjective experience that cannot be fully grasped through scientific analysis alone. While scientific knowledge focuses on uncovering the objective elements of the world, artistic understanding delves into the subjective and symbolic dimensions of human existence. Art can evoke and communicate emotional and aesthetic experiences, allowing individuals to engage with the world in a profoundly personal and intuitive way.

Cassirer emphasises that scientific knowledge and artistic understanding are crucial for a comprehensive and holistic understanding of human culture and existence. This is because science provides an analytical framework for understanding the external world. At the same time, art offers a means to explore and express our inner worlds and the complexities of human experience. This understanding brings science, art and ontology into relation with one another, deconstructing my perception of them as oppositions and dualities. Further exploration of Cassirer's thought, particularly concerning his theory of symbolic forms, is helpful to understanding how I construct music and painting and how I answer the questions posed in this book.

## Symbolic Forms

Cassirer's theory of symbolic forms is a philosophical framework presented in the three volumes of *The Philosophy of Symbolic Forms,* which examines the fundamental role of symbols in human thought and culture. According to Cassirer, symbols are not merely linguistic representations but encompass a broader range of expressive forms, including art, myth, language, religion and science. Moreover, those symbolic forms are fundamental to human cognition and serve as the building blocks through which we construct and interpret our reality. He argues that symbolic forms are not arbitrary or subjective but are deeply rooted in the human experience and collective consciousness. They enable us to engage with and comprehend the world by providing systems of meaning and interpretation. Each symbolic form has its unique structure and logic, shaping our understanding of various aspects of reality. For example, language allows us to articulate and communicate our thoughts, while art enables us to express and convey emotions and experiences.

Cassirer contends that those symbolic forms are not fixed or static but dynamic and evolving. They are shaped by cultural and historical contexts and transform as societies move forward and change. He emphasises the importance of studying the historical development of symbolic forms to gain insight into humanity's cultural and intellectual evolution. Through his theory of symbolic forms, Cassirer highlights the central role of symbols in human cognition, communication and cultural expression. He argues that those symbolic forms are not mere representations of reality but actively shape our understanding and perception of the world. By studying and analysing symbolic systems, Cassirer seeks to uncover the intricate connections between language, art, myth, religion and science, shedding light on the multifaceted nature of human culture and knowledge.

Relevant to this book, Cassirer's exploration of the relationship between science and art within his theory of symbolic forms acknowledges that science and art are distinct symbolic forms, each with unique methodologies and modes of expression. However, he argues that science and art are not mutually exclusive domains but complementary aspects of human culture where they represent different modes of engagement with reality and that despite their differences, science and art share a common origin in human cognition and symbolic thought. They both emerge from our capacity to create and engage with symbolic forms, allowing us to interpret and give meaning to our experiences.

According to Cassirer, the most fundamental and primitive form of symbolic meaning is expressive meaning. This meaning arises from the expressive function of thought, which deals with the emotional and affective significance of events in our world. It determines whether those events are desirable or hateful, comforting or threatening. This meaning is the foundation of mythical consciousness and explains its defining characteristic: the lack of distinction between appearance and reality. Cassirer posits that the mythical world does not comprise stable and enduring substances manifesting from different perspectives and circumstances. Those perspectives include everyday perceptions expressed in natural language and the mythical view of the world at its most basic level. Cassirer believes that religion and art develop from mythical thought, while theoretical science originates from natural language, specifically in what he terms the "*pure category of relation*". From the scientific perspective, modern mathematics, logic and mathematical physics are free from the limits of sensible intuition and pure relational concepts come into play. Cassirer contends that understanding this process requires equal attention to its concrete and intuitive symbolic manifestations as the "*fact of science*" is now firmly embedded within the broader "*fact of culture*".

Furthermore, Cassirer emphasises that science and art are not simply utilitarian pursuits but essential for human culture and self-understanding. For example, art's ability to evoke emotions and convey shared human experiences is vital in fostering empathy, cultural expression and exploring existential questions. Likewise, science's quest for knowledge and understanding contributes to our understanding of the natural world and informs our technological advancements. Cassirer sees science and art as complementary symbolic forms, each offering distinct but valuable contributions to human culture and knowledge. They represent different ways of engaging with reality and exploring the depths of human experience. By appreciating the unique methodologies and purposes of science and art, we understand the richness and complexity of human intellectual and creative endeavours.

In addition, Cassirer believes that every person is situated within different sign worlds and combinations of sign worlds, which shape our concepts of reality and create biased viewpoints. Those sign worlds' symbolic nature and meaningfulness filter and mould our understanding of the world. For instance, an individual whose sign-world is physics may have difficulty comprehending the perspective of someone whose sign-world is myth or religion. Both hold their interpretations of truth as per their semiotic systems. However, both perspectives hold validity, as each sign world offers a unique interpretation of truth and meaningfulness that resonates within that system. Both interpretations are valid. He also recognises that science and art often interact and influence each other. For example, scientific discoveries can inspire artistic creations, providing new perspectives and themes for creative expression. Likewise, art can stimulate scientific inquiry by challenging existing paradigms and offering alternative ways of understanding the world.

Despite the intellectual rigour Cassirer applied to his theory of symbolic forms, he is unable to identify what phenomena cause the creation of signs or where it is that signs come from; in other words, what lies beyond the sign itself, or, as Barthes wrote, what lies behind the mask. Is it signs all the way down through an infinite unfolding? I cannot locate any answers that identify where signs come from. For now, sign generation must remain a mystery. As well as not being able to explain what causes the creation of signs, Cassirer also doesn't describe how we can move between the sign worlds of the natural sciences, language, myth, art and religion with such ease and with the ability to distinguish those incommensurate semiotic systems one from the other. Nevertheless, our modes of communication and expression confirm our ability to generate signs and move easily between those systems, even without explanation. This interpretive mobility between sign systems enables art to 'speak' its truth to us individually as we interpret its meaning according to our worldviews. Within those symbolic forms, the truth of the art object, its fact, its symbolic nature and its representation hold everything necessary for the maker and receiver to experience its embedded knowledge and truth when such properties are interpreted through a hermeneutic act. Though fashioned by the artist, truth becomes independent of the artist once embedded. Art is a creative expression that necessitates interpretation from its audience. The viewer or listener must willingly engage with the artwork to generate truth.

Irrespective of the artist's intentions, artworks possess physicality and symbolic significance, providing crucial elements for receivers to derive meaning and construct their truth. This elevation of reality and physicality through art enables the emergence of experienced truth, offering insights into our internal and external worlds. Within this context, my engagement with the landscape mirrors engaging with an artwork. The landscape is an integral part of the world surrounding me and holds a central position in my artistic practice. I respond to the landscape as I would to artwork, raising whether the landscape itself can be considered an artwork and whether it contains embedded and experienced truth.

Throughout this book, the landscape assumes a significant and unifying role, as my relationship with it has evolved from a utilitarian perspective to an interpretation of it as a living artwork that encompasses and interacts with me. By regarding the landscape, particularly the English countryside, as an artwork shaped by human activity, I uncover a dynamic interplay of symbolic nature, meaningfulness and embedded truth. Guided by the principles of hermeneutics and interpretation and through my embodied experience of the landscape, I delve into its intricate tapestry of symbols and meanings, constructing truth that resonate with my artistic exploration.

As an active participant, I immerse myself in the physicality of the landscape, embracing the somatic and emotional responses it evokes. Navigating the landscape's symbolic network, I interpret it as a text, a language waiting to be deciphered, decoding signs and symbols that extend beyond utility. This active dialogue between myself and the landscape combines subjective perceptions, cultural background, personal experiences and my condition as an artist to shape understanding.

Within the hermeneutic framework, I acknowledge the landscape's embedded truths as multifaceted and context-dependent. Interpretation engages with the landscape's composite meaning, embracing the interplay of signs, symbols, physiological responses, embodiment and subjectivity. The landscape's meaningfulness is shared among all its signs, including those influenced by emotional and physiological states. Through hermeneutics, I continuously interpret those signs to construct meaningfulness. This is where my landscape truth resides.

My embodied experience of the landscape becomes the foundation for engaging with its embedded truth. Through interpretation, personal resonance and the dynamic nature of meaning-making, the landscape transcends its physicality and transforms into an artwork that speaks entirely of itself. However, considering the various semiotic systems present in art, music, painting, myth, religion, science and others I interpret the landscape through—each offering different perspectives on truth and meaningfulness, I question the relationship between those notions of truth and whether they hold universally or are merely personal constructs disconnected from factual reality. Does truth need fact to be true?

# Truth and Fact

According to Gadamer, truth is not solely determined by objective facts, but also involves interpretation and understanding. He emphasised the role of interpretation in the human experience of truth, suggesting that our preconceptions, biases and historical contexts shape our understanding of what is true. This implies that truth can encompass subjective perspectives and cultural frameworks beyond strict adherence to factual accuracy. In this way, Gadamer challenges traditional notions of truth, proposing that it is an event or encounter that transcends the individual. Unlike the conventional view that truth is determined by applying objective criteria, Gadamer argues that truth surpasses individual judgments based on such criteria. In his book *Truth and Method*, published in 1960, Gadamer delves into the realm of 'philosophical hermeneutics', drawing heavily from Martin Heidegger's influential work, *Being and Time*, suggesting that truth involves a process of understanding in which we are drawn into an event and by the time we seek to know what we should believe, we have already arrived too late. In Gadamer's words: "*In understanding, we are drawn into an event of truth and arrive, as it were, too late, if we want to know what we are supposed to believe*".[158] Gadamer critiques objective models of truth, which rely on a distanced judgment using discernible, separable and manipulable criteria. Instead, he posits a deeper, hermeneutic sense of truth not reducible to such methodological applications. Gadamer does not seek to negate the scientific method but instead aims to shed light on what enables it and the limitations inherent in its scope.

Derrida's view on facts falls under his deconstructive philosophy. He criticised the traditional notion of facts as objective and self-evident truths that correspond to an external reality. Instead, he believed that facts are shaped by language and discursive frameworks. Derrida challenged that facts can be objectively determined and universally agreed upon. Instead, he argued that language and interpretation are significant in creating facts, and that meaning depends on contextual relationships. Derrida highlighted the inherent instability and play of differences in language and meaning. Thus, the notion of a fixed, absolute fact becomes problematic. Derrida's criticism of the concept of facts aligns with his broader project of exposing the binary oppositions and hierarchical structures that underlie traditional philosophical and linguistic systems.

Although Derrida acknowledged the practical utility of facts in scientific and mathematical contexts, he emphasised the need for critical awareness of the linguistic and discursive elements that shape their construction and interpretation. He encouraged questioning and deconstruction of assumed objectivity and a recognition of the complexities inherent in producing and communicating scientific and mathematical knowledge. While Derrida's stance on facts within mathematics is a matter of interpretation, his philosophy invites critical inquiry and challenges fixed meanings and foundations.

Similarly aware of the impossibility of establishing a single, definitive meaning, Cassirer's philosophical ideas regarding truth, fact, experience and being stem from his broader exploration of symbolic forms and their role in human understanding and interpretation of reality. Adopting a nuanced perspective, Cassirer emphasises truth's dynamic and context-dependent nature. For Cassirer, truth is not an inherent property of objects or statements but is constructed through the symbolic systems and frameworks we use to interpret and represent the world. Truth emerges from our engagement with symbolic forms, such as language, art and

---

[158] Gadamer, Hans-Georg, p. 506.

science, which provide us with frameworks for understanding and articulating reality. Facts are not isolated and objective entities but are inseparable from the interpretive frameworks and symbolic systems in which they are embedded. Facts gain meaning and significance through their relationships and connections to broader conceptual frameworks. They are shaped and interpreted by the symbolic forms that we employ to make sense of our experiences.

Cassirer emphasises that experience is a fundamental aspect of human existence and knowledge, and distinguishes between immediate, individual experiences (those I describe as immanent and mediated experiences) shaped and interpreted through symbolic forms. Cassirer argues that our experiences are inherently mediated by the symbolic systems and frameworks we interpret and understand. Through symbolic forms such as language and art, we construct meanings and interpretations of our experiences, shaping our understanding of the world. Being is intertwined with the symbolic forms that define and shape human existence. He rejects the idea of being as a fixed and unchanging essence, emphasising its dynamic and fluid nature. Cassirer sees being as an ongoing process of 'becoming', where human beings actively engage with the symbolic forms to interpret and construct their reality. With significant aspects of meaning construction being based on intrasubjectivity, how is subjectivity situated in the realm of truth and fact?

## Subjectivity and Truth

Cassirer's perspective on subjectivity's relationship to truth and fact revolves around the understanding that truth and fact are not purely objective entities but are inseparably intertwined with human subjectivity and interpretation. Cassirer challenges the notion of a purely objective truth that exists independently of human perception and interpretation. He argues that our subjective experiences and perspectives shape how we understand and interpret the world, including truth and fact. Our subjectivity plays a crucial role in shaping our perception and interpretation of reality, influencing our understanding of what is factual.

According to Cassirer, our subjectivity operates within the symbolic form framework that provides the tools and structures to interpret and represent reality, shaping our understanding of truth and fact. They enable us to articulate and communicate our interpretations of the world, making subjectivity a necessary element in constructing meaning and interpreting reality. Far from being a barrier to truth, our subjectivity allows us to engage with and make sense of the world, bringing our unique perspectives and experiences to understand truth and fact. The diversity of interpretations and understandings of truth among different individuals or cultures contributes to the richness and complexity of human knowledge. While objective facts may exist, our subjective interpretations and perspectives shape how we access and comprehend those facts. Thus, human subjectivity, operating within symbolic forms, enables us to engage with truth and fact meaningfully, recognising the importance of individual perspectives and interpretations in the search for truth. Subjectivity and objectivity, therefore, are not separate entities but rather two facets of a unified whole. The objective world is not merely discovered but actively shaped through our symbolic systems and modes of representation. In contrast, our subjective experience of the world is deeply influenced by the objective structures and frameworks we encounter.

For example, in relation to art, a singular artwork stands as its entity, speaking solely for itself. It is a singularity. While various social, political, cultural, aesthetic, historical, intellectual and contextual factors surrounding embedded truths may aid in conveying their meaning to others, they do not define the truth in the artwork. The interpretations of the creator and the receiver shape their comprehension and realisation, constructing their truth based on the truth embodied in the artwork. Each interpretation is influenced by pre-existing information assimilated throughout our lives as we construct meaning. Empirical fixed truths are arguable outside the realm of pure mathematics. Instead, truth is continually created and recreated through a recursive and assimilative process of interpretation. It is through this process that we come to understand what truth is. Interpretation, as a form of thought, generates signs and interconnected networks of signs inherent to our experiences. As humans, we naturally produce signs and it is through the generation of signs and their relationships that meaningfulness is constructed. Signs shape our perceptions, experiences and thoughts, influencing our understanding of reality. These signs are continuously produced through interpretation, reason and subjective thought.

However, truth is not solely within my (our) subjective examination of the art experience. Instead, truth resides within the experience of the artwork itself and the relationship between me and the artwork, whether as the maker, viewer or both. In that moment of connection, as the maker and viewer, the artwork and I become intertwined and this experience can be revisited and reignited through the memory of the artwork. Prioritising the inherent experience of art as truth surpasses the significance of subjectivity. Subjectivity influences how I think and analyse truth after the fact rather than the lived immanent experiential phenomena that arise when encountering or creating art.

I have also come to recognise that truth reveals itself in those remarkable moments of comprehension when everything aligns and knowledge is acquired. During those instances, I often experience a 'Gestalt' moment—an 'a ha' moment or when I feel 'the penny drops'. This concept of Gestalt, rooted in psychology and perception, holds significance in understanding the recognition of truth. Gestalt refers to the holistic perception and comprehension of a situation or concept. It emphasises that the whole is greater than the sum of its parts. When experiencing a Gestalt moment, it is as if the scattered pieces of information, thoughts and perceptions suddenly come together, forming a cohesive and profound understanding. It is a moment of clarity and insight that transcends the individual elements and reveals a deeper truth. During such moments, the mind engages in a process of integration, connecting various fragments of knowledge, memories and insights. Through this integration, a Gestalt emerges, enabling me to grasp the underlying truth and see the interconnectedness of the components involved. It is a transformative experience that goes beyond mere logical reasoning and engages my intuition, emotions and perception in a unified way.

When the Gestalt moment occurs, there is often a sense of surprise, a sudden realisation that brings about a shift in perspective. It is as if a missing puzzle piece suddenly falls into place, illuminating the bigger picture and allowing me to comprehend a previously elusive truth. This recognition of truth as a Gestalt moment is powerful and impactful, as it shapes my understanding, broadens my knowledge and influences my subsequent thoughts and actions. By acknowledging the role of Gestalt in truth recognition, I embrace the idea that truth is only sometimes arrived at through linear, step-by-step analysis. Instead, it can emerge in sudden, profound moments of insight where the mind perceives the interconnectedness and wholeness of a situation. Gestalt moments give me glimpses into deeper truths and offer opportunities for personal growth, expanded perspectives and the continual evolution of my understanding. Such understanding is possible because the truth is not a fixed formula or a set of replicable conditions; it is an inherent phenomenon that I experience and filters through my perspectives. Each recollection and analysis of those experiences lead to further interpretations of truth, expanding my understanding. Truth encompasses layered experiences that continuously generate evolving concepts of truth.

A friend once told me that *"there is only one truth, but there are multiple interpretations of that truth"*. This statement becomes evident when considering the diverse applications of truth in politics, religion, science, mathematics, literature, art and other fields, where interpretations of truth are used to support different claims and worldviews. In the post-truth era, personal interpretations of truth, no matter how cynical, abound and may be considered more significant or contradictory to truth established as factual or objective. For my part, I acknowledge that the truth of a mathematical equation, such as 2+2=4, differs from the truth experienced while reading a poem by T.S. Eliot. Both instances contain truth, originating from distinct symbolic systems contributing to my understanding of reality.

Insights into the relationship between science and art, as well as considerations of truth, fact, objectivity and subjectivity, have significantly shaped my comprehension of artistic practice and guided the conclusions drawn from writing this book. At the start of writing and owing to its content comprising of objective and subjective materials, I declared this book a work of fiction. I was wrong. As subjectivity is deeply intertwined with experience and interpretation, with my emotions, beliefs and biases that shape my understanding and perception of the world, it would be challenging to conceive of a book completely devoid of subjectivity. Even selecting and organising information, choosing language and style and presenting ideas inherently involve subjective decisions. Likewise, language carries inherent subjectivity, laden with cultural and personal connotations.

Following my subsequent reading of Gadamer, Deleuze and Cassirer in particular, I would now describe *Music, Painting, Landscape and Me* as an autoethnographic book that draws upon the worlds of art, science and philosophy as an expression of symbolic forms embodying my exploration and integration of those forms, offering a multidimensional understanding and interpretation of my 'lived experience' and ideas that bridge different realms of knowledge to provide a tapestry of meaning. Drawing upon those diverse realms, I have engaged with varying modes of expression, each with a unique way of capturing and conveying meaning. Moreover, this autoethnographic approach required that I actively participated in the creation of symbolic forms—my meaningfulness networks—offering personal experiences and insights while also drawing upon broader cultural, scientific and philosophical contexts, showing the power of symbolic forms to shape my perception, stimulate my thinking and enable me to explore complex concepts from multiple perspectives. Those ideas, experiences and knowledge intertwine and overlap and do not necessarily follow a linear or hierarchical structure. Rather than categorise this book as a work of fiction, I now see it as a synthesis of my experience and understanding of the worlds of art, science and philosophy that transcends strict categorisations to be classified as a creative act of symbolic expression rather than a straightforward representation of factual information. This book is an artefact. It is its truth. It is also a material fact. It is the embodiment of my thought expressed through the symbolism of words. Its capacity to be meaningful is also a fact. However, away from whatever I associate with the book's content, its meaningfulness remains unstable and contingent upon what the reader determines.

This altered perspective of the interconnectivity between objectivity and subjectivity and the changed status of this book from fiction to synthesis is a consequence of my 'becoming'. Research, thinking and making compositions and paintings while writing has driven a transformative process characterised by constant flux and the dissolution of fixed identities that defy notions of stability and progress. My 'becoming' has involved breaking free from many binary oppositions and embracing the multiplicity of potentialities and connections in my practice, where ideas, entities and experiences intertwine, overlap and transform. As in writing this book, 'becoming' is a continuous process of creation, where new modes of existence emerge through exploring differences, 'différance' and the fluidity of boundaries. It is this constant creation process that determines *Music, Painting, Landscape and Me* as an art object.

## The Ultimate 'Why?'

The thoughts, reflections, scientific evidence and theoretical speculation I have accumulated while writing this book constitute a strong case for why I am an artist and how my artistic practice unfolds. This research and reflection shed light on the mechanisms, functionalities, processes, motivations, stimulations, inspirations and personal experiences that shape my work and interpretations. However, despite this and with the addition of ontological perspectives, I still feel something missing from the equation prevents a resolution at the core of my questions—particularly the 'why am I?' question. This lack of resolution is not helped by my understanding that there is no fixed and definitive reference point for meaning. As highlighted in Derrida's philosophy, the transcendental 'signifier'—the centre of meaning—is not a fixed entity. It is an illusion of stability and foundational meaning.

For example, in deconstruction, questions about ontology, being and reality emerge from a critique of metaphysical assumptions that seek stable foundations or definitive answers. Derrida questions the possibility of a fixed and confident understanding of being and reality. Rather than locating a lost 'transcendental signifier' as the origin of questions about being and reality, Derrida focuses on the deconstructive process. He emphasises the need to examine how language and discourse shape our understanding of being and reality, revealing the multiplicity of interpretations and the impossibility of reaching a final, authoritative meaning. While his work does engage with fundamental questions about being and reality, his approach transcends the reliance on a single lost 'transcendental signifier' as the key to understanding those inquiries. Even so, the absence of a fixed 'transcendental signifier' does not negate the existence of proof or reality nor imply that proof or reality is entirely undermined or rendered impossible.

And there you have it. The absence of a singular, absolute, stable, definitive proof or reality has troubled me throughout the writing of this book. I have been building up to this understanding for some time. As the book has progressed, I have seen it approaching. Unsurprisingly, neither science nor ontology can offer that fixed, immutable centre of meaning. There is no sign beyond the sign that signifies itself without deferral to other signs; there is no transcendental 'signifier', only mask after mask, all the way down.

In hindsight, I see what I referred to at the outset of writing as 'the missing middle' was my terminology for what I now identify as the absence of a transcendental 'signifier'. I was describing the missing centre of meaning. Having researched, thought and written about all areas of my practice and being to establish the territories that define the boundaries of 'the missing middle', at the heart of it all, I only find what is unknowable, a centre that is deferred to another centre and another and so on. Far from a reassuring 'logocentric' resolution, the answer I have found is that there are only multiple points of deferral and no centre at all.

I am undecided whether to be alarmed or comforted by this. In any event, my reaction and feelings have no bearing on the reality. I cannot change anything other than my interpretation. That interpretation may include me viewing the absence of a 'transcendental signifier' as causing uncertainty and instability, as there is no ultimate reference point or authoritative source of meaning. This lack of stability and certainty may contribute to disorientation, confusion and a breakdown of shared understandings in a dystopian context. Without a stable foundation for meaning, societal cohesion and collective values may be undermined, potentially leading to a fragmented and chaotic state.

Similarly, without a transcendental 'signifier', meanings become fluid and subject to interpretation. This creates a fertile ground for manipulation and the wielding of power. Without a fixed point of reference, individuals or groups with influence can shape and manipulate meanings to serve their agendas. This leads to dominating ideologies or suppressing dissenting voices, exacerbating social inequalities and fostering oppressive systems. However, it's important to note that the consequences of the absence of a 'transcendental signifier' are not inherently dystopian. From a positive perspective, this conclusion opens possibilities for diversity, plurality and individual agency, allowing for exploring multiple perspectives and the potential for creative and innovative interpretations. The absence of a fixed meaning can be seen as an invitation to engage in ongoing dialogue, negotiation and the continual creation of meaning, where meanings are seen as fluid, contextual and constantly shifting, dependent on a web of relations and interpretations.

This recalls and is a return to 'becoming', a concept associated with change, transformation and continual growth. It emphasises that entities and phenomena are not static but in a state of constant evolution and development. Without a fixed reference point, meaning becomes a continuous exploration and transformation process. The absence of a 'transcendental signifier' allows for the emergence of new meanings and the potential for constant reconfiguration and reinterpretation. But where does this process and understanding leave me on a day-to-day basis?

I shall continue to do what I do. Without writing this book, I would still be painting and composing. Writing and research have not necessarily made me a better artist, but it has increased my insight and knowledge about how and why I make things. However, my sense of knowing can only be speculative—an interpretation. It is not a fixed and immutable state. This knowing also embraces what I know I don't know and what I don't know, I don't know. Knowing is my best guess—my working hypothesis drawn from what I consider facts and my 'lived experience'. Although I acknowledge facts and truth, I hold some with a degree of transience. I keep an open mind. I communicate with the assumption that I am broadly understood. I operate through intentionality. I generate meaning despite any notions of 'the missing middle' and deferment.

The force that compels me to create as an artist is not based on a sense of knowing, but rather it stems from a complex interplay of genetics, biology, physics, neurology, environmental influences and social and cultural factors. This amalgamation of forces, intertwined with hermeneutics, interpretation, comprehension, subjectivity, ontology and being, ultimately shapes my understanding and fuels my compulsion to create meaningful work.

It all comes down to this: I make things. Making is real. Making is a fact. I don't know what others see or hear when they engage with my work. What I do know is that I transform thought into materiality through my body and make artworks that are singularities embodying their truth. This is meaning generation without words. It is adaptive and responsive to dynamic change and flux. It is continual growth and unfolding. It is 'becoming'. 'Becoming' is why I do what I do the way I do it.

This is my best answer. It is my interpretation and understanding—for now.

# BIBLIOGRAPHY

Aylesworth, Gary, *Postmodernism*, in *The Stanford Encyclopedia of Philosophy*, Edward N. Zalta ed., 2015.

Barthes, Roland, *The Death of the Author* (1967) in *Image-Music-Text* ed. Stephen Heath. London, Fontana Press, 1977.

Bent, Margaret, *Polyphonic mensural notation, c1260-1500 in Notation*, ed. by Ian D Bent, et al., in *Grove Music Online*, 2001.

Bird, Alexander, *Thomas Kuhn, The Stanford Encyclopedia of Philosophy*, Edward N. Zalta ed., 2018.

Bradlaugh, Adam A., Fedele, G., Munro, A.L., et al., *Essential Elements of Radical Pair Magnetosensitivity in Drosophila, Nature* 615, 2023.

Britannica, The Editors of Encyclopaedia, 'Semiotics' in *Encyclopedia Britannica*, 2020.

Campbell, Edward, *Music after Deleuze*. London and New York, Bloomsbury, 2013.

Cassirer, Ernst, *The Philosophy of Symbolic Forms*, in three volumes. Initially published 1953, trans. Steve G. Lofts. London, Routledge, 2021.

Coessens, Kathleen, Darla Crispin and Anne Douglas, *The artistic turn: a manifesto*. Leuven, Leuven University Press, 2009.

Costandi, Moheb, *Neuroscience Research Triggers Revision of a Leading Theory of Consciousness* in *Big Think*, July 2022.

Cox, Christoph, *Sonic Flux: Sound, Art and Metaphysics*. Chicago, IL, University of Chicago Press, 2018.

Crick, Francis and Christof Koch. *Towards a Neurobiological Theory of Consciou*sness in *Seminars in the Neurosciences*. Vol. 2. London, Saunders Scientific Publications, 1990.

Crispin, Darla, Preface in *Unfolding Time: Studies in Temporality in Twentieth-Century Music*, ed. by Darla Crispin. Leuven, Leuven University Press, e-book pp. 7-11, 2017.

Crispin, Darla, ed. *Unfolding Time: Studies in Temporality in Twentieth Century Music*. Leuven, Leuven University Press, 2017.

Crowther, Paul, *Phenomenology of the Visual Arts (even the frame)*. Stanford, California, Stanford University Press, 2009.

Crowther, Paul, *The Phenomenology of Modern Art: Exploding Deleuze* in *Illuminating Style* 19. London, Continuum, 2012.

Delaere, Mark, *Tempo, Metre, Rhythm. Time in Twentieth-Century Music,* in *Unfolding Time: Studies in Temporality in Twentieth-Century Music*, ed. by Darla Crispin. Leuven, Leuven University Press, e-book pp. 13-43, 2017.

DeLanda, Manuel, *A new philosophy of society: Assemblage theory and social complexity*. London and New York, Bloomsbury, 2006.

DeLanda, Manuel, *Assemblage theory*. Edinburgh, Edinburgh University Press, 2016.

Deleuze, Gilles and Félix Guattari, *A Thousand Plateaus: Capitalism and Schizophrenia*, trans. Brian Massumi. Minneapolis, MN, University of Minnesota Press, 1987.

Deleuze, Gilles and Bacon, Francis. *Francis Bacon: The Logic of Sensation*, trans. Daniel W. Smith. London, Continuum, 2003.

Derrida, Jacques, transl. Alan Bass, *Structure, Sign and Play in the Discourse of the Human Sciences* 1966 in *Writing and Difference* English translation. IL, University of Chicago Press, 1978.

Derrida, Jacques, *De la Grammatologie*, transl. Gayatri Chakravorty Spivak, revised English translation. Paris, Les Éditions de Minuit, 1967.

Derrida, Jacques, *V* in *Limited Inc*, ed. Gerald Graff, transl. Jeffrey Mehlman and Samuel Weber. Evanston, IL, Northwestern UP, 1988.

Derrida, Jacques, *Signature, Event, Context* in *Limited Inc*, ed. Gerald Graff, transl. Jeffrey Mehlman and Samuel Weber. Evanston, IL, Northwestern UP, 1988.

D'Errico, Lucia, *Powers of Divergence: An Experimental Approach to Music Performance*. Leuven, Leuven University Press, 2018.

Dieguez, Pedro R., Jéferson R. Guimarães and John P. S. Peterson, *et al. Experimental Assessment of Physical Realism in a Quantum-Controlled Device*, in *Commun Phys* 5, 82, 2022.

Dilthey, Wilhelm, ed., Rudolf A. Makkreel and Rodi Frithjof, *Wilhelm Dilthey: Selected Works, Volume I: Introduction to the Human Sciences*. Princeton, NJ, Princetown University Press, 1991.

Dimitropoulos, Stav, *Objective Reality May Not Exist at All, Quantum Physicists Say*, in *Popular Mechanics*, June 2022.

Diprose, Rosalyn and Jack Reynolds, eds., *Merleau-Ponty: Key Concepts*. London, Routledge, 2014.

Dorin, Alan, *Chance and Complexity: Stochastic and Generative Processes in Art and Creativity*, in *Proceedings of the 15th Virtual Reality International Conference: Laval Virtual*, pp. 1-8, 2013.

Edwards, Michael, *Algorithmic Composition: Computational Thinking in Music* in *Communications of the ACM* 54.7, pp. 58-67, 2011.

Eno, Brian, *Generating and Organising Variety in the Arts* in *Audio Culture*, Revised Edition, *Readings in Modern Music*, Christoph Cox and Daniel Warner eds. London, Bloomsbury, 2017.

Feld, Steven and Keith H. Basso eds. *Senses of place*. Woodbridge, England, Boydell & Brewer, 1996.

Frobenius, Wolf and others, 'Polyphony', in *Grove Music Online,* 2001.

Gadamer, Hans-Georg, *Truth and Method*, Donald G. Marshall, Joel Weinsheimer trans., London, Bloomsbury, 2013.

Gombrich, Ernst Hans, *Art and Illusion: A Study in the Psychology of Pictorial Representation*. London, Phaidon, 1977.

Gomez-Marin, Alex and Asif A. Ghazanfar, *The life of behavior* in *Neuron* 104.1, 25-36, 2019.

Goodacre, Simon, *Seven Doctoral Candidates Receive Dissertation Year Fellowships* in *News and Events* online at Brandies University, Graduate School of Arts and Sciences, 2019.

Goodman, Nelson, *Languages of Art: An Approach to a Theory of Symbols*. Indianapolis, IN, Bobbs-Merrill, 1968.

Gottschalk, Jennie, *Experimental Music since 1970* e-book. London, Bloomsbury, 2016.

Gregg, Melissa and Gregory J. Seigworth, eds. *An Inventory of Shimmers* in *The Affect Theory Reader*. London, Duke University Press, 2010.

Harvey, David Charles, Iain J.M. Robertson, Roy Jones, Thomas Carter eds., *A Creative Coast* in *Creating Heritage: Unrecognised Pasts and Rejected Futures*. Taylor & Francis, London, 2019.

Holland, Eugene W., *Deleuze and Guattari's 'A Thousand Plateaus': A Reader's Guide*. London and New York, Bloomsbury, 2013.

Ingarden, Roman, *Ontology of the Work of Art: The Musical Work; The Picture; The Architectural Work; The Film*, trans. by Raymond Meyer and John T. Goldthwait. Athens, OH, Ohio University Press, 1990.

Jaeger, Gregg, *Entanglement, Information and the Interpretation of Quantum Mechanics*. Berlin, Germany, Springer International Publishing, 2009.

Jameson, Fredric, *A Singular Modernity Essay on the Ontology of the Present*. London, Verso, 2002.

Johnson, Daniel, *Fuzzy Logic Tutorial: What is, Architecture, Application, Example, Guru99*, 2023.

Kanasevich, Gleb, *After the Genesis: Formation of Identity Through Self-Borrowing and Alternative Musical Forms and an Original Composition Found Objects for Seven Percussionists and a Sound Engineer*, diss. Brandeis University, 2020.

Klee, Paul, '*Notebooks, Volume 1: The Thinking Eye*, trans. R. Manheim. London, 1961.

Klee, Paul, *Notebooks: The Nature of Nature*. NY, Overlook Press, 1992.

Kirk, Geoffrey Stephen and John Earl Raven, *The Presocratic Philosophers: A Critical History with a Selection of Texts*. Cambridge, Cambridge University Press, 1957.

Kostelanetz, Richard, *Conversing with Cage*, 2nd. Edn. New York, Taylor & Francis, 2005. e-book, p. 122. Original material provided by Bill Shoemaker, in *The Age of Cage*, Down Beat Magazine, December 1984.

Kucyi, Aaron, et al., *Spontaneous Cognitive Processes and the Behavioural Validation of Time-Varying Brain Connectivity* in Network Neuroscience 2.4, 2018.

Lloyd, Emma Jane, *Determinacy, Indeterminacy and Collaboration in Contemporary Music-Making*, unpublished PhD thesis. University of Edinburgh, 2018.

Mack, Katie, *Yes, Everything in Physics is Completely Made Up–That's the Whole Point* in the online magazine *BBC Science Focus* published March 2023.

Mack, Katie, *We've Made a Map of Dark Matter but Still Don't Know What It Is and That's Okay* in the online magazine *BBC Science Focus* published September 2022.

Maia, João Paulo, *The Logic of Scientific Discovery*, in *Philosophy and Rhetoric of Science* from *Academia*, 1992.

Marvell, Alan and David Simm, *Unravelling the Geographical Palimpsest Through Fieldwork: Discovering a 'sense of place' in Geography* 101.3, pp. 125-136, 2016.

Matthews, William, *Masturbation Journal Paper Exposes Deeper Problems in Research* in *Times Higher Education,* 2022.

Mei, Ning, Roberto Santana and David Soto, *Informative Neural Representations of Unseen Contents During Higher-Order Processing in Human Brains and Deep Artificial Networks* in *Nature Human Behavior* vol. 6 pp. 720-731, May 2022.

Nail, Thomas, *What is an Assemblage?* in *SubStance* 46.1, pp. 21-37, 2017.

Nattiez, Jean-Jaques, *Music and Discourse: Towards a Semiology of Music.* Princetown, Princetown University Press, 1990.

Pace, Ian, *Composition and Performance Can Be and Often Have Been, Research* in *Tempo*, 70.275, pp. 60-70, 2016.

Pace, Ian, *Notation, Time and the Performer's Relationship to the Score in Contemporary Music* in *Unfolding Time*, ed. by Darla Crispin. Leuven, Leuven University Press, pp. 151-192, 2009.

Pepperell, Robert, *Connecting Art and the Brain: An Artist's Perspective on Visual Indeterminacy* in *Frontiers in Human Neuroscience*, August 2011.

Pironkoff, Simeon, *The Figure and its Dramaturgy* in *Polyphony & Complexity: New Music and Aesthetics in the 21st Century*, Claus-Steffen Mahnkopf, Frank Cox and Wolfram Schurig eds. Hofheim, Wolke, 2002.

Popkin, Gabriel, *Einstein's 'Spooky Action at a Distance' Spotted in Objects Almost Big Enough to See* in *Science.* April 2018.

Press, Clare, Daniel Yon, *Perceptual Prediction: Rapidly Making Sense of a Noisy World* in *Current Biology*, Vol 29, Issue 15, 2019.

Quinn, Carolyne. *Perception and painting in Merleau-Ponty's thought* in *Perspectives: International Postgraduate Journal of Philosophy* 2.1, pp. 38-59, 2009.

Ranade, Anagha Mayur Surana, Shivani V. Dhokne, Sudesh Gaidhani, Sharad D. Pawar, *Ayurvedic Ideology on Rasapanchak-Based Cognitive Drug Intervention* in *Medicinal Herbs and Fungi*, 10.1007/978-981-33-4141-8, 2021.

Reddy, Prishani, *The Differences Between Research Methods and Research Methodology* from DifferenceBetween.net, May 2018.

Roka, Les, *The Virtuoso as New Music Advocate: Carlton Vickers on Redefining Flute Music in 21st Century* in *The Utah Review*, 2017.

Russell, Bertrand, *History of Western Philosophy*. London, Allen & Unwin, 1946, repr. London, Routledge, 2004.

Jacques, Schnier, *Free Association and Ego Function in Creativity: A Study of Content and Form in Art'* in *American Imago*, vol. 17, no. 1. The Johns Hopkins University Press, 1960.

Schroeder, Anna M., Belén Pardi, Joram Keijser, Tamas Dalmay, Ayelén I. Groisman, Erin M. Schuman, Henning Sprekeler and Johannes J. Letzkus. *Inhibitory Top-Down Projections from Zona Incerta Mediate Neocortical Memory* in *Neuron*, 2023.

Schuback, Marcia Sá Cavalcante, *In-Between Painting and Music—or, Thinking with Paul Klee and Anton Webern*', *Research* in *Phenomenology* 43.3, pp. 419-442, 2013.

Scruton, Roger, *Representation in Music* in *Philosophy*, Vol. 51, No. 197, pp. 273-287, July 1976.

Siegel, Ethan, *Ask Ethan: How Do Fundamental Particles Create Consciousness* in *Big Think*, August 2022.

Siegel, Ethan, *Scientific Proof is a Myth* published online in *Forbes Magazine*, 2017.

Skains, R. Lyle, *Creative Practice as Research: Discourse on Methodology* in *Media Practice and Education* 19.1, 2018.

Souris andré, *Conditions de la musique et autres é crits*. Bruxelles, Editions de l'Universitéde Bruxelles, 1976.

Strenger, Carlo, *Psychotherapy and Hermeneutics Research Paper* in iResearchNet, (no date).

Sutcliffe, Daisy, *Reworlding world heritage: emergent properties of 'kinservation'*. PhD thesis, University of Glasgow, 2018.

Taylor, Janet L., *Proprioception* ed. Larry R. Squire, in *Encyclopedia of Neuroscience*. Academic Press, Cambridge MA, 2009.

Theodore, George, 'Hermeneutics' in *The Stanford Encyclopedia of Philosophy*, Edward N. Zalta ed., winter 2020.

Waikagul, Jitra and Urusa Thaekham, *Approaches to research on the systematics of fish-borne trematodes*. Academic Press, Cambridge MA, 2014.

Wallraven, Christian & Kaulard, Kathrin & Kürner, Cora & Pepperell, Robert & Bülthoff, Heinrich *Psychophysics for perception of (in)determinate art* in *Proceedings of the 4th Symposium on Applied Perception in Graphics and Visualization*, 115-122, 2007.

Watts, S. K., *Spectral Immersions: A Comprehensive Guide to the Theory and Practice of Bass Clarinet Multiphonics*. Puurs, Belgium, Metropolis, 2015.

Wiesmann, Martin and Alumit Ishai, *Training Facilitates Object Recognition in Cubist Paintings* in *Front. Hum. Neurosci*, 4:11, 2010.

Wiley, Christopher, Ian Pace eds., *Researching and Writing on Contemporary Art and Artists: Challenges, Practices and Complexities*. Berlin, Germany, Springer International Publishing, 2020.

Ximena, González-Grandón, Falcón-Cortés Andrea, Ramos-Fernández Gabriel, *Proprioception in Action: A Matter of Ecological and Social Interaction* in *Frontiers in Psychology* 11, 2021.

Yeats, Marc K., *Control, Flexibility, Flux and Complexity: A Timecode-Supported Approach to Polytemporal Orchestral Composition*. PhD thesis University of Leeds, 2021.

Zaman, Asad, *The Rise and Fall of Logical Positivism* in *Express Tribune* (online article) October 2015.

# INDEX

*A Thousand Plateaus: Capitalism and Schizophrenia*, 9
Abstract Expressionism, 158
Abstraction, 37, 64, 72, 83, 158
Acrylic (pens and paint), 103, 106, 140
Action Painting, **129-130**
*Adam's Grave No. 1*, 24
Ad Libitum, 67
Aerial (Atmospheric) Perspective, 99, 156, 161
Aesthetics, 46, 49, 123, 153
Affect, 1, 13, 22, 23, 26, 28, 32,34, 35, **36-38**, 39, 47, 51, **58-59**, 64, 65, 81, 82, 85, 88, **91-95**, **98-100**, **101-102**, **104-106**, **114-115**, 117, 123, 125, **133-135**, 137, 175, 176, 183
Affect Theory, **36-37**
Affective Weighting, 88, 91, 92, 99, 106
Affective Triggers, 91
Afferent and Efferent, 25, 88, 122, 124, **140-142**, 172, 175
Agency, 32, 113, 124, 128, 177, 190
Aleatory, **66-67**
Algorithmic Processes, 148
An Turieann Art Centre, 63
Antecedents, 1, 26, 88, 125, 126, 131, **134-138**, 175, 177
Aporetic, 173
Art Object, 4, **142-143**, 165, **172-173**, 184
Artefact, 35, 41, 42, 45, 55, 56, 78, **83,-84**, 92, 94, 106, 111, 139, 141, 143, 157, 173, 188
Artistic Practice, 1, 7, 10, 12, 13, 53, 73, 83, 112, 113, 126, 131, 134, 166, 175, 176, **177-179**, 184, 188, 189
Artist's Statements, 26, 32
*Ask Ethan*, 11
Assemblage, 62, **63-64**, 145, 147, **149-150**
Assimilation, 29, 84, 125, 136, 138
Asynchronous, **150-151**, 152
Audience, 22, 26, 42, **50-54**, 57, 61, 103, 107, 140, 165, 176, 184
Audio File Assemblage, 145, **149-150**
Audio Files, **145-146**, 149, 170
Audio Model, **145-146**, **149-150**
Aural Imagination, 101, 118, 150, 170
Auralisation, 118
Autoethnography, 6, 25, 31, 176
Automatism, 129

Barthes, Roland, 19, **44-45**, 52, **55-56**, 61, 84, 183
Basso, Keith, 2
BBC Scottish Symphony Orchestra, 60

Becoming, 1, **7-8**, 15, 22, 37, 79, 143, **160-165**, 171, 172, **179-180**, 186, **188-189**, 190
Behaviour, 1, 10, 13, 25, 39, 50, 56, 58, 66, 73, 74, 79, 80, **88-89**, 113, 120, 121, 123, **124-136**, 137, 172, 175, 177
Being (Ontology), 3, 4, 7, **10-11**, 12, 14, 38, 40, 46, 87, 88, 91, 96, 173, **176-180**, **185-186**, **189-190**
Berkshire Downs, 87, **96-100**, 101, 104, 109, 110
Bias, 4, 6, 13, **18-20**, 38, 49, 77, 80, 143, 172, 183, 185, 188
*Big Think*, 11
Bird, Alexander, 14
Blank Canvas, 170
Blindfold, 72, **126-127**
*Box Hill #2*, 169
*Box Hill #4*, 168
*Box Hill, Surrey*, 159
Bradlaugh, Adam A, **114-115**
*Bramfield, Suffolk*, 156, **163-164**
Brushstrokes, 140, **153-162**, 167

Cartesian, 4, 55
Cassirer, Ernst, **181-186**, 188
Central Nervous System (CNS), 88, 90, 93, 95, 104, 121, **140-141**, 179
Chalk, 23, **96-97**, **109-112**, 113, 114, 115, 117, **121-122**
*Chalk Downland near Winchester*, 23
Chance Procedures, 129
Choreography, 128
Cognitive, **10-11**, 40, 74, 79, 80, 88, 95, 117, 128, 131, **133-134**, **137-138**, 140, 176, **178-179**, 181
Cognitive Dissonance, 95, 100, 105
Communication, 5, **18-19**, 22, 27, 38, 55, 57, 59, **77-78**, 103, 128, 176, 182, 184
Composer-In-Residence, 100
Conceptual Landscape, 83, **87-88**, 93, 100, 102
Conditioning (Pre and Self Conditioning), 27, 28, 124, 127, 128, 138, 165, 175
Conductor (music), 47, 48, **49-50**, 59, 69, 144
Consciousness, **4-5**, 7, **10-13**, 14, 34, 40, **74-75**, 76, 79, **85-86**, 90, 95, **128-129**, 132, 133, 141, 178, 180, **182-183**
Context-Dependent, 184, 185
*Control, Flexibility, Flux and Complexity: A Timecode-Supported Approach to Polytemporal Orchestral Composition*, 48
Convention, 2, 17, 32, **42-54**, **56-60**, 65, 68, 78, 83, 96, 151, 173, 176, 180
Correlates, 25, 90, 93, 107, 111, **113-115**, 117, **120-121**, 124, 127, 137, **141-142**, 151, 185

Costandi, Moheb, 74
*Covehithe Beach, Suffolk*, 106
*Cranborne Chase No. 1*, 39
Creative Activities, 101, 178
Creative Artefacts (sonic and material), 1, 3, 5, 6, **30-31**, 33, 42, 45, 55, 92, 94, 106, 111, 141, 157
Creative Practice as Research, **5-6**
Cultural Texts, **17-19**
Culture, **17-19**, 20, 44, 55, 179, **181-183**, 186

Dance, 22, 37, 80, **112-113**, 124, **141-142**
Dark Matter, 86
Data (digital, information, neural and somatic), 1, **13-14**, 21, 26, 28, 29, 32, 33, 35, 38, **62-63**, 66, 76, 81, 87, **94-95**, 100, 104, 116, 121, 139, **140-142**, **166-170**
Deconstructed, 106, 156, 165, 173
Deconstruction (Derrida), 15, **17-18**, 20, 52, **55-56**, 185, 189
Deleuze, Gilles, 9, 37, 48, 63, 143, 188,
Derrida, Jacques, 15, **17-20**, 45, 52, 127, 180, 185, 189
Descartes, René, 4, 19
Destructive Action, 162
Deterritorialisation, 48, 51, **56-58**, 176
Différance (Derrida), 18, 20, 57, 179, 189
Digital, 24, 39, 92, 98, 100, **136-137**, 142, 145, 149, 153, **166-170**
Dimitropoulos, Stav, **40-41**
Dividing or Cutting Up an Artwork, **167-168**
Do-It-Yourself, 7
Documentation, 3, 101
Downland, 23, 96
Drawing, 24, **60-61**, 64, 68, 92, 96, **100-104**, 123, 129, 137, 140, **142-143**, **151-152**
Drip Technique, 129
Dystopia, 55, 190
D'Errico, Lucia, **53-56**

*East Kennet, Wiltshire*, 155, 158-159, 161
Effortlessness, 126
Electromagnetic Spectrum, 114
Electronic Notation Materials, 169, 170
Embedded, 18, 24, 32, 35, 47, **48-49**, 54, 55, 56, 59, 73, 76, 82, **92-93**, 96, **99-100**, 103, 105, 110, 115, **120-124**, **127-128**, 137, 142, 144, 146, 160,
Embedded Truth, 184, 186, 183, 184, 186
Embodiment, 1, 9, 13, **25-26**, 27, 30, 33, **41-42**, 56, 72, 76, 83, **89-92**, 102, 104, **111-113**, 117, **118-122**, 151, 164, **172-173**, **175-176**, 177, 178, 184, 188
Emergent Properties, 137, 147, 161
Emotional Weighting, 88
Enactive Sensorimotor Theory of Perception (ESMT), **89-91**, 107

Encoding Process, 92
*English Downland*, 96
Entanglement, 15, 27, 61, 73, 85, 125, 136, 162, 171
Environment of Possibilities (EOP), **136-138**, **139-174**
Equivalency of Meaningfulness, **27-28**, 96, 176
Erosion, 28, 72, **105-107**, 110
European Classical Music, 44, 48, 50, 51, 60, **151-152**
Event Horizon, 143
Excavation, 171
Expanded Proprioception, **115-117**, 119, **161-169**
Expressive Meaning, 183
External Modelling, 112

Fact of Culture, 183
Factual Truth, 4
Feedback Loop, 102, 112, **120-121**, 126, 140,
Feeling and Performing, 90, 107, **111-113**, **120-122**
Feld, Steven, 2
Fiction, **13-16**, 32, 177, 188
Filters, 4, 13, 23, 26, 32, 38, 49, 77, 79, 92, 94, 187
Flexible Performance Approaches, 144
Fluid, 1, 4, 26, 101, 156, 172, 186, 189, 190
Flux, **9-10**, 21, 22, 23, 29, 33, 45, 56, 57, 61, **64-66**, 69, 71, 76, 81, 85, 96, 100, 144, 175, 179, 180, 188, 190
Formatted, 25, 32, 40, 42, 89, 90, **94-95**, 99, 106, 141, 145
Free Association, 25, **128-130**, 136, 138
Freud, Sigmund, 74, 129, 136
Functional Relationships, **172-174**
Fuzzy Logic, **21-22**, 66, 73, 175, 176
Fuzzy Sets, 66, 73
Fuzzy Values, 176

Gadamer, Hans-Georg, 3, 185, 188
Gedankenexperiment (Thought Experiment), 76
Genetics, 78, 143, 175, 190
Gestalt Moment, 91, 187
Gesture, **27-28**, 32, **46-47**, 52, 53, 57, 58, 119, 124, 127, 128, 137, 140, **141-142**, 148, **154-156**, 162, **165-166**, 167
Gomez-Marin, Alex, 133
Graphic Notation, **68-69**
Gregg, Melissa, 36

Hallucination, **79-82**, 176
Heidegger, Martin, 17, 185
Heisenberg, Werner, 29
Heraclitus, 34

Hermeneutic Circle, 3, 139, 141
Hermeneutic Situatedness, 87, 103, 123, 175
Hermeneutic Immersion, 35
Hermeneutics, 2, **3-4**, 9, 13, **26-27**, 31, 33, 35, 37, **43-44**, 50, **55-59**, **60-61**, 68, **78-79**, 81, **92-94**, 102, 106, 172, 176, 179, 184, 190
Heterogeneous, 59, **62-63**, 123, 125, 136
Holistic Understanding, 182
Homogeneous, 9, 48, 124
Horizons, 29, 35, 82, 115, 158, 172
Human Indeterminacy, 57, 71
*hyīran*, 148

Icon, 2, 25, 32, 83, 96, 157, 158
Identity (musical and painting), 46, 48, 50, 53, **63-64**, 119, 123, 138, 148, 168
Identity (ontological), **177-179**
Image Generation, **166-169**
Imagination, 2, 57, 96, 101, 118, 121, 130, 139, 143, 150, 152, 156, 169, 170, 173, 176, 182
Imagined Landscapes (see also Remembered Landscapes), 117
Immanence, 35, 37, 141, 172, 176
Immanent Experience, 4, 16, 26, 94
Immersion, 35, 36, 87, 93, 111
Impulse-Driven Behaviour, 128
Indeterminacy (see also Ad libitum, Aleatory, Graphic Notation, Human Indeterminacy, Indeterminacy and Fuzzy Sets, Indeterminacy of Form, Instrumental Indeterminacy, Jelly, Notational Hierarchy, Painting Techniques and Indeterminate Outcomes, Pitch Indeterminacy, Structural Indeterminacy, Temporal Indeterminacy and Timbral Indeterminacy), **38-39**, 42, 57, 59, **64-66**, 69, **70-71**, 73, 176
Indeterminacy and Fuzzy Sets, **64-66**
Indeterminacy of Form, 71
Index (indexes), 2, 163
Individuality, 71, 125
Indivisibility of an Artwork (cutting up or dividing), 142, **167-168**
Inspiration, 26, **94-95**, 143
Instability, **9-10**, 81, 100, **105-106**, 185, 189
Instrumental Indeterminacy, 71
Instrumental Writing, **118-121**
Intentionality, 9, 19, **24-25**, 32, 38, **44-50**, 52, 54, 58, 72, 85, 101, 112, 118, 122, 124, **137-138**, **141-143**, 164, 176, 178, 179, 190
Interiority, 16, 136
Interpretation, **2-7**, 13, 17, 19, **22-27**, **31-32**, 33, 35, **37-38**, 39, **42-43**, **45-46**, **47-55**, **57-58**, 61, 62, 64, 66, **68-69**, **78-79**, 81, 85, **87-88**, **92-94**, 95, 96, 102, 112, 117, 122, 123, **139-143**, **146-147**, 150, 152, **153-155**, 157, 160, **162-164**, 165, 166, 168, 170, **172-174**, **175-176**, **179-180**, 181, **182-184**, **185-188**, **189-190**

Interpreter and the Interpreted, 172
Interpretive Equivalency, 172
Intersubjectivity, 172
Intrasubjectivity, 177, 180, 186
Isorhythm, **148-149**
Iteration, 65, 144, **163**,-**164**, 170
Iterative Images, 167

Jelly (see Indeterminacy), 65
Johnson, Daniel, 21
Journey (painting), 158, **160-164**
Journeying, **7-8**
Jungian Symbology, 129

Kanasevich, Gleb, **119-120**
Kessingland (Suffolk, England), 104
Keyhaven Harbour (Hampshire, England), 101
Kinetics, 30, 155
Klee, Paul, 27
Knockholt (Kent, England), **111-112**
Knowledge, **5-6**, 10, **12-17**, **18-20**, 24, **32-33**, **41-42**, 49, 50, 55, 77, 101, 104, 118, 135, **176-177**, **178-179**, **180-184**, **185-188**, 190
Kucyi, Aaron, **133-134**
Kuhn, Thomas, 14

Landscape Configurations, 93, 96, 98, **104-105**, 115, 154
Language (see Deconstruction and Metaphysics of Presence), 3, 4, 7, 10, **17-20**, **22-23**, 27, **36-38**, 52, 55, 62, 74, **77-78**, 79, 83, 85, 103, 112, 179, 181, **182-184**, **185-186**, 188, 189
Layering, 64, 162, 171
Learning on the Job, 6
Lenses, 4, 7, 14, 77, 79
*Letcombe Bassett, Oxfordshire*, 84
Lighting, 99, 100, 104, 115, 137
Linguistic Systems, 185
Lived Experience, 4, 10, **12-13**, 14, 33, 73, 82, **84-85**, 92, 95, 113, 121, 133, 135, **175-179**, 181, 188, 190
Lloyd, Emma Jane, **66-71**
Located Work, 102, 104, 139
Logic Pro, 139, **145-146**, 150
Logocentric (Logocentrism), **4-5**, **17-20**, 189
*Look In, Look Out*, 100
Low-Resolution, 118
*Lyme Bay*, 157
Lymington Marshes (Hampshire, England), 87, **100-101**

Mack, Katie, 86
Magnetoreception, 114
Magnetosensitivity, 114
Maia, João Paulo, 14

Making (paintings and musical compositions), 1, 6, 13, 22, **26-27**, **32-33**, 34, 38, 61, 63, 64, 72, 79, 81, 84, 88, **91-92**, 95, 101, 104, 112, 115, 121, **123-125**, **126-128**, 130, 135, 137, 138, **139-143**, 151, **153-160**, **161-164**, 166, **169-171**, **172-174**, 175, **178-180**, 190
Making Techniques, 27, 140, 154, 172
Manuscript, 136, 153, 171
Mapping, 7, 35, **87-96**, **97-100**, **105-106**, 111, 115, 123, 139, 141, 151, **175-176**
Maps, 29, 35, 87, **92-93**, 96, **97-98**
Mark-Making, **27-28**, 35, 37, 39, 62, 100, 102, **124-127**, 137, 142, **153-171**, 172
Marker Pens, 156
Massingham, H. J., 96
Material Existence, 25
Material Generation, 172
Materiality, 32, 43, 46, 49, 53, 87, **92-94**, 96, 107, 113, 117, **118-119**, 128, 137, 141, 152, 176, 177, 179, 190
Matthews, William, **31-32**
Maxwell Davies, Peter, 30, 181
Meaning (meaningfulness construction or generation), **2-5**, **6-8**, **9-10**, 11, 13, 14, 15, **16-20**, 22-29, **31-32**, **33-34**, 35, 37, **38-40**, **42-49**, 52, **54-56**, **58-59**, **60-61**, **62-63**, **68-69**, 76, **77-79**, 81, **82-85**, 92, 95, 96, 100, 103, **113-115**, 121, **139-143**, 152, **153-154**, 157, 158, 160, 168, **170-171**, **172-174**, **175-177**, **178-180**, **182-184**, **185-187**, 188, **189-190**
Meaningfulness Equivalency, 140, 176
Meaningfulness Networks, 154, 156, 157, 167, 171, **172-173**, 188
Memory, 2, 29, **33-35**, 74, 87, 91, **95-96**, 100, 115, 117, 118, 121, 123,124, 126, **127-128**, **133-135**, 139, 161, 166, 170, **175-176**, 187
Mental Map, 98, 126
Mesearch, 6, **31-32**
Metaphysics, 7, 11, 12, **16-18**, **19-21**, 40, 45, 47, 51, 52, 181
Metaphysics of Presence (Derrida), 20, 52
Methodology, 5, **59-60**, 76, 104, 149, 180,
Metronome, **43-44**, 45, 144
Mind, 11, 16, 20, 26, 41, 62, 73, 74, 76, 81, 88, 94, **95-96**, 107, 118, 122, 125, 128, 130, **132-134**, 136, 139, **141-142**, 150, 173, 179, 187
Missing Middle, **13-14**, 21, 77, 86, 189, 190
Mistakes, 121, 138, 164, 176
Mobile Phones, 166, 170
Mock-Up, 118
Modernism, 64,
*movement towards no.4*, 155, 157, 158
Multidimensional, 2, 134, 188
Multivalent, 26, 52, 56, 104
Muscle Memory, **127-128**, 135, 154, 160

Music and Painting (the connection between), 1, **3-4**, **6-7**, 25, 29, 42, 66, 90, **120-122**, **140-142**, 175, 178, 182
Music Composition, 58, 66, **77-78**, **143-153**, 166, 165, **169-171**, **175-176**, 178
Music Notation (including standard European classical and Western classical music notation), 29, 43, 46, 47, 50, 52, 53, 54, 69, 140, 141, **151-152**
Musical Score, 24, 29, 43, 44, 46, 61, 67, 144, 180
Musical Time, 30, **46-47**
Myth (mythology), 15, 55, 111, 181, **182-183**, 184

Nattiez, Jean-Jaques, **45-46**, 48
Natural Sciences, **3-4**, 6, 10, 183
Nature of Being, 4, 7, **11-12**, 177, 179
Naughty Corner, 160, 163
*Near the River Blyth, Blythburgh, Suffolk*, 60
Neuromuscular Memory, 127
Neuroplasticity, 10, 132
Neuroscience, **10-12**, 20, 38, 74, **76-77**, 96, 113, 115, **133-135**, 175
Non-Fungible Tokens (NFTs), 168
Notation (music), 19, 29, **42-54**, **56-60**, **67-71**, 76, 106, **118-120**, **136-137**, 139, 140,141, **143-152**, **169-170**
Notational Hierarchy, **67-68**
Notational Signification, **50-51**, 118, 119, 141, 143, 146

Obfuscation, 65, 125
Objectivity, 9, **13-16**, **22-27**, 28, 32, 53, 74, 101, 128, 176, 180, 185, 186, 188
*obscure sorrows*, 70
Observation (also self-observation), 10, **13-17**, 29, 31, 32, 40, 41, **75-77**, 80, 83, 86, **100-101**, 103, **105-107**, 118, **123-124**, 132, 170, 176, 180, 181
*observation 2*, 148
*Observatory 1h, Near Winchester, Hampshire*, 103
Observer Effect, 11, 85, 176
Oil Paints, 156
*On a Theme of Hermès*, 150
Ongoingness, **36-37**, 139
Ontology, 7, **10-13**, 16, 28, 40, 57, 172, **177-178**, **180-182**, **189-190**
Ordinance Survey Maps, 97
Orkney Islands Landscapes, 157
*Oros*, **151-152**
Out of Awareness, 88, 117, 123, 125, **127-128**, 135, **140-141**
*Overton Downs, Wiltshire*, 116, 155

Painting, 1-8, 13, **18-19**, **22-26**, **28-31**, **34-35**, **37-38**, **39-40**, 42, 45, 57, **60-61**, **62-63**, 64, 66, 68, **72-73**, 76, **77-78**, **82-85**, 87, 89, 90, 91, 96, **100-101**, 104, **106-107**, 109, **112-113**, **116-117**, 120, 122, **123-124**, **126-127**, **129-130**, 135, **136-137**, **139-143**, **153-171**, 172, 175, **177-178**, 182, 184, 190
Painting Techniques and Indeterminate Outcomes, **72-75**
Palette, 72, 155, **165-166**
Palimpsest, 64, 72, 127, 165, 171
Partial Truth, 21
Parts (musical), 59, **61-62**, 63, 65, 70, **144-147**, 152
Peirce, Charles Sanders, 2
Pepperell, Robert, **38-40**, 64, 72, 83
Perception, 14, 16, 23, 29, 31, 33, 38, 46, 49, 61, 63, **64-65**, 78, 81, **88-91**, 94, 95, **98-99**, 101, 105, **111-112**, 113, **114-115**, 120, **121-122**, 133, 134, 137, 143, **175-176**, 177, 178, 180, 181, **182-183**, 184, **186-188**
Perception-Action loops, 91, 120
Performance Approaches, 43, **49-50**, **56-60**, 58, 144
Performative Pieces, 101
*William Mumler's Spirit Photography*, 67
Performer (and performance), 25, 26, 32, 42, 44, **46-48**, **50-58**, **60-61**, 62, **67-71**, 76, 81, 119, 121, 141, 144, 149, 152, 165, 170, 176, 178
Performing Drawings and Paintings, **24-25**, 56, **60-61**, **68-69**
Phenomenology, **4-5**, 10, 17, 26, 89, 111
Philosophy, 7, 9, 14, 16, 17, 29, 53, 128, 176, 177, 181, 182, 185, 188, 189
Photo-Realistic, 154
Photographs, 33, 35, 87, **92-93**, 98, 100, 101, 104, 107, 117, 137, 166, 170
Pironkoff, Simeon, 62
Pitch Configurations, 148
Pitch Indeterminacy, 70
PK Coupling, **88-95**, 101, 102, 103, 107, **111-113**, **114-115**, **116-117**, **118-122**, 123, 124, 127, 137, 139, 141, 175
PK Perceptual Experience, **89-90**
PK-Self-Ecological, 89, 91
PK-Self-Other Interactions, 89
PK-Sensorimotor Contingencies-Self, 89, 91
Place-Specific, 34, 117
Platonic Image, 54
Play and Playfulness, 126, 136, 147, 147, 150, 153, 156, 170, 179
Poems (Marc Yeats), 10, 22, 31, 33, 36, 37, 42, 77, 78, 80, 81, 82
Pollock, Jackson, **129-131**
Polyphony (musical), **61-64**, 149
Polyphony for the Ear, **61-63**, 176

Polyphony for the Eye, **61-63**, 176
Polyphony Through Complexity, **61-64**
Polytemporality, 29, **58-60**, 65, **69-70**, 71, 101, 119, **143-147**, **150-152**
Positivism (Logical Positivism), **63-65**
Postmodern (Postmodernism), 15, **17-21**, 32, 44, 45, 52, **55-56**
Poststructuralism (Derrida), **17-20**, 44
Potential-Rich Phenomena, 136
Potentiality, 166
*Powerstock, Dorset*, 162
Practice (artistic and performance), 1, **4-7**, 10, **12-13**, **21-22**, 25, 27, 31, **33-32**, 53, 54, 56, 61, 63, 64, 66, 72, 73, 77, **83-84**, 87, 89, **90-91**, 93, **95-96**, 101, 103, 112, 113, 118, 119, **123-124**, 125, **126-127**, 129, 131, **133-136**, 138, **139-140**, 153, **164-171**, **172-174**, **175-180**, 184, 188, **188-189**
Practice-Based Research, **5-6**
Preconceptions, 4, 99, 137, 156, 164, 172, 185
Predetermination, 138
Predetermined Iterations, 127
Predictability, 132, 173
Press, Clare, 80
Prints (digital), **166-169**
Programming (self and neural), 24, 38, 81, 82, 103, 126, 132, 135
Projection (perceptual), 3, 55, 73, 94, 98, 115, **118-119**, 121, 125, 139
Proprioception, 30, **88-90**, 113, **114-117**, 119, 122, 126, 175
Proprioception-Kinaesthetic (PK), 89
Prototype, 149
Psyche Inducing, 138
Pure Category of Relation, 183

Quality Control, **123-125**
Quantum Entanglement, 85
Quantum Mechanics, 11, 20, **40-42**, **75-77**, 85
Quotation (Barthes), 44

Random, 66, 89, 129, 135, 148, 149
Reading (landscape and artwork), 2, 13, 17, 19, 20, 23, 28, 29, 33, 56, 59, 60, 68, 87, **93-94**, 98, 127
Reality, 4, 10, 13, **16-17**, 19, 20, 21, 24, 31, 33, 38, **40-42**, 55, 58, 73, 74, **75-77**, **78-83**, 92, 94, 95, 96, 100, **105-106**, 119, 176, **177-181**, **182-184**, **185-188**, 189
Recursive, 3, **25-27**, 47, 72, 91, 102, 120, 123, 127, 137, 141, **145-147**, 160, 172, 187
Referent, 2, 18, 22, 25, 32, 78, 83, 95, 96, **116-117**, 123, 125, 139, **153-154**, **156-158**, 161
Referent Paintings, 157

Remembered Landscape, 83, **87-88**, 91, 92, 94, **95-96**, **98-100**, 101, **104-105**, **116-117**, 123, 137, 166, 171, 173, 175
Rendition, 48, 50, 51, **53-54**, **60-61**, 70, 119, 121, 145, 150, 170
Research, **5-6**, 11, 13, 28, **31-32**, **38-41**, 53, 54, 64, 74, **75-77**, **87-88**, **89-90**, 96, 101, 104, 113, **114-115**, 118, 120, 130, **133-135**, 142, 151, 170, 175, 189, 190
Residency, 35, 87, **100-104**
Resonance, **33-35**, 36, 84, 100, 111, 113, 114, 134, 137, 171, 173, **175-176**, 183, 184
Reterritorialise, 35, 48, 95
Reviewing Work, 140, 150, 164, 170
Rhizome, 9, 27, 136
Rhythmic Entities, 148
Rituals, 87, 95, 100, 123, 142, 172, 175, 177

Schnier, Jacques, 129
Science Domain, 8
Science Fact, 16
Scraping, 72, 107, 156, 160, 171
Scriptor (Barthes), 44, 84
Seigworth, Gregory J., **36-37**
Self-Awareness, 7, **11-13**, 74, 131, 133, 177
Self-Borrowing, 6, 119, **145-148**, **151-152**
Self-Conditioning, 124, 127
Self-Defining, 131
Self-Fulfilling Artistic Prophecy, 82
Self-Referential, 6, 17, 78, 95, 123, 125
Self-Similar, 147
Semiotic Systems, 13, 56, **183-184**
Semiotics, **2-3**, 4, 13, 32, 43, 54, 55, 85
Sense of Place, **1-2**, 13, 22, 35, 38, **63-64**, 90, 92, 94, 96, 100, **104-107**, 115, 112, **175-176**
Sense of Significance, 92
Sensed Sound, **114-115**, 118, **121-122**
Sensing, 88, 101, **111-113**, 117, 119, 122, 124, 127, 132, 141, 142, 151, 172, 175
Sensorimotor, **89-91**, 93, 102, 111, 117
Serendipity, 47, 126, **135-138**, 149, 153, 160, 176
Seth, Anil, **10-11**
Shared Making Processes, 139, **169-171**
Sibelius Notation Software, 139, 144, **145-147**, **149-150**
Siegel, Ethan, **11-12**, 15
Sign Theory, 2
Sign Worlds, **183-184**
Signature (gestures), 127, 128
Significance (meaningfulness), 3, **6-7**, 10, 20, **23-28**, 31, 33, 37, 43, 45, 60, 64, 71, **92-96**, 102, 113, 115, 123, **128-129**, 153, 156, 158, 161, 166, 175, 178, 181, **183-184**, 186, 187
Signified, 2, **18-19**, **24-25**, 27, 29, 43, **45-47**, 48, **51-52**, 53, 85, 92, 141, 144, 146, 149, 156
Signifier, 2, 18, **189-190**

Signs, **2-3**, 17, 18, 28, 43, 96, 178, **183-184**, 187, 189
Simulacra, 50, **51-54**, **57-58**, 82, 158
Simulation, **79-82**, 176
Situatedness, 4, 19, 50, 58, 87, 94, 103, **116-117**, 119, 123, 125, 175
Skains, R. Lyle, 5
Sketches, 101, 104, 151, 171
Somatic Data, 94, 100, 116, **140-141**
Somatosensorial Cortex Correlate, 89
Sonic Building Blocks, **149-150**
Spatiotemporal Self-Orientation, 90, **120-121**
Species-Typical Body, 113
Speed Drawing, 103
Spontaneity, **126-136**, 153, 156, 160, 176, 179
Spontaneous Cognition, 133
Spontaneous Thought, **133-135**, 137
Starting Points and Finishes (of artwork), 7, 77, **101-102**, 124, 125, 129, 130, **142-143**, 150, 153, 160, **163-165**, **173-174**
*stillness in movement*, 63, 157, 167
Stimuli, 22, 25, 35, 55, 56, 57, 62, 73, 79, 80, 82, 85, 95, 107, 112, 114, 127, **133-140**, 172
Stopwatch, 59, 71, 144
String Quartets, 104
Strong Embodiment, **89-91**, 102, **111-112**
Structural Configurations, 106
Structural Indeterminacy, 71
Structuralism, **17-18**, 58
Studio, 91, **123-124**, 139, 160, 170, **172-173**
*sturzstrom* (a landslide event for voices), 69
Style, 43, 46, **50-51**, 56, 82, **123-126**, 127, 129, 160, 163, 166, 179, 188
Style-Building, 123, 126
Stylistic Fingerprints, 123
Stylistic Values, 124
Subjectivity, 4, 7, **13-14**, 28, 32, 35, 53, 58, 73, 78, 141, 178, 181, 184, **186-189**, 190
Suffolk Coastline, **104-107**
Superposition, **41-42**, **74-76**, 85
Surrealists, 129
Symbolic Expression, 83, 188
Symbolic Forms, 7, 93, 157, 173, 177, 181, **182-186**, 188
Symbolic Networks, 93, 117, 142
Symbolic Representation, 42, 82, 88, **92-93**, 96, 100, 101, 106, **116-117**
Symbolic Systems, 29, 181, 182, **185-186**, 188
Symbols (symbolic), 27, 29, 31, 37, **43-50**, 53, **59-60**, **68-69**, **77-79**, **82-83**, 85, 87, 88, **92-96**, 98, 100, **101-102**, **106-107**, **116-117**, 123, 129, 142, 143, **153-154**, 156, 162, 166, 168, 171, 173, 177, **181-184**, **185-186**, 188
Synaesthesia, 25

Technology, 150, **166-170**

Tempo Transformations, 147
Temporal Activity, 29, 59, 139
Temporal Flexibility, 144, 147
Temporal Flux, 29, 71
Temporal Indeterminacy, **59-60**, **69-70**
Temporal Trajectory, 144
Temporality, 62
Territory, 1, 9, 35, 48, 51, 87, 93, 95, 98
The Centre of Meaning (see Transcendental Signifier), **17-18**, 189
*The Berkshire Downs*, 97
*The Death of the Author*, 19, 44, 45, 52, 55
The Model, 65, **145-146**
*The North Sound*, 30
*The Observatory*, **100-104**
The Observer (The Observer Effect), 11, 41, 74, **75-77**, 85, 176
The Perpetual Symbol (see Transcendental Signifier), **77-86**
The South Downs National Park, 87, **100-104**
The Viewer, **24-25**, 31, 39, 42, 63, 64, 72, 76, **83-84**, 140, 162, 164, 179, 184
Theory of Evolution, 15
Thermodynamics, 132
Thought, 7, 9, 13, 20, 21, **22-23**, 26, **27-28**, **29-30**, 33, 35, 36, **37-38**, 42, 45, 52, 59, 73, 74, 76, 77, **78-79**, **81-82**, **84-86**, 95, 101, **132-135**, **136-137**, 139, 143, 151, 164, **172-174**, 175, **177-179**, **181-183**, **186-189**, 190
Thought Experiment (Gedankenexperiment), 76
Timbral Indeterminacy, 71
Timecode, 29, 48, **59-60**, **63-65**, **69-70**, 71, 119, **143-147**, **149-151**
Timecode-Supported Polytemporal Music, 60, **69-70**, **143-147**, 150
Titles (see also Artist's Statements), 31, **38-40**, 176
Tollaksen, Jeff, **75-77**
Topographical Configurations, 1, 88
Total Deterritorialisation, 51, 54 **56-58**
Trace, 19, **43-47**, 61, 77, 96, 127, 128, 137, 156, **165-167**, 166, 170
Transcendence, 8, 22,
Transcendental Signifier, **17-18**, **189-190**
Transduced to Materiality, 141
Transduction, **28-33**, 56, 63, 78, 119, **141-145**, **175-176**
Transformation, 7, 47, 63, 87, **144-145**, **147-149**, **151-152**, 166, 172, 179, 190
Translation, 23, 32
Transmission, 1, 10, 13, **18-19**, 22, **23-26**, **28-33**, 38, 42, 46, **47-48**, 51, **52-53**, 57, 59, 78, 84, 92, 176
Trial-and-Error Testing, 139
Tripartite Relationship, **46-48**

Truth, **13-20**, **21-22**, 31, 33, 52, **55-56**, 73, 81, 129, **185-189**
*Truth and Method* (Gadamer), 185
Truth and Objectivity, **13-16**
Truth Values, **21-22**, 73, 172, 176

Understanding, **3-4**, **6-7**, **13-14**, 20, 22, 24, 28, **32-33**, 37, 38, 48, 50, 52, 59, **77-78**, **81-82**, 85, 93, **102-104**, **112-113**, **114-115**, 127, 133, **135-136**, 139, **143-144**, 160, 164, 166, 170, **172-173**, **175-176**, **178-184**, **185-190**
Unfolding, 23, 37, 78, 94, 160, 171, 183, 190
Unforeseen Outcomes (see Chance Outcomes), **172-173**

Vertical Harmonic Relationships, 147
Video (video diary), 33, 64, 87, 92, 98, 101, 104
Visual Complexity, 28
Visual Indeterminacy, **38-39**
Visualisation, 93, 96, 98, 123, 142
*Vulgar Gorgon*, 68

Walking, 5, 13, 89, **90-92**, 94, 104, 107, **111-112**, 120, 136, 139, 142, 149
*Wastwater*, 83
Weak Embodiment, 89
Weald Geology, 109
Weather, 1, 35, **99-100**, 104, 105, 115, 116
Wenhaston (Suffolk, England), 104
Wenninger, Markus, 29, 56, **119-120**
Workspace Theory of Consciousness, 74

Ximena, González-Grandón, **89-91**, 113, 122

Zaman, Asad, 14